Helmand Mission

By the same author

Wall of Steel: The History of 9th (Londonderry) HAA Regiment, RA (SR); North-West Books, Limavady, 1988

The Sons of Ulster: Ulstermen at war from the Somme to Korea; Appletree Press, Belfast, 1992

Clear the Way! A History of the 38th (Irish) Brigade, 1941–47; Irish Academic Press, Dublin, 1993

Irish Generals: Irish Generals in the British Army in the Second World War; Appletree Press, Belfast, 1993

Only the Enemy in Front: The Recce Corps at War, 1940–46; Spellmount Publishers, Staplehurst, 1994

Key to Victory: The Maiden City in the Second World War; Greystone Books, Antrim, 1995

The Williamite War in Ireland, 1688–1691; Four Courts Press, Dublin, 1998

A Noble Crusade: The History of Eighth Army, 1941–1945; Spellmount Publishers, Staplehurst, 1999

Irish Men and Women in the Second World War; Four Courts Press, Dublin, 1999

Irish Winners of the Victoria Cross (with David Truesdale); Four Courts Press, Dublin, 2000

Irish Volunteers in the Second World War; Four Courts Press, Dublin, 2001

The Sound of History: El Alamein 1942; Spellmount Publishers, Staplehurst, 2002

The North Irish Horse: A Hundred Years of Service; Spellmount Publishers, Staplehurst, 2002

Normandy 1944: The Road to Victory; Spellmount Publishers, Staplehurst, 2004

Ireland's Generals in the Second World War; Four Courts Press, Dublin, 2004

The Thin Green Line: A History of The Royal Ulster Constabulary GC, 1922–2001; Pen & Sword Books, Barnsley, 2004

None Bolder: A History of 51st (Highland) Division 1939–1945; Spellmount Publishers, Staplehurst, 2006

The British Reconnaissance Corps in World War II; Osprey Publishing, Oxford, 2007

Eighth Army in Italy: The Long Hard Slog; Pen & Sword, Barnsley, 2007

The Siege of Derry 1689: The Military History; Spellmount Publishers, Stroud, 2008

Ubique: The Royal Artillery in the Second World War; The History Press, Stroud, 2008

Helmand Mission

With The Royal Irish Battlegroup in Afghanistan, 2008

Richard Doherty

Pen & Sword
MILITARY

First published in Great Britain in 2009 by
Pen & Sword Military
an imprint of
Pen & Sword Books Ltd
47 Church Street
Barnsley
South Yorkshire
S70 2AS

ISBN 978-1-84884-148-2

A CIP catalogue record for this book is available from the British Library.

Typeset in 11pt Ehrhardt by
Mac Style, Beverley, E. Yorkshire

Printed and bound in the UK by CPI

Pen & Sword Books Ltd incorporates the imprints of Pen & Sword Aviation, Pen &
Sword Maritime, Pen & Sword Military, Wharncliffe Local History, Pen and Sword
Select, Pen and Sword Military Classics and Leo Cooper.

For a complete list of Pen & Sword titles please contact
PEN & SWORD BOOKS LIMITED
47 Church Street, Barnsley, South Yorkshire, S70 2AS, England
E-mail: enquiries@pen-and-sword.co.uk
Website: www.pen-and-sword.co.uk

Dedication

To the memory of those who have lost their lives in Afghanistan, among whom are numbered these men of the Royal Irish Regiment

'They shall grow not old, as we that are left grow old ...'
Ranger Anare Draiva
(1 September 2006)

Lance Corporal Paul Muirhead
(1 September 2006)

Lance Corporal Luke McCulloch
(6 September 2006)

Ranger Justin James Cupples
(4 September 2008)

Not only are they commemorated by columns and inscriptions in their own country, but in foreign fields there dwells also an unwritten memorial of them, graven not on stone but in the hearts of men.

Faugh A Ballagh!

Contents

Acknowledgements

In producing this book I had the support and assistance of a remarkable group of men. The men of the Royal Irish Regiment are a credit to their Regiment, the Army and their country. They carried out a most difficult task in Afghanistan with patience, humour and understanding and they also showed those qualities to me as I researched this account of their service on Operation HERRICK VIII. To all of them, I say thank you very much. Special mention must be made of Lieutenant General Sir Philip Trousdell KBE CB, whose idea the book was, Lieutenant Colonel Ed Freely, Commanding Officer, 1st Bn The Royal Irish Regiment, for his unfailing courtesy, hospitality and kindness, Lieutenant Colonel Andrew Cullen, Commanding Officer, 2nd Bn The Royal Irish Regiment, for his enthusiastic support, Captain Brian Johnston MBE and his team for their unstinting efforts on my behalf when they had so much more to which to attend, and all those with whom I spoke, who provided information on their time in Helmand, those who provided photographs and Captain Andy Shepherd, Unit Press Officer, for his support. Where I have quoted the words of others I have indicated this clearly but I must make special mention of the blogs written by Lieutenant (now Captain) Paddy Bury and which have already seen publication in print. These are superb accounts of his time in Afghanistan and will, I believe, stand as classics for future generations; he is a modern John Shipp.

Photographs are included by courtesy of The Royal Irish Regiment except as indicated otherwise.

Richard Doherty
March 2009

Foreword

Lieutenant General Sir Philip Trousdell KBE CB
Colonel, The Royal Irish Regiment

In 1816 Ensign John Shipp joined the 87th Regiment (later the Royal Irish Fusiliers) just in time to take part in the campaign against the Gurkhas in Nepal. He was an experienced 31 year old soldier who at the end of the hard fought campaign wrote:

> I must confess I do love to be on duty on any kind of service with the Irish. There is a promptness to obey, a hilarity, a cheerful obedience, and a willingness to act, which I have rarely met with in any other body of men; but whether in this particular case, those qualifications had been instilled into them by the rigid discipline of the corps, I know not …, but I have observed … in that corps (I mean the 87th Irish Regiment) a degree of liberality amongst the men I have never seen in any other corps – a willingness to share the crust and drop … with their comrades, an indescribable cheerfulness in obliging and accommodating each other, and an anxiety to serve each other, and to hide each other's faults. In that corps there was a unity I have never seen in any other; and as for the fighting, they were the very devils.

In March 2009 when the honours and awards for Afghanistan were published in which the Regiment were well represented The Sun newspaper carried a banner headline:

"THE PLUCK OF THE IRISH"

This account of the part the Royal Irish Regiment played in the Afghanistan campaign in 2008/2009 reflects in detail the characteristics which John Shipp so accurately noted and the courage which The Sun so clearly recognised. These are the enduring traits of our regiment and all those Irish regiments which we honour as our forefathers. They do not exist because of some natural right. They exist because we strive to achieve the highest level of professionalism in all we do. We recognise the need to trust each other and in the bleakest moments to be confident of success. We cherish our history and our traditions but do not allow them to be a barrier to change and evolution.

Richard Doherty has skilfully caught the difficulties and dangers of the Afghan operation. He, too, has captured the flavour of service in the Royal Irish Regiment when faced with its most demanding fighting since Korea. It is an inspiring tale.

Faugh-a-Ballagh

Introduction

This is the story of a remarkable unit doing a remarkable job. Training soldiers of a foreign army, with a radically different culture and traditions, as well as a language barrier, is no easy task. To perform that task in the front line in a harsh environment and with a dedicated enemy attacking at every opportunity and from any direction makes the task all the more difficult. In other times and other places, it is a task assigned to special forces, men such as the Army's Special Air Service Regiment or their US equivalents. Operation HERRICK, the British contribution to the international effort in Afghanistan has seen that task given to infantry battalions, who have discharged it with credit. During HERRICK VIII, in 2008, the Royal Irish Battlegroup undertook the role and carried it out so well that three of the soldiers involved in training, or mentoring, the Afghan National Army earned the Conspicuous Gallantry Cross, the first time that any unit has received three of Britain's second highest gallantry decorations in one tour of duty.

The account that follows is the story of the Royal Irish in Afghanistan, a compelling story of professionalism, empathy with the Afghans, humour typical of the Irish soldier, and raw courage. These men, and women, were from both the Regular and Territorial Armies, and from both sides of the Irish border, and all carried out their duties to the highest standards, following in a long tradition of service that marks the Irish soldier out as a unique figure. And for those who are not Irish by birth, their service in the Regiment makes them Irish by adoption, whether from Fiji, South Africa, Scotland or England.

In St Mary's Churchyard, Cloughcor, four miles north of Strabane in County Tyrone, rest many of my predecessors. Some lie below a headstone erected by Sergeant John Doherty of the 87th Royal Irish Fusiliers. Thus my family has an association with The Royal Irish Regiment that dates back to the late-nineteenth century. John Doherty was my late father's great-uncle and my father, J J Doherty, followed him into the ranks of the Royal Irish Fusiliers; too old to be an infantryman in 1939, J J spent the war with the Royal Artillery in North Africa, The Sudan and Italy. One of my father's uncles, Hugh Sweeney, served in the Connaught Rangers before and during the Great War and another, Denis Sweeney, in the Royal Navy during the Great War and the Merchant Navy in the Second World War. It was, therefore, a labour of love for me to research and write this book and to see that the spirit of the Irish regiments is as strong today as ever.

It may be too soon for this book to be described as a history of the Afghan conflict but it is to be hoped that, in the future, it will contribute towards an objective history of NATO involvement in that campaign and show clearly the involvement of the Royal Irish in Helmand in 2008.

Richard Doherty
Co. Londonderry
St Patrick's Day, 2009

Chapter One

In the Heart of Asia

Afghanistan is a country apart. Although the modern state of Afghanistan was founded by Ahmad Shah Durrani, the 'Father of Afghanistan', as recently as 1747, the country was home to some of the earliest farming settlements in the world, while the noun Afghan has been in use for over a millennium. Its strategic location within Asia – the country's national anthem describes it as the 'heart of Asia' – means that it has provided a crossroads between various civilizations; this, in turn, has led to Afghanistan being fought over for centuries. The country's immediate neighbours include Iran, Turkmenistan, Uzbekistan, Tajikistan, China and Pakistan. Other regional neighbours include Kazakhstan, Kyrgyzstan, Mongolia, Russia and India, emphasizing the diversity of influences on Afghan history.

A further reflection of that diversity is to be found in the many ethnic groups in the country. The largest is Pashtun, or Pathan, said by many to be synonymous with Afghan, with more than four of every ten Afghans claiming such ethnicity. In fact, the Pashtuns can claim to be the largest such 'family' grouping in the world; they also claim descent from Qais, a friend of the Prophet Mohammed, with the two dominant Pashtun tribes, Ghilzai and Abdal, tracing their lines back to the sons of Qais. Tajiks, with slightly over a quarter of the population, come next, followed by Hazaras, many of whom can claim direct descent from Genghis Khan, and Uzbeks, at 9 per cent each, with Aimaks (4 per cent), Turkmen (3 per cent) and Baluchis (2 per cent), while other smaller groupings contribute the final 4 per cent.

Afghanistan has seen the armies of Alexander the Great of Macedon and of Genghis Khan of Mongolia while, in the nineteenth century, the country became a buffer in the 'great game' between Britain and Tsarist Russia. It remained under nominal British control until 1919 when, with the end of the third Anglo-Afghan War, Afghanistan became fully independent under King Amanullah Khan. One legacy of British influence was the Durand Line, which divided ethnic Pashtun territories and remained a source of friction between Afghanistan and British India and, after 1947, Pakistan. This friction, dubbed the 'Pashtunistan debate', continues today with twice as many Pashtuns on the Pakistan side of the border, a border that they do not acknowledge.

However, for a time Afghanistan dropped out of the international picture as it enjoyed a lengthy period of relative stability during the reign of King Zahir Shah from 1933 until 1973. Towards the end of that era, Afghanistan even found itself the destination for the 'beautiful people', the hippies of the flower power generation of the 1960s, many of whom travelled there in their iconic Volkswagen camper vans. However, Zahir Shah's reign was brought to an end by his brother in law, Mohammed Daoud Khan, who deposed his king in a bloodless coup in 1973 to become Afghanistan's first president, declaring the country a republic. Five years later, Daoud Khan's government killed Mir Akbar Khyber, also known as Kaibar, a prominent member of the People's Democratic Party of Afghanistan (PDPA), and the days of relative peace were all but over. Leaders of the PDPA were imprisoned, leading the party to conclude that Daoud Khan intended to kill them all. As a result, those PDPA leaders who escaped imprisonment set about organizing a rebellion through their military wing.

Led by Hafizullah Amin, Nur Mohammad Taraki and Babrak Karmal, the PDPA-led rebellion was known as the Great *Saur*, or April, Revolution. Mohammad Daoud Khan and his family were killed and a new government was formed with Taraki as president, prime minister and general secretary of the PDPA. On 1 May the country became the Democratic Republic of Afghanistan, a clear sign that the new regime in Kabul favoured the Soviet Union. Soon after this, Soviet military advisers arrived. On Soviet advice, Taraki shared the ministries in his avowedly communist government between members of the two factions of the PDPA, *Khalq* (Masses) and *Parcham* (Flag). Included in the government's agenda were religious freedom, land reforms and greater rights for females, with women being able to enter political life. While some welcomed these changes, especially in cities and major towns, the majority of people in rural areas rejected them and preferred a traditional Islamic lifestyle with its restrictions on females and on many other aspects of everyday life.

Such tensions caught the eye of the United States where the Carter administration saw an opportunity to use Afghanistan against the USSR in a twentieth century version of the great game. With the Soviets pouring aid into Afghanistan, Carter allowed the Central Intelligence Agency to start covert propaganda operations against the Afghan government. This was to be achieved by providing funds to anti-government forces, generally known as '*Mujahideen*', a loose coalition of traditionalist Islamic groups with a common theological standpoint. President Carter's National Security Adviser, Zbigniew Brzezinski, suggested that the outcome of this action might be Soviet intervention in Afghanistan and the policy continued in spite of the 1978 Soviet–Afghan Treaty of Friendship, Cooperation and Good Neighbourliness. Brzezinski believed that Afghanistan could become the USSR's equivalent of Vietnam.

In March 1979 Taraki was succeeded as prime minister by Hafizullah Amin who also became vice president of the Supreme Defence Council; he retained the rank of field marshal in the army. Although Taraki remained as president, a figurehead position, and head of the army, he was deposed six months later by Amin who then had him murdered by a palace guard. Then, on Christmas Eve, the Soviet Fortieth Army intervened in Afghanistan, ostensibly to support the *Parcham* faction, long favoured by the Soviets and controlled to some extent by Soviet intelligence. To justify their invasion Moscow cited the Treaty of Friendship, Cooperation and Good Neighbourliness and claimed that they had been invited in by the Afghan government. More than 100,000 Soviet troops invaded the country, supported by as many again. On completion of their mission, it was stated, they would withdraw. Welcomed by the *Parcham* faction, the invasion led to the installation of Babrak Karmal as president; Amin was murdered with his wife, seven children, a nephew and twenty aides. Amin had been of the *Khalq* faction and the KGB believed that he had come under American influence.

During the period of Soviet occupation, resistance was led by the Mujahideen, who received support from the United States, Pakistan and the People's Republic of China. The bitter war between the Russians and the Mujahideen led to great disruption in Afghanistan with several million civilians fleeing the country while at least a million Afghans died. According to official Soviet figures, almost 15,000 Soviet troops were killed in the war but the true figure may be twice that. Afghan resistance was fierce, as may be gleaned from even the lowest estimate of Soviet deaths, but the Soviets left even more Afghans dead in their wake. Not surprisingly, any Soviet soldier unfortunate enough to be captured by the Mujahideen suffered a prolonged and painful death. For centuries the Afghans played a game called *buzkashi*, which is closely related to polo and in which the 'ball' was the body of an enemy. In recent history, a freshly-slaughtered, decapitated goat was used instead but, during the Soviet era, there was at least one instance of reversion to tradition with a Soviet soldier being used as the ball – and the man was still alive when the game started. This cruelty towards enemies was nothing new, as British soldiers had learned during the nineteenth century's two Afghan wars, a cruelty summed up by Kipling when he wrote:

> When you're wounded and left on Afghanistan's plains,
> And the women come out to cut up what remains,
> Jest roll to your rifle and blow out your brains
> An' go to your Gawd like a soldier.

Allied to the brutality of the war, which the Red Army had never been equipped or trained to fight, international pressure mounted for a Soviet withdrawal and, almost ten years after the invasion, their forces began to quit Afghanistan. The Americans saw this as a psychological victory; it was perceived as part of the overall western victory that saw the Soviet Union collapse. By mid–February 1989 Soviet withdrawal was complete. Before the end of the year the USSR was dying.

Although their forces had left Afghanistan, the Soviet government still backed President Najibullah's regime but that support ceased in 1992 when the new government in Moscow declined to sell petroleum products to Kabul. Najibullah's fall came quickly thereafter as a coup organized by Ahmed Shah Massoud, the 'Lion of Panjshir', and Abdul Rashid Dostum took control in Kabul and established an interim Islamic Jihad Council. That council paved the way for a new regime, with Professor Burhanuddin Rabbani as president. Rabbani set about suppressing dissent but failed to eliminate the Pashtun leader Gulbuddin Hekmatyar, who set up Hezb-e-Islami, through which he received substantial aid from both the USA and Pakistan.

Western nations showed no real interest in Afghanistan after the Soviet withdrawal, thereby losing the opportunity to influence events in the country. Little effort was made by western governments to assist in rebuilding the country after the ravages of war. Instead, Afghanistan was allowed to become destabilized, which led to many more Afghans fleeing the country. Having played a pivotal role in evicting the Soviets, the Mujahideen coalition crumbled as its leaders started fighting each other and warlords gained control in many areas. Vicious fighting among those warlords left many dead, with over 10,000 perishing in the capital, Kabul, alone in 1994. But a more cohesive force was also developing in the form of the Taliban (seekers of truth), an Islamic fundamentalist organization, which took control of Kabul in 1996 to establish the Islamic Emirate of Afghanistan. The Taliban controlled almost all of Afghanistan by 2000. Taliban follow a strict code of Wahhibism, as practised by Osama bin Laden, whereas most Afghans belong to the non-hierarchical Hanafi school of Sunni Islam, which has no centralized authority.

Taliban rule meant the denial of many freedoms for Afghan citizens with women forbidden to work and girls denied the right to education. Although women were still permitted to work in healthcare, there would be no new female doctors and nurses in future as the laws on education were enforced. Male doctors were not allowed to see women in a state of undress, or to touch them, unless a chaperone was present so that, effectively, women ceased to have access to proper medical care. Afghans with communist sympathies were persecuted and a very hard line was taken with any lawbreaker. No distinction was made between moral law and civil law, as a result of which adulterers could be put to death and thieves could have their right hands hacked off. An Islamic dress code was enforced for both sexes; men had to grow beards and shun western clothing. Televisions were banned as were other forms of entertainment including, famously, kite flying.

The Taliban also moved to eliminate opium production in the country, seeing the drug in the same light as alcohol, which was also banned. Then followed a remarkable *volte face* as the new rulers realized that much money could be made from the opium trade and decided to allow the cultivation of poppies for this purpose. Not only had they come to see that this was an easier option for farmers than growing fruit, but it also kept the powerful and influential truck driver lobby on their side while providing funds for their *jihad*, or holy war. (Since Afghanistan is one of the few countries without a rail network, lorry drivers are a very important part of the national infrastructure and have an almost Mafia-style organization.) Thus the Taliban anti-drug officials claimed a new rationale for opium production: since the drug was not used in Afghanistan but only by infidels in the corrupt west, it was not immoral to produce it. By 2000, when they controlled most of Afghanistan, the Taliban had another rethink and once more banned the production of opium. This had two immediate effects: it increased the value of the opium that the Taliban had stored, while gaining much sympathy, goodwill, and cash aid from across the world. The vicious trade went on, with the former Soviet states providing routes to the new markets of Russia.

When al Qaeda (the base) terrorists attacked targets in New York and Virginia on 11 September 2001, focusing US attention on al Qaeda training camps in Afghanistan, the US government authorized Operation ENDURING FREEDOM to wipe out those camps. (The operation was initially dubbed INFINITE JUSTICE by the Bush administration, a title that was changed with alacrity when clerics pointed out that only God can deliver infinite justice and the title was, therefore, an affront to the beliefs of Muslims everywhere.) When the Afghan government, led by Mullah Omar, rebuffed US demands that al Qaeda's leader, Osama bin Laden, and several of his lieutenants be handed over to the Americans, it led to a US threat to topple the Taliban regime. Before long the Americans were making good their threat, supporting the anti-Taliban Northern Alliance, a Mujahideen militia accorded recognition by the United Nations as the legitimate government of Afghanistan. Among the leaders of the Northern Alliance – the United Islamic Front for the Salvation of Afghanistan – were Massoud, who was assassinated by two al Qaeda members disguised as cameramen, and Dostum while Rabbani was its political leader. The Alliance, a coalition of Hazaras, Tajiks and Uzbeks, controlled many northern provinces, thus giving it the popular name by which it became known.

American support for the Northern Alliance included sending specialist teams of US Special Forces, and CIA members, to Afghanistan. At the same time, US air power was deployed to strike at Taliban and al Qaeda targets, with aircraft ranging from the mighty Cold War Boeing B-52 Stratofortresses, Rockwell B-1B Lancers and Northrop B-2 Spirits to carrier-based Grumman F-14 Tomcats and Boeing F/A-18 Hornets striking at camps and other targets. In addition, Tomahawk cruise missiles were launched from US and Royal Navy warships. (US aircraft had struck at suspected al Qaeda training camps in Afghanistan in 1998 following terrorist attacks on US embassies in Africa.) With American support, and much sympathy from

Afghans, the Northern Alliance captured Kabul and overthrew the Taliban regime. Many local warlords switched their allegiance from Taliban to Northern Alliance as the campaign progressed. Western ground forces, including American, British, Canadian, Norwegian and Australian, continued the land battle against the Taliban and the search for al Qaeda and its elusive leader, Osama bin Laden.

While the military campaign was underway a political initiative was also being pursued, with Afghan exiles and former Mujahideen leaders gathering in Bonn in Germany in December 2001 where they agreed on a plan that would lead to a new democratic government for Afghanistan. An Afghan Interim Authority was established with Hamid Karzai as its chairman. Karzai, from the southern city of Kandahar, is a Pashtun from the same Durrani tribe as the former Afghan royal family. In 2002 a *Loya Jirga*, or council of elders, from across Afghanistan selected Karzai as his country's interim president. There followed a constitutional *Loya Jirga* in 2003 which drafted a new constitution that was ratified in January 2004. Ten months later a national election led to Karzai becoming President of the Islamic Republic of Afghanistan. In September 2005, elections were held for the National Assembly which met for the first time in December. This was the first such assembly elected by universal suffrage in free elections since 1973 and the results mirrored the degree of democracy accorded the people of Afghanistan with many women elected.

Operation ENDURING FREEDOM continued as a joint US/Afghan operation, but other western nations were to become involved as an International Security Assistance Force (ISAF) was established under United Nations Security Council Resolution 1386 on 20 December 2001; this was one of the outcomes of the Bonn Agreement. Eighteen countries agreed to contribute to ISAF, which was expected to increase to about 5,000 personnel. The initial ISAF mandate was restricted to securing Kabul and its immediate hinterland, thereby allowing the establishment of the interim authority free from interference from the Taliban, al Qaeda or any warlords sympathetic to either organization.

ISAF remained restricted to the Kabul area for almost two years with the newly-created Afghan National Army (ANA) responsible for security throughout the rest of the country. However, in October 2003, the Security Council voted to extend ISAF's role; UN members followed this by agreeing to deploy troops to Afghanistan. Among the first so to do was the German government but the Canadians, already ISAF members, declared that their troops would not operate outside Kabul. By now, ISAF was under operational command of the North Atlantic Treaty Organization (NATO).

The initial ISAF headquarters was based on HQ 3rd (UK) Mechanised Division with a brigade of three battlegroups operating in Kabul as the Kabul Multinational Brigade. As well as ISAF HQ under Major General John McColl, the UK also provided the brigade HQ and an infantry battalion. With expansion of its role, not only did national contingents of troops arrive in the country, but ISAF also took command of Provincial Reconstruction Teams (PRTs), which were intended to improve security and allow reconstruction to begin in the country's provinces, of which there are thirty-four. The United Kingdom was among the lead nations in this scheme and was responsible for Mazar-e-Sharif PRT in Balkh, in the north of the country, before handing this province over to Sweden in March 2006 and assuming responsibility for Helmand province in the south with the PRT at Lashkar Gah. A second UK-led PRT in Meymaneh, also in the north, was transferred to Norwegian control in September 2005.

With expansion of ISAF continuing, and the emphasis on reconstruction, the UK deployed HQ Allied Rapid Reaction Corps (ARRC) to Kabul to lead ISAF for nine months from May 2006, during which time the force expanded into southern and eastern Afghanistan. In these areas the task facing them was an even greater challenge. In the south, sixteen nations assigned a total of 18,000 troops with Britain, the United States, Canada and The Netherlands leading PRTs in Helmand, Zabol, Kandahar and Oruzgan provinces. Additional forces for these regions came from Denmark, Estonia, Australia, Lithuania, Poland, the Czech Republic, Bulgaria, France, Slovakia, Singapore, Georgia and Romania. By the end of 2006 ISAF was operational across all Afghanistan for the first time with about 10,000 Coalition troops, mainly from the USA, coming under its command to increase troop numbers to 31,000.

The British contribution to ISAF also increased with John Reid, then Defence Secretary, announcing on 26 January 2006 that 3,300 UK military personnel would deploy to Helmand for at least three years; British forces already in the country would hand over their existing PRT areas to Sweden and Norway as noted already. Reid also commented that the UK force might quit Afghanistan at the end of three years 'without having fired a shot'. Initially, the expanded British deployment was to be led by HQ 16 Air Assault Brigade. It was under 16 Air Assault Brigade that the Royal Irish reinforced 3 Para Battlegroup with 112 men in 2006 on Operation HERRICK IV. Since then Britain's contribution has increased to over 7,000 personnel in southern Afghanistan. Deployment of UK forces to Afghanistan has, since 2004, been designated Operation HERRICK. The earlier deployments were known as Operations VERITAS, which included Task Force JACANA, and FINGAL, the British leadership of, and contribution to, ISAF in Kabul. Since its initial deployment in Helmand the British contingent, which is rotated on a six-monthly cycle, has carried out many operations, ranging from small-scale actions to much larger ones, all of them designed to improve security in the province. The overall aim is to increase the size of the secure area, thereby enabling development and reconstruction to take place, while allowing indigenous forces to assume the lead in security operations, thus giving local people greater confidence in their government and more hope for a stable future.

However, this aim has to be achieved in the face of harsh and determined opposition, represented by the Taliban. So who or what are the Taliban?

We have already seen that the name Taliban means seekers of truth, or teacher in a religious context. The truth that they seek is rooted in Islam and those who do not seek the truth, who are not of the faith, are classed as infidels. Islam, as practised by the Taliban, is a fundamentalist faith, an area in which it has parallels in the western world with certain fundamentalist Christian groups. However, the Taliban see no common ground with Christian fundamentalists, nor would the reverse be the case. They are opposed to the modern, western way of life, which they view as corrupt and corrupting of young people, and they also believe that they have a duty from Allah to spread the message of Islam across the world. None of these beliefs are in any way threatening but they assume a threatening nature when those professing them consider that they are entitled to use violence, even extreme violence, to spread their message. Thus the destruction of the World Trade Centre in New York would have been welcomed and applauded by Taliban members. Their views are held with the rigidity that characterizes fanatics and their armed campaign in Afghanistan illustrates clearly their fanaticism.

When John Reid announced that British troops would go to Helmand, he expressed an aspiration that their role would not be chasing the Taliban through the mountains as well as his hope that they would return from Afghanistan in three years without having fired a shot. He reckoned without the Taliban, who went on the offensive against British troops in Helmand and ensured that millions of shots would be fired. Initial Taliban opposition usually took the form of attacks using small arms, machine guns, mortars, rocket propelled grenades (RPGs) and Chinese 107mm rockets. The Russian AK47 assault rifle is their favourite weapon while their machine guns are also, usually, the products of Russian factories. These include the 7.62mm weapon and the brutal Dushka, a Soviet DShK 12.7mm heavy machine gun originally designed as an anti-aircraft weapon, that will shred a human body and tear through brick and concrete as well as light armour. During Operation HERRICK VI in 2006, early Taliban attacks were made by large groups of fighters, numbering between fifty and 100 men. Later attacks were generally made by small groups of men, and the Taliban also began developing what the Army termed 'shoot and scoot' attacks, in which a few men would fire a handful of shots and withdraw quickly, sometimes using a motorbike in both attack and withdrawal.

Taliban training was generally basic. This showed in their lack of tactical skills although it was noticeable that they learned something about tactics from British troops. In his book *Into The Killing Zone*, Sean Rayment notes that, having watched British troops operating, the Taliban began working in ten-man groups, usually 'commanded and coordinated by a senior, experienced Taliban fighter'. However, as they were suffering heavy casualties, they adopted another tactic, the use of the improvized explosive device, IED, which soon proved its effectiveness against coalition forces. Those Royal Irish soldiers who served on both HERRICK IV and

HERRICK VIII commented that the IED was almost non-existent in the earlier tour but dominated HERRICK VIII.

The Taliban, sometimes known as Terry Taliban to the British soldier, has another tactical advantage: he has no fear of death. With no body armour, no combat helmets, in sandalled feet and flowing robes, these men are prepared to take on the best trained and equipped soldiers in the world. To them death in battle against the infidel guarantees entry into paradise, an attitude almost totally alien to a modern western mind.

It was against this background and to face this foe that the Royal Irish Battlegroup deployed to Afghanistan and Helmand province on Operation HERRICK VIII in March 2008.

Chapter Two

Destination Helmand

Helmand lies in the south-west of Afghanistan and its southern border abuts the Pakistani province of Baluchistan. Geographically, Helmand is about half the size of England although its population, at 740,000, is not much greater than that of County Antrim. The province is divided by the Helmand river, at some 715 miles the longest in Afghanistan, which rises in the Hindu Kush mountains to the north and eventually flows into Lake Hamun, close to the Afghan-Iran border. Throughout the year, this river presents a significant obstacle. Along it may be found towns and villages, while its waters nourish the Green Zone, which is fed by irrigation canals from the river, the three principal such waterways being the Boghra, Shamalan and Darweshan. It is this irrigation system, the product of an American aid programme in the 1960s and 1970s, that prevents the province reverting to its natural desert state. The Helmand river also provides the energy for a hydroelectric scheme at Kajaki where a dam harnesses that energy and converts it into electricity for much of southern Afghanistan while its tributary, the Arghandab, powers another hydro-electric dam near Kandahar. Further development of the Kajaki hydro-electric scheme was planned and its implementation would draw soldiers of the Royal Irish Battlegroup into a major operation.

About 46,000 people, some six per cent of Helmand's population, live in the provincial capital of Lashkar Gah, a name derived from the Persian for 'army barracks'; the site of the town was once the barracks for soldiers protecting the Ghaznavid nobility in their winter capital of Bost. Lashkar Gah is located between the Helmand river and its tributary, the Arghandab. Bost is now the site of an airfield with a gravel runway. There are few tarmac roads in Helmand, other than Highway 1, the main highway in Afghanistan although there are roads from Lashkar Gah to Kandahar, Herat and Zaranj. Highway 1, built with US aid, is virtually an orbital road around the country. Afghanistan has no railways, the only attempt to build one foundering with its German operator in the 1920s.

In the south of Helmand, miles of flat desert come to an end against a mountain range that lies along the border with Pakistan – and which shows the folly of the Durand Line – while, in the north, are to be found the towns of Sangin, Musa Qaleh,

Nowzad and Kajaki, all names that would become familiar to the soldiers of the Royal Irish during their time in the province.

This is a harsh land, a fact underlined by the range of temperatures to be found there. In the winter the thermometer can drop to as low as minus 15 degrees C while summer months see the mercury rise to almost 50 degrees C. There can also be wide variations between day and night-time temperatures. Not since the Second World War have British soldiers been on extended operational duties in such a climate, although today's soldiers have the benefit of much better equipment and logistical support than was the case with their forebears. Interestingly, one of those pieces of equipment is Osprey body armour, which has saved many lives – some examples of which will be encountered in this story – but risk assessments by health and safety advisors suggest that, due to its weight, the armour should not be worn for more than four hours when the temperature is in the 40s. Commanders and soldiers have a more pragmatic approach to 'risk assessment', summed up in the words 'would you want to be hit by a 7.62mm round when not wearing Osprey?'. The answer to that question is a resounding 'no'.

Of Helmand, former Prime Minister Tony Blair said that 'This piece of desert … in the middle of Afghanistan, in the middle of nowhere … is where the future of world security in the early twenty-first century is going to be played out'. And in spring 2008 the men and women of the Royal Irish Regiment Battlegroup became part of the playing out.

The Battlegroup was built around 1st Battalion The Royal Irish Regiment, which is part of 16 Air Assault Brigade. This brigade had deployed to Afghanistan before in Operation HERRICK IV from May to November 2006, an operation in which a company from 1st Royal Irish strengthened 3rd Parachute Regiment. (During HERRICK IV the Royal Irish operated as three platoons within Para companies rather than as a discrete company; this led to the Regiment receiving less credit than was its due for the work of Ranger, Somme and Barrosa Platoons.) For HERRICK VIII, the brigade included, in addition to the Royal Irish Battlegroup, a reconnaissance squadron of the Household Cavalry Regiment; two battalion battlegroups of the Royal Regiment of Scotland – the Royal Highland Fusiliers, the regiment's 2nd Battalion, and the Argyll and Sutherland Highlanders, the 5th Battalion – two battalion battlegroups of the Parachute Regiment – 2nd and 3rd Battalions – with 7th (Parachute) Regiment Royal Horse Artillery; 23rd (Air Assault) Regiment, Royal Engineers; 13th (Air Assault) Support Regiment and 6th Supply Regiment, Royal Logistic Corps; 16th Close Support Medical Regiment, Royal Army Medical Corps; and 7th Battalion, Royal Electrical and Mechanical Engineers. The Brigade's artillery also included a battery from 32nd Regiment with UAVs (unmanned aerial vehicles) and a troop from 176 (Abu Klea) Battery of 39th Regiment with Guided Multiple Launch Rocket System (GMLRS) equipments. Also under command of 16 Air Assault Brigade HQ was 216 Signal Squadron, Royal Corps of Signals; the Pathfinder Platoon; 156 Provost Company, Royal Military Police and further elements of the Royal Armoured Corps, Royal Artillery, Royal Engineers, Royal Corps of Signals, Royal Logistic Corps and Army Air Corps. Elements of three Fleet Air Arm squadrons – Nos 845, 846 and 847 Naval Air Squadrons – were also in support as part of the Joint Helicopter Force structure.

Preparation for deployment to Afghanistan began long before the Battlegroup left Britain for Kandahar. The Commanding Officer, Lieutenant Colonel Ed Freely, conducted his earliest command reconnaissance to Helmand in September 2007 to shape the preparatory training and plan the development of his Battlegroup. He was able to identify the strengths and weaknesses of the fledgling Afghan National Army and meet the senior officers with whom he would be working. Extensive training for deployment took place both in the United Kingdom and in Kenya where, in temperatures similar to those of Afghanistan, the Royal Irish prepared for all that the terrain and the Taliban could engage them with. Lieutenant (now Captain) Paddy Bury, from County Wicklow, described some of the training in Kenya.

> As temperatures touched 50 degrees Celsius in the mid-day sun, Ranger Company, 1st Battalion, The Royal Irish Regiment, prepared to make their final assault. As 7 Platoon moved through a myriad of dried up riverbeds towards our line of departure, all eyes were focused on the granite mountain that towered over the surrounding plateau of bush. There could be no doubt as to where our objective was. It was the steepest, rockiest feature for miles around. And 7 Platoon would have to shake out and assault straight up it. As our mortars crashed onto the hill we waited nervously in the wadi for the command to attack. Our combat uniforms stuck tight to us, soaked through with sweat and sealed heat from our body armour. Up to 30 kilos of water, ammunition, radios, gun sights, spare barrels, med kits, cleaning kits and rations hung defying gravity from our shoulders. And that was light. We had already tabbed through the night and over a mountain to drop off heavy ammunition to the machine guns that would fire us in on the attack. The mortars lifted. The platoon let out a collective groan as calf muscles strained to pull each soldier to his feet. Like staggering drunks 7 Platoon swayed into position. Bound by bound the sections moved forward to close with the enemy…

The training in Kenya took place between September and November 2007 under the banner of Exercise GRAND PRIX. Strictly speaking, this Overseas Training Exercise (OTX) in Kenya was not an element of the Battalion's preparation for Afghanistan but the culmination of its Adaptive Foundation (AF) training to confirm its conventional skills at war fighting in any war, rather than being specific to

Afghanistan. Nonetheless, courtesy of HQ 16 Air Assault Brigade, there was a mission-specific Full Spectrum Operations element that, although it might have been presented as a surprise to the Royal Irish left them unfazed; the Battlegroup adapted in their customary manner.

With 900 personnel in the Royal Irish Battlegroup, this was the largest British training exercise ever undertaken in Kenya. It was also notable for two firsts: use of the Army's new Bowman radio system, and deployment of the RAF's new AgustaWestland Merlin medium-lift helicopters in support of the Battlegroup, although Merlins had yet to deploy to Afghanistan. Two Merlins operated with two Westland Lynx helicopters at various stages of the exercise. Thanks to a generous 50,000kg airfreight allowance – no economy fares here – the Battlegroup was able to take out its full complement of Bowman radios.

Kenya, with its varied topography, its heat and environmental conditions, was an excellent preparation ground for Helmand. During Exercise GRAND PRIX, the Battlegroup was able to develop live-fire battle skills and joint effects employment. Company groups conducted all-arms exercises with each company rotating its personnel through a programme of live firing, patrolling and air assault training. Mortars and machine guns, together with the 105mm light guns of C Battery, 3rd Regiment Royal Horse Artillery (3 RHA), enriched the live-firing training and ensured highly realistic joint fires at company level. C Battery 3 RHA was also to provide the Battery Commander, Major Richard Clements, for the Royal Irish Battlegroup in Kenya; and Major Clements' C Battery gunners provided the nucleus for the Combat Support structure that was to be so important in Helmand. There was also considerable manoeuvre training, all of which culminated in two Battlegroup combined-arms live-fire exercises. These exercises were extremely demanding but proved that the Battlegroup was more than capable of the task it would face in Helmand. A CALFEX, or combined arms live firing exercise, was the penultimate element of the Battlegroup's training and was conducted in the Kamanga mountains. During this phase Merlins and Lynxes moved men and equipment about as necessary, with the Lynxes also evacuating casualties back to the Battlegroup base at Forward Operating Base Masterson, named for the Faugh sergeant who, at Barrosa in 1811, seized the first French Eagle to be captured in battle by a British unit.

It is worth recording the Operations Officer's summary of the finale of this element of the exercise, an attack on the Ol Kanjao feature. The Permanent Range Team and the Royal Engineers had 'spared no effort in producing the final four kilometres of extensive positions not to mention the depth training camp a further two kilometres beyond, for 1 R IRISH to assault'. Captain Lee Shannahan went on to note that

16 Brigade had openly tried to break 1 R IRISH and they had come close. Every man was thoroughly exhausted as we approached the final objective sixteen hours after starting the twenty-six kilometre insertion march. As I sat alongside the CO we launched A Coy into the enemy training camp. Major Shirley (OC A Coy) let his dogs off the lead and our spirits soared. A Company burst into life. Many battle cries were shouted, mostly unrepeatable but all synonymous with our Regimental motto. They cleared the final position as if it was their first. Deputy Commander 16 Brigade turned to me and asked if I thought 1 R IRISH could manage another mission. Of course I accepted on behalf of 1 R IRISH.

Such exercises are never without danger and all armies suffer casualties during them, not only from live firing but also from other causes including vehicle collisions, environmental factors and misunderstandings. For 1st Royal Irish, one of the most serious casualties was caused by a snake. This was not just any snake but a Black Mamba, the longest snake in Africa. A tree snake, the Black Mamba moves extremely fast and has exceptionally dangerous venom that can be fatal for humans since it attacks both the central nervous system and the heart. The victim of this Black Mamba was Ranger Flynn, who had been targeted and bitten by the snake, which held on to inject its venom. However, Captain Mike Stacey, the Regimental Medical Officer (RMO), saved Flynn's life by his skilful treatment and the unfortunate Ranger was evacuated from the approach to the Engwaki feature for further treatment. Another casualty that might have proved fatal also occurred near the Engwaki feature. Navigating in darkness, with neither artificial light nor moonlight to illuminate the route, the Regimental Sergeant Major, WO1 Jon Miller, plummeted fifteen feet into a dried-up riverbed. Subsequently, he described how he felt a sensation of weightlessness during his brief freefall. Although Captain Stacey was keen to evacuate him for treatment, the RSM insisted on remaining with the Battlegroup; even RMOs hesitate to give orders to RSMs. As it turned out, WO1 Miller's injuries were more serious than he believed and it took some time to reach full recovery. Another Ranger is unlikely ever to forget his close encounter with a very large member of the feline family. Ranger Devine was carrying out a close target reconnaissance and had decided that he needed a different viewpoint from which to acquire more information on his target. To do so, he began turning slowly, as he had been trained to do, only to find himself looking into the eyes of a leopard. Whether *Panthera pardus* was more surprised than Ranger Devine we shall never know but he, or she, did have faster reactions, hooking off Devine's kneepad and bolting away into the darkness.

With Exercise GRAND PRIX complete, there was an opportunity for adventurous training and some safaris were also organized. This element of the Kenya experience was not to be enjoyed by the Battlegroup Headquarters planning team, which had to return quickly to Britain for Operation HERRICK brigade briefings and planning sessions at Colchester. This emphasized the frenetic pace of events for the command team, who had also squeezed in a reconnaissance trip to Helmand before the deployment to Kenya.

In England the Battlegroup trained in Norfolk and on Salisbury Plain and conducted live firing at Warcop, Lydd and Hythe. Once again Paddy Bury recorded the scene.

> Ranger Company is manning a Forward Operating Base (FOB). Of the 120 or so men in the Company, thirty are manning the sangars that defend the base. Another thirty are out on patrol in the area, supported by dog handlers, interpreters, Forward Air Controllers, snipers and even Apache attack helicopters. The operations room buzzes as the boss and his second-in-command monitor the patrol's progress. A Quick Reaction Force sits ready to deploy at a moment's notice should anything happen. Another lucky thirty men are asleep in the shelters.
>
> Then there is the distinctive crump of a mortar firing. The alarm wails. Everyone runs for cover, bar those in the sangars, who can only hope for the best. Huge blasts sound within the camp, then silence. Someone screams. The stretcher party is confronted with an amputee squirming in his own blood. There is shock on their faces, but they quickly get stuck in. Over the net the patrol says it has been fired on by the enemy and is looking to call in the Apaches. Suddenly a sangar reports a suspect vehicle moving at speed toward his location ...

Reading the two accounts from Paddy Bury in retrospect, one might assume that they describe events that occurred in Afghanistan. However, Ranger Company's attack took place in Kenya in October 2007 while the events in the FOB happened in Norfolk during a British winter. Both formed part of the pre-operational training and development which the Royal Irish Battlegroup underwent before deployment. The training was meant to prepare them for Afghanistan; it was testing to ensure that they were ready to go. Exercises presented Ranger Company with highly realistic conditions, the most authentic that were possible in training, which included the many adrenalin-spiking stresses and frictions of war as it was being fought in Afghanistan.

Another critical element of such training, which included all the attachments to Ranger Company for the tour, was that it allowed everyone to familiarize themselves with the way their comrades operated, as well as the specialities they brought to the company. Ranger Company, based on C Company, was to operate with the 2nd Parachute Regiment Battlegroup (Battlegroup North) in Sangin and so had personnel attached from the other companies of the 1st Battalion, including 6 Platoon of B Company. In the build up, there was a marked increase in the tempo and intensity of the training; new tactics and techniques had to be learnt and absorbed; information on Afghanistan and its people had to be digested; and there were also courses to be completed. Following tried and tested military tradition, personnel from units that had just returned from Afghanistan passed on the lessons that they had learned the hard way. The Army has long described such teaching as passing on 'lessons learnt'. Those who had 'done the business' most recently were placed ideally to pass on advice; and such advice was sought keenly and listened to just as keenly. Needless to say, best wishes for a safe tour were also passed on.

While Ranger Company, under Major Graham Shannon of C Company, augmented to about 130–140 strong (its total strength as a company group, with personnel attached from other units and the United States Marine Corps, was 180), was to operate with Battlegroup North, the bulk of the Battalion was to undertake an operational mentoring and liaison role with the Afghan National Army (ANA). To do so the Battalion provided Operational Mentoring and Liaison Teams (OMLTs – pronounced 'omlettes'). Specifically, it was to perform this task with 3 Brigade of 205 Corps, or 3/205 Brigade; the ANA does not have a divisional level of command. In this role the Battalion would be broken down into small teams working with ANA units and sub-units. In every case, Royal Irish personnel would be charged with raising the operational standards of their Afghan colleagues, a task that fell on the shoulders of officers and NCOs from the Commanding Officer down to corporals. In some cases, as we shall see, even the most junior of soldiers would perform the mentoring role with considerable distinction and élan. 'Mentoring and liaison' may sound a safe option to civilian ears but the critical word in the Battlegroup's role was 'operational'; they would perform their task with Afghan units in the field in the toughest part of Afghanistan. At all times the tension between the immediate tactical imperative and the training role required considerable skill and diplomacy to resolve. There is also little doubt that this task was the most important element of 16 Air Assault Brigade's mission in Helmand. This was no easy option.

Before the pre-deployment training began, the Battalion's order of battle (orbat) had to be revised to deal with this role. OML Teams, built around the cores of A, B and D Companies, were formed while a fourth OMLT was created from attached elements of the Battlegroup with a core of Royal Irish personnel cementing the team together. As already noted, C Company formed the basis of the Ranger Company Group with Battlegroup North. Interestingly, Battlegroup North, the 2 Para Battlegroup, was commanded by a former Royal Irish officer, Lieutenant Colonel Joe O'Sullivan. (During the course of HERRICK VIII, a further battlegroup would be created, based on 2nd Princess of Wales's Royal Regiment, 2 PWRR, the theatre reserve battalion which had been based at Dhekelia in Cyprus; this was Battlegroup South, commanded by Lieutenant Colonel Doug Chalmers, CO of 2 PWRR, but, as with Joe O'Sullivan, commissioned and 'brought up' in the Royal Irish.)

The mentoring and liaison role means that the story of the Royal Irish in Afghanistan is not a straightforward one to narrate but, nonetheless, it illustrates the professionalism of the Battlegroup and its willingness to learn, adapt and teach while fighting an implacable foe. Put simply, the senior officers of the Royal Irish worked 'one up' with Afghan officers: Lieutenant Colonel Ed Freely worked with Brigadier General Mohaiyodin, the brigade commander, while his company commanders worked with ANA *Kandak*, or battalion, commanders, platoon commanders with company commanders, and so on down the chain of command. By its nature, the OMLT role meant that the soldiers of the Royal Irish Battlegroup would work in small multiples of six or eight men alongside companies of Afghan soldiers. Interpreters, mostly civilians, ensured that the language barrier was overcome as far as possible, thereby reducing one obvious friction of such operations. The language barrier itself was doubly complex: the language of the Afghan Army and officer corps was Dari, whereas that of Helmand and the south was Pashtun. Thus the officers of the Royal Irish did their best to get to grips with the fundamentals and key phrases of Dari that would assist relationship building, whilst also learning basic greetings in the local vernacular. Soldiers were swift to learn simple phrases in Pashtun, such as 'good day' 'thank you' and 'stop'. Apparently, the Afghan Army mastered the Royal Irish Gaelic motto 'Faugh a Ballagh!' (Clear the Way!) with similar ease.

That the OMLT role fell on the Royal Irish is a remarkable tribute to the Battalion. Perhaps the fact that the Commander of 16 Air Assault Brigade, Brigadier Mark Carleton Smith, was an Irish Guardsman, and therefore familiar with the nature of the Irish soldier, had a part to play in that choice, but the fact remains that the Brigade Commander considered that, of the units under his command, the Royal Irish were best suited to a task that involved working so closely with soldiers whose language, culture and traditions were so different, not to say alien. Not only had he identified the special character of the Battalion, but he had also seen for himself the quality of its junior commanders. Another critical aspect is that 1st Royal Irish is one of the Army's most operationally mature battalions. Since 1998 there has been only one year – 2007 – when the Battalion has not deployed in whole or in part on an operation; these have included Northern Ireland, Kosovo and Sierra Leone as well as Operation TELIC, the invasion of Iraq, in 2003.

For the mentoring teams, pre-tour training also had to take account of their role. One Warrant Officer commented that this 'was not all relevant to the OMLT role but it's difficult to see how this could be represented in training'. However, he added, 1st Grenadier Guards, the OMLT Battlegroup on HERRICK VI, 'gave us a good heads up' while soldiers from 2nd Yorkshire Regiment, back in the UK on R&R (rest and recuperation; a period of leave during an operation) from HERRICK VII, visited the Battalion to help build up the current picture; this was the unit that the Battalion would relieve in Afghanistan. Part of the OMLT role was to convert the Afghan National Army from its old Soviet-era weaponry to new equipment, which entailed Royal Irish personnel who would conduct the conversion training becoming familiar with weapons that were not in the Battalion's inventory. These included the Kalashnikov AK47 rifle, which the Afghans were phasing out, and the American M16 rifle, which was replacing the AK47, although it was found that the Afghans preferred the Russian weapon. Soldiers had to become familiar with weapons from a 9mm pistol to the Javelin anti-armour missile; Warrant Officer 2 Billy Roy recalled that his team later fired five Javelin missiles from Patrol Base Attal. One OMLT Lance Corporal agreed that while the training was not always relevant, it was a help. Philosophically, he commented that the training was 'a work in progress' that prepared everyone for Afghanistan but 'learning on the move was critical'. Another soldier said of the training's value that 'You can't hit the nail on the head until you actually do it'. Acting as Afghan soldiers during the training in England were men of the Royal Gurkha Rifles who 'were very good'; their primary role was to duplicate the problems arising from issuing orders via interpreters to indigenous forces.

An important ingredient in the Battalion's preparations was the successful visit of Brigadier General Mohaiyodin and two of his Kandak Commanders to Tern Hill in February. This achieved an early and positive start to the vital business of relationship building between Ed Freely and his Afghan counterpart. Adapting the Afghan code of *pashtunwali*, Freely hosted the Afghan commander in his home with his family, as a demonstration of hospitality, trust and openness. Pashtunwali is a traditional code that predates Islam and has its roots in Mosaic law: its central elements are independence, justice, self-respect, hospitality, love, forgiveness and tolerance for all, but especially for guests or strangers. By inviting Mohaiyodin to be a guest in his own home, Freely had bound the Afghan commander to the Royal Irish. During his visit General Mohaiyodin spoke eloquently and with passion about his country and the importance of the Royal Irish mission to groupings of the Battalion's officers, senior ranks and indeed the families. This was a key element in forging early bonds that would withstand the inevitable tensions that would develop over the forthcoming eight months. No one expected the training programme to produce all the answers but it did provide excellent preparation which, allied with the Battalion's professionalism, ensured that HERRICK VIII held no real surprises for the Royal Irish.

There was a third element to Ed Freely's command: Imjin Company. With a strength of 140, Imjin Company was based on volunteers from 2nd Battalion The Royal Irish Regiment. This is the Regiment's Territorial Army (TA) battalion, based in Northern Ireland and known, until July 2007, as The Royal Irish Rangers. Some

112 soldiers of 2nd Royal Irish, under Major Mark Hudson, formed Imjin Company, which was fleshed out with a platoon from the 1st Battalion and some personnel from other units and corps. Early, and brief, mobilization of Imjin Company took place over two days at RTMC Chilwell, the reserve forces training and mobilization centre, in Nottingham. This short period was followed by months of integration and training at Tern Hill with their sister Battalion. It was a crammed period but it led to rapid integration of the TA soldiers with their Regular counterparts and, in the words of the Commanding Officer, was 'a hugely successful model of Reserve support to Regular Army operational deployments'. Relations between the 1st and 2nd Battalions were close and cooperative, in part because Ed Freely had been a fellow subaltern with the Commanding Officer of the 2nd Battalion, Andrew Cullen, and had known him well for twenty-three years. Furthermore, Major Mark Hudson was well known to the 1st Battalion, having served alongside them previously in Iraq, and Captain Eddie McMillan, Imjin Company's second in command, had regular Royal Irish pedigree stretching back many years. This mobilization was the largest in the history of 2nd Royal Irish or their predecessors, the Royal Irish Rangers, and it saw Imjin Company provide more than 10 per cent of all mobilized personnel in the UK in 2008. For many Company members it was their second mobilization as they had served in Iraq on Operation TELIC in recent years. Imjin Company deployed a manoeuvre support platoon, two rifle platoons and a company headquarters, which included chefs, clerks, mechanics and the other specialities needed to sustain a company on active service.

The Imjin Company title reflects a battle honour earned by one of the Royal Irish Regiment's predecessors, the Royal Ulster Rifles, in 1951 during the Korean War. The title was especially apt as Afghanistan has provided the Army with its most intense fighting since Korea, the first war fought under a United Nations mandate. In Afghanistan, Imjin Company was assigned the task of force protection for Camp Bastion, the huge British logistical base in Helmand, the largest overseas military camp built by UK forces since the Second World War; it measures four miles by two miles and includes an airstrip that can take C-17s, a hospital, barrack accommodation and many other facilities, as well as the storage of the supplies needed to sustain Operation HERRICK. To Major Hudson's men fell the task of securing the main entry point into Camp Bastion, manning sangars overlooking the surrounding area and patrolling into the desert to detect and interdict would-be attackers. Imjin Company was also responsible for providing a medical emergency response task force (MERT), or Incident Reaction Team (IRT), to operate with the helicopters that would evacuate casualties. Later, as a recognition of Imjin Company's high standards and professionalism, a platoon operated from FOB Robinson and the town of Now Zad while company members also mentored ANA soldiers at FOB Keenan in the hostile Gereshk Valley.

It would be most unfair not to mention at this stage a further vital element of the Royal Irish team, the Rear Party. Not everyone in the Battalion went to Afghanistan and some seventy personnel remained at Tern Hill under the command of Major Ricky Kane, ably assisted by the Rear Operations Sergeant Major, WO2 Denis Haighton. Lieutenant Jim Berry, a casualty of Operation HERRICK IV, was the Rear Party Adjutant and maintained the Regimental website – a vital communications tool. Included in the Rear Party was the Welfare Officer, Captain Nigel Bradley QGM, whose task was to work with the families of soldiers in Afghanistan on everyday problems that might arise through separation, and to deal with the trauma caused by casualties. No one expected the Battalion to be immune from casualties and the Rear Party was ready to process casualties, work with their families and outside agencies, and ensure that as much as possible of the burden of such circumstances would be lifted from families. Captain Bradley and his assistant, Colour Sergeant O'Neil, continued supporting those injured on the previous Afghanistan tour whilst covering the current operation. Of course, they would also have the unenviable job of performing the same role in the case of fatalities. Finally, the Rear Party dealt with individual reinforcements passing through the system to join the Battalion in Afghanistan, as well as recruits wanting to join the Royal Irish; and the fact that the Battalion was deployed operationally meant an increase in numbers wishing to enlist.

As with all things in the military life, there were some uncertainties that led to rumours. Again, this is an age-old reality with only the place names changing: Ranger Company was going to Musa Qaleh. No, it was Sangin. It was going on the twelfth. No, it was the first. And someone always knew someone who knew someone who knew. But, eventually, orders were confirmed, although, of course, these could change if the situation on the ground in Afghanistan changed. Nonetheless, this was the time to increase insurance cover. With wills being completed, the reality of what lay ahead became clear: this was something from which some might not return alive. That was emphasized when boxes had to be ticked showing whether a soldier wanted a military or civilian funeral in the event that he, or she, did not survive. With training and preparation complete, a last spell of leave was spent with families. Then it was back to Clive Barracks where, on 5 March, the Battalion celebrated Barrosa Day with the Barrosa Dinner, recalling the 1811 Battle of Barrosa, near Cadiz in Spain, where one of the Regiment's predecessor units, the 2nd/87th (Prince of Wales's) Irish Regiment had taken the first French Eagle ever captured in battle by a British regiment. Since the 87th became the Royal Irish Fusiliers, the Faughs from their regimental battle cry *Faugh A Ballagh!*, or Clear The Way!, it was appropriate that the last Commanding Officer of 1st Royal Irish Fusiliers, Major General The O'Morchoe, should be the guest of honour. General The O'Morchoe had also commanded 16 Brigade and thus his attendance was doubly appropriate. Incidentally, the Royal Irish Fusiliers' battle cry and motto is, as reported before, the motto of the Royal Irish.

Then it was time for Saint Patrick's Day. The Saint's memory was celebrated in traditional style by the officers, men and families of 1st Royal Irish Regiment albeit a day early on the 16th, but Irish regiments have a special dispensation to change the date of the celebrations to meet operational requirements. The Colonel of the Regiment, Lieutenant General Sir Philip Trousdell, inspected five guards of Royal Irish soldiers in desert combats, ready to deploy. Afterwards, Fiona Freely, the Commanding Officer's wife, presented shamrock to the Officers and Warrant Officers. Thus the day also served as a poignant farewell parade and party for the families of those deploying to Afghanistan. Some personnel had already left a week before as the Advance Party and were en route to Asia as the echoes of the celebration of Barrosa Day were dying quietly. After the Paddy's Day party, it was time for RAF Brize Norton and the air bridge to Kandahar.

Chapter Three

So this is Helmand

The Royal Air Force operates an airbridge from the UK to Afghanistan to support Operation HERRICK, which, with support for Operation TELIC in Iraq, represents the largest proportion of the RAF's overseas transport commitment. While, at first glance, the airbridge resembles the workings of a civil airline, the environment in which the RAF's strategic transport aircraft, Lockheed Tristars and McDonnell-Douglas C-17 Globemaster IIIs, work is often hostile and with no civil counterpart. Since HERRICK began in 2004, RAF aircraft have carried more than 115,000 personnel – more than the population of the city of Cambridge – to Afghanistan. Included in those figures are the personnel of the Royal Irish Battlegroup.

The flight to Afghanistan was summed up by Lieutenant Paddy Bury of Ranger Company.

The RAF Tristar jet reluctantly pulls itself into the Oxfordshire sky. On board are the men of Ranger Company, 1st Battalion the Royal Irish Regiment, bound for Afghanistan. This is a flight like no other. All those on board are wearing desert fatigues, carrying helmets and body armour. Along the side of the cabin, in rows, are the empty stretchers for returning the wounded from theatre. But spirits are high as the soldiers joke about the (lack of) quality of the in flight service. We are finally on our way and with that comes a sense of relief. Thoughts can now focus on the task in hand. Some even manage to sleep. As we approach Afghanistan the pilot warns us to don our body armour and helmets. For the final few minutes we will be in missile range of the Taliban. The plane creaks as it dives steeply toward the ground. Through the port hole I see an Apache attack helicopter hovering in the distance. And then we're down.

That the Tristar seemed reluctant to leave Brize Norton's runway may have been due to its age. The RAF's Tristar fleet was not purchased new but bought on the used market and most of the airframes are now over thirty years old; the author recalls Tristars serving the Belfast-Heathrow shuttle in the mid-1970s and some of those

British Airways machines found their way into RAF service, having been retired by their civil owners in the mid-1980s.

On the approach to Kandahar, the aircraft face the danger of missile or machine-gun attack by the Taliban. The threat from shoulder-launched surface-to-air missiles (SAMs) is taken seriously and explains the reason for donning body armour and helmets and the diving approach. Captain Markis Duggan recalled that his pilot made the announcement that 'we will shortly be landing in Kandahar. Please ensure that your seatbelts are securely fastened and your seat is in the upright position', which was not unusual until he added 'Ensure that your body armour is fitted and put your helmets on now'. When civilian guests, including journalists, travelled out to visit the Royal Irish they experienced the same procedure. The steep approach is designed to counter SAMs but it also works against machine guns and small arms since it makes it extremely difficult for any terrorist to lock on to the target. However, it is a stomach-churning experience for passengers. The presence of AgustaWestland Apache AH Mk 1 helicopters is a further deterrent to any would-be SAM- or machine-gun-armed Taliban fighter whose first round or burst of fire would draw the full horror of the Apache's nose-mounted 30mm chain gun. For that reason the Taliban call the Apache the 'mosquito', since it has a most unpleasant sting.

From the Tristars the Royal Irish disembarked at Kandahar International Airport

into a night world of kerosene fumes and flashing safety sirens that illuminate the dust clouds. It doesn't feel too hot. We move to a holding area and get our kit. The sergeants are barking commands, organizing the troops into neat formations for the helicopter ride. We wait some more and fall asleep.

Kandahar is but a waypoint from which helicopters – specifically Boeing CH-47 Chinook HC2 or HC2As of No. 1310 Flight from the RAF's 904 Expeditionary Air Wing, based at Kandahar – or Lockheed C-130 Hercules transport planes carry the soldiers to Camp Bastion, where a detachment of No. 1310 Flight is based. For Ranger Company and Paddy Bury, the onward flight to Camp Bastion was to begin in the light of a new day, their first full day 'in theatre'.

With the pale blue hue of dawn comes our first sight of Afghanistan. Rocky. Dusty. Barren. The heat begins to rise, and although it is still March, there is an ominous ferocity to the sun. It is not our friend. From over our shoulders comes the low whicka-whocka of the approaching helicopters. They touch down on the dirt pads, sending slow, enveloping tidal waves of dust toward us. Engulfed, dust pours down the back of any exposed necks, chests and into eyes. A hand signal gives us the OK to board and we move through the downdraft quickly, past the heat of the engines and into the relative quiet of the cabin. The engines' pitch roars and we watch the ground disappear. To our left huge mountain ranges can be seen. To our right, desert. Apaches buzz around like lethal hornets, ready to sting anything that has a go.

It is a relatively short trip to Camp Bastion, 'in the middle of nowhere' in Tony Blair's words. But the journey emphasizes the rugged nature of this country with its mountains and deserts and its sparse population. It also illustrates that colourful Afghan explanation for the topography of their land: God created Afghanistan from what was left over after He had created all the other countries by dumping this detritus in a part of the world that no one wanted.

As we descend I lose sight of the mountains and we become surrounded by a desert moonscape. We arrive in Camp Bastion, the headquarters of British forces in Afghanistan and the home to some 4,000 troops. It is huge. A sprawling suburb of reinforced concrete walls, HQs, accommodation blocks and vehicle parks. It is in the middle of nowhere and I wonder how far the sangars can see out to. We pack our kit for tomorrow's training, discuss how we will go about things with the Corporals and Sergeants, talk and joke with the soldiers and eventually get some sleep. During the night the continuous roar of aircraft and helicopter engines roll through the desert like a ferocious thunderstorm. We sleep fitfully.

Bastion was not the end of the journey for Ranger Company whose final destination was Sangin, some fifty miles away. But there was a short interlude of three days at Camp Bastion. Those days, the Reception, Staging and Onward Movement and Integration (RSOI) package, were full of purpose as the soldiers trained hard for the task they would undertake at Sangin.

Storming purpose built Afghan compounds. Breaking contact from ambushes. Casualty evacuations. Calling in air support. How to spot Improvised Explosive Devices in the ground. Remind and revise. Remind and revise. The adrenalin is up from the live ammunition compound clearances. We all understand that this is only one small step from the real thing. We get a little more familiar with the alien landscape. And almost as soon as it starts, our final period of training is over.

Once again it was aboard the helicopters for the flight to Sangin, the final leg of an odyssey that began half a world away. Sangin is

where Ranger Company will spend the next six months. It is a town we have heard much of in intelligence reports over the past few months, a town where men from 1 Royal Irish and indeed from my platoon, have fought and died in before. I approach with mixed emotions, my heart in my mouth and my head repeating and repeating what will happen if we land in a hot landing zone. We touch down. Into the fire...

* * *

But it will be remembered that the Advance Party of the Battlegroup had left Britain for Afghanistan after the celebration of Barrosa Day. Under Major Max Walker, second-in-command of 1st Royal Irish and Chief of Staff to the Battlegroup, the Advance Party was based in Camp Shorabak, next door to Camp Bastion, in Helmand, where they had celebrated Saint Patrick's Day as they awaited the arrival of the main body. Major Walker's team had prepared the ground for the Battlegroup's arrival and the handover, or transfer of authority, from 2nd Yorkshire Regiment, formerly the Green Howards, to the Royal Irish. The handover week was a frenetic round of briefings and visits for Lieutenant Colonel Freely and commanders at all levels. The pair of Royal Irish Quartermasters, Major Hughie Benson (QM Maint) and Captain Brian McNabb (QM Tech) immersed themselves in checking, accounting and taking responsibility for the various accounts: accommodation, stores, specialist equipments, weapons, rations, interpreters, vehicles and communications assets. Across the Battlegroup the Royal Irish team grilled their predecessors and milked them for information. Introductions to the ANA opposite numbers were a critical part of the process. Gradually, Royal Irish OMLTs were relieving their Yorkshire forebears out in the deployed areas of operation (AOs). The Commanding Officer and the RSM were whisked away to Kabul by the Commanding Officer of 2 Yorks to meet the key British members in ISAF's Chain of Command and the Embassy staff. This also afforded the Commanding Officer the opportunity to get a feel for the US CSTC-A (Combined Security Transition Command – Afghanistan) perception of how the British had been performing in the south. All was not well with the relationship and perceptions would need to be improved. CSTA-C was but one of the three chains of command to which Lieutenant Colonel Freely would have to work over the next six-plus months. CSTA-C was the American-financed and led organization driving the development and equipment programme for the creation and expansion of the Afghan National Army and Police; it would, therefore, dictate the Security Sector Reform agenda. Whilst in Kabul they also visited the Kabul Military Training Centre (KMTC). Both organizations would have significant influence on how the Battlegroup operated over the coming six months as the HQ OMLT would report to CSTC-A via one chain of command while it would receive some of the 1,200 trained soldiers, who were passing out from KMTC every fortnight. During those early days, the mentors from Battlegroup HQ had spent increasing amounts of time with their Afghan counterparts as they built up positive working relationships, a process lubricated by 'endless cups of chai' that helped 'ease the natural frustrations caused by cultural and language barriers'. Chai – or tea, a word corrupted to 'char' by generations of British soldiers in India – would play an important part in the relationships between Royal Irish soldiers and their Afghan comrades, and with civilians in their operational areas.

With a better picture of the current situation, and the majority of the Royal Irish in theatre, change of command, or transfer of authority, occurred on 25 March. A simple raising of the Royal Irish flag, accompanied by Sergeant Bradley on the pipes, saw the Commanding Officer shake hands with his Yorks' counterpart in front of the Battalion's sign at Camp Shorabak. With the low key ceremony complete, the Royal Irish Battlegroup soon had its feet firmly on the ground in the first of its three roles in Afghanistan – providing operational training and support to 3/205 Brigade of the Afghan National Army (ANA) across Helmand. Ranger Company were also off to Sangin for their role as part of Battlegroup North while Imjin Company was to remain at Camp Bastion with four main duties, which would be carried out on a weekly rotation.

Those duties were to:

1: provide the Helmand Reaction Force (HRF), which would be at an hour's notice to deploy anywhere in the province where it might be needed; when not being called out, the soldiers undertook fitness training, range work, weapons handling, medical and signals training.

2: guard the main entrance point to Camp Bastion by providing cover and protection for the gate as well as controlling the search bays through which civilian vehicles arriving at the camp had to pass before being cleared; this gave protection against vehicle-borne suicide bombers.

3: provide an incident reaction team (IRT) to extract casualties from any part of Helmand. The IRT had to be ready at any time to board Chinooks to pick up battlefield casualties, frequently from 'hot' landing sites, i.e., under fire from the enemy.

4: provide a quick reaction force (QRF) at Camp Bastion, the main duty of which was to perform escort duties between Camps Bastion and Shorabak. These escorts were undertaken in Snatch Land Rovers. The QRF had to be ready to respond to any situation arising outside the boundaries of either camp. QRF duty also included a further role, that of protecting the tactical landing zone (TLZ) at Bastion, when flights were due to land or take off. This role was performed in Wimiks[1], in which the soldiers deployed around the Bastion area, and during it the QRF team would spend some sixteen hours 'out on the ground'.

As the OMLT Battlegroup, the Royal Irish would be reinforced by numerous individual officers and senior non-commissioned officers from Regiments and Corps across the Army. The business of mentoring indigenous forces, particularly rank-conscious Afghans, required attention to the relationship and rank and status of mentors. Thus this particular role required much more by way of 'rank' than normally available in 1st Royal Irish. Many of the Royal Irish team were wearing rank one or, in some cases, two levels above that to which they were entitled in order to give them the right influence and authority. Probably the last occasion on which this role play was enacted had been in Austria in 1945 when, in the immediate aftermath of war, Brigadier Pat Scott, Commander 38 (Irish) Brigade, had been passed off as a major general by his corps commander for the benefit of visiting Red Army officers.

The initial phase of the Battlegroup's deployment included the training known as RSOI (Reception, Staging and Onward Integration) at Camp Shorabak. This involved briefings – including many from the outgoing Battlegroup – range packages and various drills that would be put into practice during the deployment. At the same time, the Battlegroup was taking over patrol bases, equipment, stores, accounts, jobs, computers, files and all the other paraphernalia needed to execute their task. And, of course, the various elements of the Battlegroup were finding the rhythm of life on Operation HERRICK. This period also allowed the Royal Irish command team to establish the necessary esprit de corps and mutual understanding with those who had only recently joined the Battlegroup.

During the first week there were challenges, including reminders of the ubiquitous threat. At this time, the Battlegroup HQ OMLT was getting involved with meeting and mentoring their Afghan counterparts in 3/205 Brigade HQ and finding that the Afghan brigade HQ was a much smaller organization than a British equivalent. Members of the HQ OMLT were doubled up with their Afghan counterparts: Lieutenant Colonel Freely was mentor to the brigade commander, Brigadier General Mohaiyodin, while his second-in-command, Major Max Walker, mentored the brigade executive officer, or deputy commander. This was repeated across the HQ of 3/205 Brigade although the Battlegroup Operations Officer, who had a very heavy workload, retained his own role and the mentoring of the brigade operations staff devolved on another officer, acting Major Jonathan Toomey, who was supported by US advisors from a specialist company (Military Professional Resources Incorporated or MPRI), run by former military personnel. During those early days, the CO and Battlegroup Chief of Staff, Major Max Walker, visited Kandahar and three important elements of the separate chains of command that the OMLT Battlegroup would need to satisfy. First was Regional Command (South), or RC(S), the multinational NATO two-star superior HQ that sits above the British Task Force Helmand. This strand was concerned primarily with the conduct of the counter-insurgency campaign. Second, and also based within the Kandahar HQ area, was the Afghan Regional

Security Integrated Command (South), or ARSIC(S), the regional arm of CSTC-A, which promulgated policy and monitored advances on the Security Sector Reform line of operations. Third, and perhaps most importantly for the Royal Irish, was the HQ of the Afghan 205 Corps, the superior HQ of 3/205 Brigade. As the sovereign force, this would have influence over where and how the ANA in Helmand operated. HQ 205 Corps was also based in Kandahar but a little way beyond the relative security of the vast allied Kandahar Air Base set up. It became clear rapidly to Freely and Walker that the chains of command and their associated complexity and inevitable different outlooks would present significant tensions and challenges.

The personal relationship with Commander 3/205 Brigade was critical to the progress and degree of cooperation between the Royal Irish and the ANA – indeed the relationship would naturally have an impact on the extent that the Afghan Brigade worked with or apart from the British Task Force Helmand. General Mohaiyodin Ghori was a thoroughly experienced and respected Afghan warrior. Ethnically a Tajik, whose family hailed from Ghor Province in the high mountains east of Herat, he was descended directly from the notorious warrior Ghorid dynasty which, in the twelfth century, had crossed the Khyber Pass and dominated much of what is now northern India. Mohaiyodin had an impressive track record: staff trained by the Soviets at the Frunze Academy outside Moscow, he had fought long and hard over the past twenty-eight years. An acolyte of Shah Massoud, he was fiercely anti-Taliban. He was in his third year of constant operations in Helmand, and Ed Freely was his fifth UK Battlegroup Commander mentor. Freely said this of him:

> Mohaiyodin was undoubtedly a talented, courageous and charismatic leader. I admired and respected him enormously. However, at the same time he could be mercurial and deeply frustrating. It was hard at times to follow his logic. He could at once be perceptive and analytical – and then all of a sudden make statements without any recognizable military foundation of logic. Despite his experience and stature in Helmand, he had two key weaknesses: his health and his impatience. He was extremely tired, both physically and mentally. This was understandable, bearing in mind he had been effectively at war for nearly twenty-nine years. Originally, he had been told that he would only be posted to Helmand, arguably the toughest province, for six months. His impatience made it a regular struggle to try to convince him of the merits of UK and US counter-insurgency doctrine and the need to secure the people of Helmand. Mohaiyodin's past and natural inclination was for grand, fast, brutal sweeping acts of manoeuvre, rather than committing men to numerous bases in amongst the population to develop a longer term security relationship.

Soon after the Battlegroup's arrival, OMLT 1 was established in Sangin, with the advance parties of OMLTs 2 and 4 in Musa Qaleh and Gereshk respectively. OMLT 3 remained at Shorabak training Kandak 3, which had just returned there; part of OMLT 3 had already deployed to Kajaki. Meanwhile the CS OMLT was getting to grips with Soviet-era D30 122mm howitzers, trying to find the CS Kandak's reconnaissance element and preparing for the training of sappers. The CSS OMLT had already undertaken an eventful, but successful, resupply convoy to Musa Qaleh. All of this occurred within the first week, a busy, tiring but good seven days. Battlegroup personnel felt a buzz as they got to grips with their new roles, vehicles, equipment and the Afghan way of life.

At Shorabak, OMLT 3 was down to work immediately. Its tasks included converting Kandak 3's soldiers from the AK47 to the M16 rifle as well as training them in counter-insurgency and other skills. The Kandaks would rotate through the training programme at Shorabak and through the bases at Musa Qaleh, Gereshk and Sangin as General Mohaiyodin, determined that his men would not become rooted in any location, had adopted such a policy. Mohaiyodin's fear was that becoming too familiar with an area would lead to corruption and slackness; the OMLTs would move with their Kandaks. In addition to the four infantry OMLTs, each of about fifty men, there were also Combat Support (CS) and Combat Service Support (CSS) OMLTs, which linked up with their respective ANA Kandaks to develop their particular specializations. The CS Kandak included the brigade's supporting arms of artillery, engineer and reconnaissance, each of which was mentored, while the CSS Kandak included signals, medical support, maintenance, supply, and transport elements, with each of those also mentored. However, since the supporting arms were both poorly equipped and trained, the CS Kandak often operated in the infantry role. The CSS Kandak had an even greater problem: it was so stretched in trying to re-supply 3/205 Brigade in its various bases throughout Helmand that there was little time to conduct training. The overall effectiveness of the Kandak was reduced by its situation.

The Commanding Officer, his Second-in-Command, Major Max Walker, and Captain Lee Shannahan, the Operations Officer, were working in overdrive, attending meetings and making visits as they sought to further their understanding of the Afghan National Army's capabilities and how future operations would be conducted. They also had a visit from the Danish Battlegroup (Battlegroup Centre), who suggested joint operations.

As 16 Air Assault Brigade settled in, so too did Helmand province's new governor, Gulab Mangal. Appointed only in early-March, he was young, energetic and had a more pragmatic approach than the man he succeeded; he was also a former Taliban member. Governor Mangal's first security *Shura*, or meeting, gave him the opportunity to lay out his approach to tackling both the insurgency and the development of sound civil governance and of the economy. In the person of Mangal, and his approach to his role, many saw grounds for optimism for Helmand but it was realized that progress would be slow.

Ed Freely also had the opportunity to assess the conditions in which his soldiers would be operating and noted that 'some of the outstations are poorly served with communications facilities and are what we would term "bare bases"'. He was determined that the scale of satellite welfare phones would be increased but noted that soldiers could still use the old-fashioned system of communicating with home, the 'bluey' or airmail letter; there was also some e-mail access. In the meantime, a planned rotation of Kandaks by the ANA would bring OMLT 1 back from Sangin, where OMLT 3 would relieve it, and OMLT 4 from Gereshk, where it would be relieved by the CS OMLT, thus giving OMLTs 3 and 4 'some time in the relative luxury of Camp Shorabak'. The impending changeover of Kandaks in Sangin and Gereshk led to a busy time for many, not least the CO, the Ops Officer, Captain Shannahan, and the RSM, WO1 Jon Miller, who had their first opportunity to visit both Ranger Company and OMLT 1 in Sangin where they joined soldiers on patrol and visited the bases. The CO was pleased that the troops were settling in well and 'working hard to get to know their opposite numbers in the ANA' as well as the local area.

Of the Battlegroup's operational areas, Musa Qaleh had only recently come under coalition control, having been wrested from the Taliban by ISAF a mere five months earlier in Operation MAR KARADAD. Earlier, it had been the scene of especially vicious fighting during Operation HERRICK IV, in which soldiers of the Royal Irish distinguished themselves while serving under command of 3 Para Battlegroup. It was in Musa Qaleh that the men of Somme Platoon relieved 16 Air Assault Brigade's Pathfinders and reinforced the Danish Reconnaissance Squadron. Subsequently, when the Danes were relieved in their turn, Barrosa Platoon joined Somme and, with the addition of a company HQ element from 3 Para, formed E Company of 3 Para. In fact, 90 per cent of that company wore the green hackle and shamrock rather than the paras' maroon beret. It was in Musa Qaleh, too, that Somme Platoon lost Ranger Anare Draiva and Lance Corporal Paul Muirhead, both killed by a mortar round that landed on a sangar: Ranger Draiva died instantly while Lance Corporal Muirhead died later from his wounds. Lieutenant (now Captain) Paul Martin and six men were injured seriously when another round landed close to their position. In addition to the two deaths at Musa Qaleh, Lance Corporal Luke McCulloch died after a mortar attack on Sangin where Ranger Platoon was based.

In September–October 2006, the people of Musa Qaleh, through their elders, brokered a peace deal, which they undertook to police themselves; no Taliban would be allowed to enter the town. As their contribution to this arrangement, the British HQ agreed to withdraw troops from the town and their departure took place, by road, on 17 October. However, following the death of a Taliban leader in a USAF strike, the

Taliban returned to Musa Qaleh, retook the town and remained there at the beginning of Operation HERRICK VI in October 2007. It was planned that Musa Qaleh would be taken by NATO troops in spring 2008 with the return of 16 Air Assault Brigade but Operation MAR KARADAD was brought forward to December 2007 when, following a lengthy air bombardment, the town fell to NATO forces; Afghan soldiers were placed in the forefront of the operation so that it could be said that the ANA had retaken Musa Qaleh.

Not surprisingly, the Taliban were anxious to regain control of the town and, in the meantime, do as much as possible to disrupt the life of the area, attack coalition forces and undermine attempts to establish civil governance. Thus the coalition had a difficult task to perform and had to balance achieving and maintaining security with winning the confidence of the local people, of the new town governor, Mullah Salam, and his executive *Shura*, and kick-starting both civic development and the local economy. Assigned to garrison and protect Musa Qaleh was Kandak 2 of 3/205 Brigade of the Afghan National Army with, alongside it, a Royal Irish mentor team, OMLT 2, commanded by Major Dave Kenny who, as the key military adviser to Kandak 2's commander, was pivotal in the story of Musa Qaleh. His relationship with that commander, and with the local chief of police (ANP – Afghan National Police), Mullah Wali Koka, as well as the National Directorate of Security (NDS), the Afghan intelligence service, was critical to the smooth working of the alliance and the development of governance in Musa Qaleh. Almost as soon as it arrived in Musa Qaleh, OMLT 1 was busily cultivating relationships with the ANA and the local population, which was helped by the fact that a number of planned Taliban attacks were thwarted while some enemy equipment was uncovered and several arrests were made. These, and other arrests, were made by the Afghan National Police as ISAF troops had no power of arrest.

Major Kenny developed very quickly and effectively a productive and consensual forum of Afghan security force officers. Based firmly on mutual trust, commitment and shared interest in the future of Afghanistan, through this forum, and his own commitment, Kenny created a co-ordinated joint Afghan security effect that met the UK Battlegroup Commander's intent. Working tirelessly to increase his understanding of the complexities of local Afghan matters, he forged strong and valuable bonds with Salam, who could be a very difficult individual, without deviating from the highest standards of integrity. He made certain that the many agencies involved, including the Police Mentor Team, SAS, stability advisers and CIMIC (civil and military cooperation), were incorporated fully into an Afghan-led area of operations, which developed around the Musa Qaleh District Centre (DC).

Simultaneously, Kenny led his fifty-strong mentor team with courage, skill and grip. Having a perfect grasp of the situation and threat, as well as of the tactical approach necessary, he led through clear example, repeatedly placing himself in harm's way in an area with a constant and varied range of Taliban threats. When the Battlegroup North West commander, the commanding officer of the Argyll and Sutherland Highlanders (5 Scots), was shot and evacuated in June, Kenny had to develop in his successor the required understanding of the extremely complex local picture. He did so with an determined approach that was co-operative, modest and pragmatic – a variation on his mentoring of the Afghan Kandak commander.

Having identified the Taliban intent at an early stage, Kenny skilfully located, established and manned new patrol bases to provide a more effective security perimeter that allowed his mentors, alongside ANA and ANP, to fight hard from firm bases. This allowed them to interdict and rebuff the Taliban's ambitions to overthrow the DC. He also led numerous offensives to obtain intelligence and defeat Taliban advances and, by July, it was acknowledged widely that the Taliban had suffered such losses that they had to revise their intentions. General Mohaiyodin singled out Kenny for praise, noting the success of his methods, which had demonstrated empathy with local people as well as being industrious and effective. Meanwhile there were noticeable results in the town where he had prevented any IEDs being placed for months, thus allowing the bazaar to thrive and new shops to open. The local population became more and more receptive to the ANA and the idea of governance. Overall, a new and heightened degree of security was achieved by the OMLT in Musa Qaleh.

Major Kenny's accurate analyses, his moral courage and his strong leadership ensured that his troops suffered no casualties at all while ensuring an impressive security development in Musa Qaleh alongside a similar development in the Afghan security forces. His work supported the executive *Shura* in line with 16 Air Assault Brigade's main effort and his contribution to Musa Qaleh, the development of the ANA and the advancement of the campaign aims were all remarkable. Kenny and OMLT 2 remained in Musa Qaleh until the end of June when they returned with Kandak 2 to Shorabak. His achievements at Musa Qaleh have since been recognized with the Queen's Commendation for Valuable Service.

Throughout Helmand the atmosphere was comparatively calm as the Battlegroup settled in but a surge in Taliban activity was expected as the winter lull came to an end. A clear example of what could be expected in the days, weeks and months ahead was experienced on 25 March, the very day on which the Royal Irish took over from the Yorks. That day, OMLT 1 personnel were working with a patrol of ANA near Barakzai village in Sangin district; this was a routine security patrol in the most difficult of the districts in Helmand. As the patrol moved along the south bank of a canal, Taliban fighters opened fire from the north. The engagement was vicious and at close quarters. So intensive was the initial enemy fire that the patrol was pinned down. Moreover, the difficult ground did not lend itself to launching a quick attack that might have wrested the initiative from the Taliban. However, one Royal Irish soldier, Ranger Garry Bradshaw, the junior mentor team member, proved to be a man with initiative and calm courage.

Bradshaw was armed with a light support weapon (LSW), a 5.56mm automatic weapon based on the Army's standard SA80 rifle but with a longer and heavier barrel that permits a higher muzzle velocity and greater accuracy than the rifle. Although in the centre of the enemy's killing zone, the place of greatest danger in an ambush area, Ranger Bradshaw remained calm and returned fire immediately on the Taliban. This had the desired effect of forcing some of them to keep their heads down and cease firing, which allowed Bradshaw to identify some of their firing positions. Maintaining fire, he moved to a rallying point where he was able to indicate clearly to his patrol commander the locations of several enemy targets. This allowed an extraction plan to be made quickly.

However, when it became obvious to him that this rallying point did not provide a position from which the enemy fire could be suppressed effectively, Bradshaw moved to a fresh position and from there was able to put down accurate fire on the Taliban positions. Throughout the firefight, he continued to give his patrol commander clear target indications and to suppress the Taliban with accurate and effective fire. His actions allowed the patrol to move into positions from which it could quit the ambush position with no casualties. Ranger Bradshaw's calm and self-assured actions demonstrated not only an innate talent for leadership but also the skills of a junior NCO, although he was a comparatively junior soldier of three years' experience. The ANA soldiers recognized this leadership talent by following Bradshaw's example. He had also shown excellent situational awareness together with observation and communication skills that contributed greatly to the positive outcome of the engagement.

Bradshaw's immediate reaction to the ambush illustrated the quality of the training he had received, especially as he had been under heavy and effective fire from a determined enemy. However, it was as the battle developed that the young Ranger showed his real mettle, through his quite remarkable initiative and calm courage in a very dangerous and kaleidoscopic action. In particular, his move from cover to seek a better position from which to support the patrol's extraction was an excellent example of courage and clear-thinking initiative. His patrol commander believed that Ranger Bradshaw's actions were critical to the safe extraction of the patrol and were an inspiration to his comrades, both British and ANA.

Thus OMLT 1 had their brutal introduction to war in Helmand. Although the tempo of Taliban operations was still slow, it was less than two weeks before the team sustained its first serious casualty. The injured man was the OMLT commander, Major Simon Shirley, OC A Company, who was injured severely by an improvised explosive device (IED), an augury of a major feature of the Battlegroup's time in Afghanistan. Major Shirley was also the Battlegroup's first severe casualty. He became the victim of an IED on 6 April as a two-vehicle patrol from Sangin DC travelled north on Route 611. The first vehicle, in which he was travelling, was blown up by a concealed IED, Shirley was injured seriously and the others in the vehicle, including his driver, Corporal Chris Rushton, were incapacitated by the shock of the blast. It was at this stage that another young soldier of A Company demonstrated his personal courage and initiative.

Lance Corporal Alister Sutherland, a Glaswegian, was a patrol medic travelling in the second vehicle. While his comrades debussed immediately to protect the wounded, Sutherland dashed forward to treat them. He did so in spite of the obvious threat from the Taliban and the fact that there may have been either a secondary device or an attack with machine guns or rocket-propelled grenades (RPGs). In treating the casualties, Sutherland had to work alone as his comrades, of whom there were only two, were providing protection for the scene. There were three injured men but he ascertained quickly that two had sustained wounds that were comparatively minor whereas Major Shirley's injuries were life threatening and so he concentrated his attention and skills on the OMLT commander. His initial treatment of the wounded major ensured that Simon Shirley did not die from loss of blood and that he could be evacuated by the Medical Emergency Response Team to Camp Bastion for surgery. The surgeons at Bastion later praised the care that Sutherland had given his OC, commenting that his immediate, skilful efforts, ignoring the dangers of the situation, were instrumental in saving Simon Shirley's life.

Nor was this the sole occasion on which Al Sutherland demonstrated his medical skills. He did so on several occasions during the tour while, at the same time, playing a full part in mentoring ANA soldiers in infantry skills; Sutherland was also a GPMG gunner. In fact, it was less than a day before his medical skills were again in demand. On 7 April, as an Afghan police patrol prepared to leave Sangin DC, there was an explosion that left two policemen dead and six more injured seriously. The blast had not been a result of enemy action, as thought initially, but the detonation of an RPG round carried by a patrol member. Since there were other RPGs lying around, there was a real danger of further detonations but, ignoring this risk, Sutherland began triage on the casualties. He gave them immediate treatment that allowed them to be moved to a makeshift operating theatre, improvized from the Medical Centre, the TV room and the landing area. There his treatment ensured that the men did not lose their lives in spite of the severity of their injuries: two lost two limbs each and three lost single limbs. All were evacuated for treatment and surgery at Camp Bastion. Until then Sutherland monitored their conditions and re-assured them. During this entire emergency, Lance Corporal Sutherland had taken control of the vicinity and delegated tasks to those around him. At all times he remained calm and cool and his behaviour provided inspiring leadership while his medical skills were outstanding.

These three incidents, occurring within a two-week period, were a portent of things to come and a clear indication of the type of warfare the Battlegroup would experience in Helmand. This was not conventional war fighting, with clearly defined front lines on either side, but what is known as asymmetric, or 360-degree, warfare where enemy attacks can come from any direction at any time. With its lengthy experience in Northern Ireland, the British Army is prepared better than most for this style of fighting; but the Taliban present a much more ferocious and determined foe than the various factions of republican terrorists ever did. Even throughout the winter lull there had been a constant but low level of violence and this was now expected to increase.

On the Chinook that evacuated the casualties of that explosion on 7 April was Lance Corporal Haggan of Imjin Company. He had taken over as Incident Response Team watchkeeper only three hours before being alerted by the Bastion Force Protection watchkeeper of a major incident at Sangin. Alerting his section commander, Haggan also immediately instructed IRT section to move to the Chinook flight line as he appreciated the seriousness of the incident. When the Chinook's loadmaster learned that there had been a so far unexplained explosion in Sangin DC, he decided that he could take only one member of the IRT as he would be carrying an EOD team as well as the MERT members. At this point, Haggan volunteered to be the IRT member on the flight as he was a qualified team medic and had the electronic countermeasures (ECM) kit and UGL to protect the Chinook.

When the helicopter landed at Sangin, Haggan debussed first and, with no enemy threat, reverted to assisting the medical team as they loaded the casualties on to the Chinook. When the machine left Sangin he helped to treat three of the ANA soldiers and continued doing so as the helicopter flew on towards Bastion, devoting considerable attention to the worst injured of the three men. This unfortunate had suffered severe leg injuries and Haggan applied a dressing to the remains of his left leg, and a tourniquet close to the wound, as well as cleaning the area so that fresh bleeding might be seen more readily. The most responsive of the three injured was checked by him for breathing and pulse on a regular basis while he prepared a full report on the treatment of the third man who had sustained major wounds to his groin and thigh. When the Chinook touched down at Bastion, Lance Corporal Haggan completed his report for the medical team, changed his bloodstained clothing for a fresh uniform and went back to his duties as IRT watchkeeper.

The Commanding Officer, Operations Officer and the RSM had been visiting and getting a feel for Sangin during the period of concentrated attacks detailed above. It was apparent that the Taliban were having significant success in restricting the freedom of manoeuvre of the ANA, OMLT and the ISAF Company, now Ranger Company of 2 Para Battlegroup. The base locations that the Royal Irish had inherited in and around Sangin were too linear and focused primarily on Route 611, which traversed north–south through the centre of Sangin, parallel to the Helmand River. The Royal Irish command team also observed that patrols were reactive, predictable and insufficiently innovative; the ANA were generating too low a presence for their manpower. Complacency had set in during the winter tour, and the Taliban seemed to have the initiative. Much more could be done and would be done to disrupt and dominate the enemy's control of movement in and around Sangin. It was vital to wrest the initiative from the Taliban in order to provide a real sense of security in the area. That said, the situation was complex, as was discovered by the Commanding Officer in early April:

> I was stuck on the edge of a cordon in Sangin as an IED was being dealt with and I began to engage some local elderly gentlemen in conversation. Asking one particular man what he did for a living he responded that he was a farmer. I asked him, 'what do you farm?' He was very open and responded that he farmed opium for heroin. I asked him what he thought about the Taliban. Again, he was very open, saying he disliked the Taliban. However, he would certainly join and support them if his agricultural produce was threatened or destroyed by the authorities.

The pattern of violence was not constant across Helmand. Each area of operations (AO) showed variations with localized violence tending to reflect the local situation. In Sangin there was an especial problem. The area had not seen much development, many of the population had left and not returned, and the Taliban were harassing movement with IEDs and ambushes. Indeed, the IEDs were often linked with ambushes, the detonation of a device leading to an attack with small arms, including machine guns, and RPGs, on a shocked patrol or convoy. Likewise, Musa Qaleh endured a high level of Taliban activity, especially since the area had been wrested from their control by the Allies a mere five months earlier. In the Musa Qaleh AO the B Company-based OMLT 2 set about strenuous efforts to deny the Taliban the facility of approaching the town with malevolent intent through the establishment of an additional satellite base to close the gap in the defences through which the enemy had been infiltrating. Taliban activity in the general area remained high with engagements on a daily basis as Kandak 2 and Major Dave Kenny's OMLT 2 kept the opposition at arms length so that daily life could continue in Musa Qaleh with efforts to increase the quality of that life for its residents.

OMLT 1 was relieved in Sangin by OMLT 3, which had completed the conversion training of Kandak 3 to the American M16 rifle. OMLT 3 left Shorabak with a protective and logistics convoy bound for Sangin, whence OMLT 1 would move to Shorabak to take their part in the training cycle. In the meantime, OMLT 4 had also begun M16 conversion training for Kandak 4, although a team from the OMLT, under Captain Doug Beattie MC, had flown up to Kajaki to assume protection duties on the northern flank.

In both Sangin and Musa Qaleh, the security problem was relatively straightforward: the Taliban presented the principal threat to stability. By contrast, Gereshk was a different picture. Due largely to geography, this is Helmand's most prosperous town: it is situated on Highway 1 and on the Helmand river. While the Taliban were involved in violence in the Gereshk area, there were numerous other elements in the mix, including local warlords, straightforward criminals, corrupt local officials – including civil servants and policemen – and local militias. Many of these groups sought control over, or pecuniary gain from, both the illegal drugs and the transport trades. (For this reason, NATO tends to classify all opposing groups in Afghanistan as anti–coalition militias (ACM).) As an opium provider, Helmand beats Myanmar by a considerable length, and there is much money to be gained from this trade in human misery. It was some time before a clear picture emerged of the varied problems and the key elements in those problems in Gereshk.

Helmand is the world's single largest source of opium and it was almost time for the poppy harvest as the Royal Irish Battlegroup settled in. In mid–April the harvest began. In the two to three weeks before harvesting, the local population made every effort to ensure that as much water as possible was directed to the fields so that they might have the best yield. This season also sees migrant workers from across Afghanistan and Pakistan arrive to assist in the harvest. Thus only low-level enemy violence was anticipated during the month as the Taliban realized that aggression in the area would affect the prosperity of local farmers which would not inspire those farmers to support the Taliban; rather it would make them more likely to look to the Afghan government and their allies for support and defence. Furthermore, the Taliban continued profiting from the poppy harvest as they 'taxed' many growers. Even so, there was a Taliban ambush on a Warrior column of The Highlanders (4 Scots) on 1 April in the Musa Qaleh AO. This led to a saturation of the ground by troops followed by a Taliban attack on Patrol Base South-West in an effort to draw off some of those troops. Of this battle we shall see more. In general, however, the month was quiet in comparison to what lay ahead.

'Quiet' does not mean that April passed without incident and that Taliban attack on the Highlanders' Warrior column provided but one example of an incident that helped to define the relative nature of that adjective. A mentor team of eight had deployed in two vehicles at 9.00am that day and, for most of the day, had been giving flank protection to the Warrior column as it fought the Taliban in Musa Qaleh wadi. As darkness approached, the patrol was returning to base, some 1.5 kilometres from Musa Qaleh; the patrol base (PB) was home to forty ANA soldiers as well as the mentor team.

Both vehicles had come to a halt in the PB and the team were debussing when some twenty Taliban, in two groups, attacked with small arms fire. The last man to debus from the second vehicle was Ranger William Galloway, an eighteen-year-old soldier who had been in the Regiment only since the previous December. Galloway was still wearing his full protective Osprey kit in which he had been clad for nine hours. As the attack was launched, Galloway reacted immediately and, without awaiting orders, raced to an exposed rooftop position inside the compound. As the first British soldier in position, he took command of eight Afghan soldiers whom he rallied to join him on the rooftop. He disposed these men into tactical positions from which they put down suppressing fire on both attacking groups.

Although the base sustained four direct hits from RPGs, as well as many strikes from small arms fire, Galloway did not quit his exposed position but continued engaging the enemy with no apparent concern for his own safety. In spite of being a junior soldier, one of the most junior in the Battlegroup in fact, his behaviour was that of a veteran. He gave accurate target indications to his fellow soldiers and used tracer to assist the other members of his team to assume combat positions and engage the attackers with effective fire. When the Taliban closed on the PB, they moved out of Galloway's arcs of fire and, knowing that he could no longer provide suppressive fire, he left his position, once again showing remarkable initiative for such an inexperienced and young soldier. With darkness falling, he collected night vision aids for his team, even though he had to expose himself to enemy fire while so doing. His disregard for his own safety was demonstrated most clearly when he moved to the southernmost rooftop to take night vision aids to his comrades. Here he had to climb a ladder in full view of the enemy who were still advancing.

Galloway's comrades were now engaging their foe with heavy machine-gun fire, the effectiveness of which increased considerably with the arrival of the night vision aids. The Taliban closed to within 250 metres of the PB before being forced to withdraw and there can be little doubt that Ranger Galloway's swift and courageous response to the initial contact played a significant part in their defeat. Galloway's behaviour, his quick reactions, his anticipation of events, his devotion to duty and to his comrades, allied with his bravery in the face of a most determined foe, acted as an inspiration to the ANA soldiers in the base.

Later in the month there was another major engagement, this time in the Gereshk area. The ANA unit deployed to Gereshk was the Combat Support Kandak, operating, as it often did, in the infantry role and it faced a dangerous and complex threat, as already noted. One of the many dangers in the area was that presented by IEDs while there were also suicide bombers. IEDs were especially prevalent along Highway 1 east of Gereshk. This meant that, before convoys could travel along it, the road had to be swept for such devices. A number of critical resupply convoys were scheduled to travel via Gereshk on 17 April, using Highway 1, in preparation for which the road was checked by a UAV (unmanned aerial vehicle).

This survey identified an individual near a culvert whose behaviour suggested that an IED might have been planted. As a result, and just over three hours before midnight, the Joint District Co-ordination Centre OMLT was ordered to check if an IED had been planted at the culvert. Since time was short, specialist search teams could not be deployed and two ANA companies with mentors were assigned. Neither the ANA Kandak nor the mentors had been long in Gereshk and they had carried out only daylight patrols. Moreover, they had not received training in the specialist search role, which they were going to have to conduct in darkness without any prior rehearsal.

Following a swift planning conference, orders were issued and both companies and their mentors deployed at 10.25pm. With an outer cordon in place to the west of the culvert, WO2 Bruce Dickson, of 23rd Engineer Regiment and mentor Company Sergeant Major (CSM) to the ANA CS Kandak, led fifteen ANA soldiers towards some buildings south of the culvert. His task was complicated by several factors: the ANA lacked night vision equipment, had no radio communications and no experience of night-time operations, and nor was an interpreter available.

To reduce the threat to others, Dickson decided to search the buildings alone. When he had completed this search, he moved on to clear an 80-metre-long lane towards the culvert from an area that was known to be safe. This hazardous and exhausting procedure demanded both great patience and courage while operating against the clock and in complete darkness. Having finished his initial sweep with a metal detector and basic search techniques, WO2 Dickson carried out a meticulous search of both ends of the culvert, which he found to be clear. However, since UAV information suggested that the grid reference originally provided may have been wrong, additional searches were necessary. Once again, Dickson worked alone, eventually searching a number of culverts along an 800-metre stretch of road. When he had completed this exhausting task, the area was declared safe five minutes after midnight. The cordon was then collapsed. Although no IEDs were uncovered, the searches confirmed that the route was safe and there is no doubting the sheer courage and cool nerve of WO2 Dickson. He was the epitome of a professional soldier that night, working, regardless of the danger to himself, in most difficult conditions to ensure the safety of others.

In late-April, Governor Gulab Mangal demonstrated his determination to improve life for the people of Helmand through a Super *Shura* held in Lashkar Gah. To this gathering the governor invited high-ranking officials from both Kabul and Kandahar and succeeded in gaining the attendance of the Minister of Defence, Mr Wardak, as well as the ISAF commander, General Dan McNeil, various senior government figures and other key officers from ISAF, the ANA and ANP. They came, at Mangal's request, to discuss how to improve the security of Helmand and its economy. Their attendance was seen as a major coup for Mangal and suggested that he had made a good impression in the highest echelons of government.

Late April also saw 16 Air Assault Brigade's commander,[2] Brigadier Mark Carleton-Smith, pay his first visit to Battlegroup HQ where he met the staff of both the Battlegroup and 3/205 Brigade. He was briefed on the situation and on the nature of the Royal Irish role. At the same time, Major Walker had produced the Battlegroup's first detailed analysis of the performance of 3/205 Brigade and its Kandaks, a document that would travel up the US chain of command until, finally, it landed on the desk of the commander-in-chief in the Oval Office of the White House.

With violence rising in May, the Battlegroup had engagements on a daily basis with the enemy while IEDs were an increasing menace. The Taliban were showing a marked preference for this weapon which came in many forms. IEDs might be detonated by pressure pad, by command wire or radio control, and could even take the form of suicide bombers, whether on foot or in a vehicle. They might be the prelude to an ambush or lurk as the unseen enemy lying in wait for as long as it took to claim an unsuspecting victim. There were many forms of IED, including 'daisy chains' where a number of devices were linked for maximum effect. A 'daisy chain' might include two or more 105mm shells that had been linked together. Any form of munition would suffice and one operation carried out by Explosive Ordnance Disposal (EOD) personnel during HERRICK VIII was a search for a bomb dropped by a USAF B-1B Lancer but which had not exploded. The search was mounted so that the weapon could be recovered or destroyed to prevent its falling into Taliban hands and becoming the core of an IED. Many IEDs showed fiendish ingenuity. One NCO recalled an IED that included a pressure cooker in which the explosive charge was surrounded by scrap metal that included gear cogs: had it exploded it might have claimed many lives but it was detected by a patrol and defused by an EOD officer.

In the centre of Helmand, on the Helmand river where Highway 1 passed over that waterway, is the town of Gereshk, the richest in the province. However, with its prosperity came a complicated security picture with threats not only from the Taliban but also from various militias and drug barons, the so-called narco-khans, while corruption in the Afghan National Police further complicated the picture. Part of the picture was a struggle between several of those groupings to control checkpoints along the main routes through Gereshk. At these checkpoints, 'taxes' were levied on those passing through with goods, especially opium. Although the exact involvement of the Taliban in this struggle was not clear, it was one where violence was no stranger; in late-April a suicide bomb attack was made on the town's main police station. Major Richard Clements commanded the CS OMLT in Gereshk and, towards the end of April, he hosted a visit from the Battlegroup HQ and General Mohaiyodin. That visit included a patrol through the desert to PB Sandford, recently taken over from the Danish Battlegroup Centre by Captain Dave Landon's team and its ANA colleagues. From Gereshk, the Commanding Officer and his team 'also ventured into the Green Zone east of the river to take in PB Barazki where Captain Russ Archer and his Sappers are mentoring ANA engineers'. Freely, Mohaiyodin and their staff also spent an evening at a *shura* with local leaders where they enjoyed a traditional Afghan floor supper.

Such was the situation in the Gereshk valley that 16 Air Assault Brigade launched Operation OQAB STERGA (Eagle's Eye) to clear an area of the valley of Taliban and bring it under coalition control. Central to the operation were 1st Royal Irish and 3/205 Brigade, which deployed OMLT 4 and Kandak 4 in the Green Zone, although this was actually in the Danish Battlegroup OA; Lieutenant Colonel Freely deployed with his Tactical HQ, some of OMLT 1 and the CSS OMLT, in addition to OMLT 4. During the planning of the operation, Major Max Walker, the second in command, Captain Lee Shannahan, the Operations Officer, Captain Tom Forrest, the Intelligence Officer (IO) and Captain Jon Toomey, the Regimental Signals Officer (RSO), had accompanied the Commanding Officer to Camp Bastion to meet the planning staff of Task Force Helmand and the other Battlegroups – the two Para Battlegroups – and finalize plans for the ANA's role in the operation. Following this, the CO and General Mohaiyodin, accompanied by RSM Jon Miller and his team, travelled to Gereshk to attend Shuras with key local leaders to outline the ANA plans for the operation. These meetings were held in a new Shura Hall, on the outskirts of Gereshk, where the group met local people, representatives of the local administration and Afghan National Police officers.

The Shuras completed, Freely and Mohaiyodin flew to Lashkar Gah to discuss their plans with the Task Force Helmand Commander. Soon after the party landed at Lashkar Gah, there was a major dust storm across Helmand and they were unable to fly back to Camp Shorabak, thus missing the ANA orders for the operation. However, the other members of the team at Shorabak were present and witnessed 3/205 Brigade's Operations Officer, Colonel Sarwar, make an impressive presentation of orders to the ANA chain of command and soldiers.

The elements from OMLT 1 and Kandak 1 involved in Operation OQAB STERGA worked with the two Para Battlegroups east and west of the Helmand river whilst the Royal Irish Battlegroup HQ OMLT co-ordinated the clearance of eight kilometres of Taliban-dominated Upper Gereshk Valley Green Zone as far north as the enemy stronghold near Shurakay. Kandak 4 and OMLT 4 deployed from Shorabak in a huge convoy en route to the Danish Forward Operating Base, Armadillo, where Major Rob Armstrong, the OMLT commander, and his team made their final preparations. Danish troops also took part in OQAB STERGA with their Leopard II tanks providing a screen and guard for the western flank of the advance. Armoured personnel carriers took troops, including an ANA mobile force, into the valley floor on D-Day, 9 May.

Once underway, Operation OQAB STERGA made good progress and developed according to plan, pushing Taliban fighters northward up the Helmand river's west bank and away from Gereshk town. Operations were conducted in temperatures that touched 45 degrees in the desert and the Green Zone and saw the ANA enter for the first time areas that had been dominated by Taliban and anti-coalition militias. Initial resistance was less than expected, which suggested that the scale of the ISAF operation had caught the enemy off-balance. There were, however, many IEDs and caches of IEDs in wadis and the desert approaches while some small arms and RPG fire was directed at the advancing forces. Although motivating the personnel of Kandak 4 created some problems for the mentors, as did co-ordinating the movement of their companies, the operation was a morale booster for the Kandak which, by 12 May, had not only exploited up the valley but had also gained some seven kilometres of ground. There was, however, a price to be paid by the ANA with two soldiers killed and six others injured in IED explosions.

Morale amongst the soldiers on the ground was high while, at Shorabak, the Operations Room staff put in long hours to ensure that those deployed received the support they needed. Men such as Captain Gordon Mahood, WO2s Robbie O'Farrell and Noel Pearson, Colour Sergeant 'Spud' McCaw and Lance Corporal Brendan Hanna performed their roles with little respite. The CSS OMLT also worked hard to support the deployment; Major Nick Brady, commanding this OMLT, was forward based in FOB Armadillo while Captain Martin Leach with his team at Shorabak made certain that there was no reduction in support to Sangin, Musa Qaleh and Gereshk.

OQAB STERGA was a long hard slog through the constant heat of mid to late May. Progress was slow through the Green Zone with the Royal Irish having to cajole and encourage the ANA to maintain the momentum of the clearance of compounds, villages, fields and orchards. The threat from IEDs was constant; the Taliban exploited the slow advance with RPG and small arms attacks, but were unable to flank the tight, broad formation as it edged north, gaining one to two kilometres per day. The whole advance and consolidation took approximately two weeks. The end result of Operation OQAB STERGA was that another area of the Gereshk valley had been cleared of Taliban; to ensure that it remained clear, a new forward operating base (FOB), called Attal, was built, from which a company of ANA with their OMLT 4 mentors would operate. A site for the base was reconnoitred and two mud-walled compounds were requisitioned to be 'hardened' by the Sappers with Hesco walls, sangars for observation and many, many sandbags to increase protection for the occupants. This new base allowed the ANA and OMLT 4 to build up a relationship with the people of the area, assuring them that their security was improved greatly by the Taliban being held to the north and that a more normal life could be enjoyed on a daily basis. Most local people were positive about the eviction of the Taliban from their immediate area but there were expressions of concern that the Taliban would carry out reprisals against those they believed had assisted the ISAF troops. The presence of the new base was an assurance for them.

At the same time, the Royal Irish Battlegroup continued overseeing the rotation of ANA Kandaks from their forward operating areas to Shorabak for M16 conversion and further individual and collective training. As a result of such rotations, some OMLTs eventually experienced action in three or even four areas. The most important factor, however, was that the ANA's professionalism was growing steadily, with a clear improvement in strength, confidence and operational capability. Of course, there would still be problems, but it must be remembered that this was a new army and the progress that it had made thus far was remarkable. To give but some examples, when the Royal Irish arrived the ANA had not been conducting joint patrols but these became a standard operating procedure during HERRICK VIII; night patrolling was also introduced by the Battlegroup. Further aspects included joint AOs with the police and other coalition elements while, as the tour progressed, the Battlegroup gradually handed over responsibility for control of weapons, ammunition and POL (petrol, oil and lubricants) to the ANA, even though this created some problems and further challenges for the mentors. Hitherto, these essentials had been under control of the OMLT Battlegroup and had been issued to Afghan units only as they were needed.

The conversion and training programme at Shorabak received a boost when, on D-Day for Operation OQAB STERGA, 9 May, General Bismillah Khan, the ANA Chief of the General Staff, visited Camp Shorabak. With the Commanding Officer in the field, Major Max Walker and the Regimental Quartermaster Sergeant, WO2 Richard Sheridan, greeted the Afghan CGS with, as Major Walker commented, Ranger Billy Bittles and his camera recording the occasion. Following a briefing by 3/205 Brigade HQ staff, General Bismillah addressed those soldiers of the brigade who were in Shorabak before moving to the ANA cookhouse where he watched the chefs prepare *nan-e-Afghani* bread, the traditional staff of life in Afghanistan. The visit was not confined to Shorabak, however, as the general then boarded a helicopter to visit forward bases at Sangin and Musa Qaleh, where he met soldiers from Kandaks 3 and 2, as well as OMLTs 3 and 2. Overall, this visit boosted morale in 3/205 Brigade and its timing, to coincide with OQAB STERGA, enhanced further the confidence of the ANA soldiers.

As we have seen already, Taliban activity increased during May as the poppy harvest was complete. There followed the wheat harvest; this brought its own problems as workers migrated across Helmand in search of employment and, since it was now the 'fighting season', there was always the possibility that Taliban fighters could be moving under the guise of migrant workers. Temperatures were also rising and soldiers were having to adapt to operations in conditions much hotter than they had experienced before, although Kenya had been good preparation.

The May offensive against the Taliban included a surge south of Musa Qaleh, which was commanded by the Commanding Officer of 23rd Special Air Service

Regiment. Included in this surge was a company of ANA soldiers with their eight-man mentor team of Royal Irish. Disrupting the Taliban and assuring the local population were among the objectives of the operation in which Afghan National Police were also involved; a Warrior company provided support. Acting second-in-command of the mentoring team with the ANA Company was Lance Corporal Jone Bruce Toge, a Fijian, who found himself in charge of the team when his commander became incapacitated. Toge is a man of great character and imposing physical appearance; at over six feet in height and built in proportion, he would put both Arnold Schwarzenegger's Terminator and Sylvester Stallone's Rambo to shame.

On 10 May the ANA Company reached the village of Deh Zohr E Sofla where it was learned that the Taliban warlord, Abdul Bari, was leading a force to the south of the village. When, at 9.00am, the ANP were engaged by Taliban, the ANA and their mentors deployed immediately in support. Having formed a firebase from which to suppress some twenty Taliban, Lance Corporal Toge's team came under heavy fire from rifles and RPGs. After an hour and a half of this engagement, Toge received orders for the ANA Company to advance with two platoons forward. With the support of another lance corporal and two rangers, he rallied the ANA soldiers, who were now settled in their defensive positions, and urged both platoons forward, supported by two Warriors.

With the Warriors giving direct support, the platoons and their mentors advanced through the Taliban killing area to engage the foe at close quarters. As they closed on the enemy, Toge maintained a firm grip on the tactical situation, exhorting the ANA soldiers at every bound, and switching from firing to leading the ANA, to make sure that they did not go to ground under the fierce enemy fire. During the advance, Toge also had the tactical presence of mind to advance his platoons in such a way that their supporting Warriors were not exposed to RPG fire. Mindless of his own safety – and he made a very large target – he repeatedly put himself in the way of enemy fire to maintain the impetus of the advance. That every man followed him was testimony to his courage and inspirational leadership.

In the searing midday heat, the Warrior with which Toge advanced was targeted by Taliban and hit at least ten times by RPG rounds, one of which injured seriously the ANA lead sergeant and knocked Toge off his feet. In spite of this, he got up, carried the injured ANA sergeant to cover and administered first aid before returning to the fray to deal with the Taliban. Toge then led the advance, with grenade and rifle fire, to within 100 metres of the enemy where a further four ANA soldiers were wounded. Each injured man was carried out of danger by Toge, who also dealt with their immediate treatment, showing both great physical strength and selflessness. After half an hour his ANA Company had pinned down at least twenty enemy fighters and he was then ordered to fight back to a point beyond the danger zone of fast air support.

This withdrawal in contact was carried out quickly, in spite of the difficulty of having to co-ordinate the evacuation of three seriously and two slightly wounded ANA personnel. However, the intervention of the fast air support ended the engagement. At least two Taliban had been killed with five wounded while the remainder fled. Never again was the enemy seen in such numbers around Deh Zohr E Sofla, which allowed CIMIC development to go ahead.

Lance Corporal Toge's actions demonstrated the professionalism of the Royal Irish. In normal circumstances, a lance corporal would not command a company group, especially of another nation's forces, but Toge had done so in circumstances that were far from normal. In the most challenging and dangerous conditions, and against a determined, well-equipped and brutal enemy, he showed not only raw courage and inspirational leadership but also tactical acumen and what has to be described as almost superhuman strength. Not surprisingly, he was awarded the Conspicuous Gallantry Cross, an award second only to the Victoria Cross.

In the operations in the Upper Gereshk valley, Lance Corporal Andrew Cairns was a patrol medic with a mentor team. A TA junior NCO with 16th Close Support Medical Regiment, he proved to be a soldier of great courage whose calm dedication to his medical role saved many lives in several engagements. Not least of these was an engagement on 19 May during the move of ANA vehicles and men from the Green Zone, which was dominated by the Taliban, to a new patrol base. The patrol departed the Green Zone in the early afternoon to begin the hazardous southward journey.

At about 5.00pm it was found that the route was blocked by an IED and a number of men suspected of being Taliban were spotted in a nearby compound. Two operations were then undertaken, one to clear the compounds and the other to prepare a by-pass. Cairns, with another mentor, led four ANA soldiers to clear the compound while the by-pass was made by blowing irrigation ditches and filling trenches. This was a lengthy task since it was necessary to route the by-pass beyond the blast radius of the IED while difficult terrain added to the complications.

As the patrol moved off again, Cairns took up the lead position, on foot, to scout for further IEDs, ignoring the real danger that he might be shot by a gunman. With the onset of darkness the patrol embussed in their vehicles so that they might make better progress but, as they drove through the night, an ANA vehicle fell victim to a buried IED. At the same time, in a typical Taliban tactic, the patrol came under fire from several concealed positions. Taliban fighters engaged the vehicles with automatic fire and a storm of RPGs but the latter fell short although still showering lethal splinters in the direction of the trapped men. The ANA and their mentors reacted immediately and a bitter firefight developed with Lance Corporal Cairns engaging the enemy from the centre of the stalled convoy. A number of Taliban were killed, prompting the enemy to fall back. But this was only to allow them to regroup, ready for another onslaught. Nonetheless, a brief lull ensued, which Cairns used to advantage to dash to the damaged ANA vehicle and assist the injured.

The most badly injured soldier had been propelled some twenty feet from the command vehicle and lay, unmoving, in a dried-up ditch. Soaked in blood, the unfortunate man had had his right leg all but severed above the knee. Such was his blood loss that he was in imminent danger of dying and so Cairns concentrated his attention on him, applying a tourniquet to stem the bleeding. As he did so, the Taliban opened fire again but the thirty-one-year-old medic continued treating his patient. When several Kalashnikov bursts struck the bank near the wounded man, Cairns turned to protect the casualty by shielding him with his own body. As the engagement continued, the mentors and ANA soldiers increased their volume of fire to pin down the enemy which allowed Cairns to carry the wounded soldier to a vehicle that was still intact.

For another five hours the battle continued with undiminished ferocity as the patrol fought its way to relative safety and out of the Green Zone. En route, four more IEDs had to be dealt with; these were all detonated where they lay. Throughout this lengthy battle, Lance Corporal Cairns remained with the casualty, even when under fire. At times moving the injured man to safer positions, he continued to treat him until the patrol met up with Danish medics whose team had advanced to secure a helicopter landing site from which the man could be evacuated. By then it was some ten hours after the patrol had left its base. Lance Corporal Cairns' outstanding actions had been instrumental in saving the wounded soldier's life; Cairns' steadfast bravery under fire and his complete dedication to his task were inspirational.

At the same time, Sergeant Darren Esdale, a mentor team commander in Musa Qaleh, was taking part in a surge into Taliban territory north of Musa Qaleh. Esdale was an experienced B Company Sergeant with a strong Royal Irish family pedigree. He was accompanied by another mentor, and a ten-man section of Afghan soldiers, as a company of Royal Welsh advanced on the enemy-dominated area. It was on the morning of 19 May that Esdale and his squad led the Royal Welsh company forward; the squad's task was to clear five kilometres of ground into the Taliban area.

The Taliban were watching the company's advance, as intercepts of their radio communications made clear, and, as he moved northwards, Esdale spotted several Taliban fighters crossing the Musa Qaleh wadi. Although they were some distance away they were moving in his direction. On the company commander's orders, he led his men in line with the company that was advancing in parallel on the other side of the wadi. By now the heat was growing more intense as the morning wore on.

Sergeant Esdale and his men had advanced a further 600 metres when they were ambushed by a party of Taliban, estimated at some twenty-five strong, who poured rifle and RPG fire at them. Immediately, Esdale rallied his ANA into cover and formed a firebase to bring accurate return fire on the enemy, even though this meant moving frequently amongst the men of his squad. The Taliban knew exactly where

Esdale's soldiers were located and showered RPGs and small arms fire on them. A ferocious firefight developed, in which the remainder of the company were unable to help the leading squad due to the terrain and the fact that they were also under heavy suppressive fire from the enemy. Over the following twenty minutes, Esdale, by his tireless leadership and strength of character, co-ordinated the fire of the ANA to such effect that the Taliban could not push home their attack. The enemy had lost the initiative and Esdale's ANA soldiers had won the firefight.

It was time to organize the withdrawal of the ANA squad to link up with the company but, as they started moving, the Taliban opened up with 82mm mortars and heavy machine guns. Identifying a suitable firing point, Esdale dashed through the hail of enemy fire to retaliate. Once in position he opened fire on the enemy to suppress their fire but he had not realized that his new position was exposed to Taliban fire from the east flank and, before long, rounds were striking around him, posing an immediate threat to his life. In spite of this heightened danger, he continued returning fire and organizing the move of his squad into a nearby compound where they had some protection. His actions allowed the remainder of the company to re-organize and provide effective fire support, which, in turn, allowed Sergeant Esdale and his men to join the company. With the ANA squad and Royal Welsh company able to bring down more fire than the enemy could match, the Taliban were forced to retreat, allowing the company to consolidate its position overnight.

Next morning, the 20th, the company received orders to move south but, early in that move, it came under heavy fire from a force estimated at about twenty Taliban. However, Esdale with his squad had remained in a compound to cover the move of the lead elements of the company and their presence was unknown to the enemy. Appreciating the danger facing the Royal Welsh, Sergeant Esdale took the initiative by counter-ambushing the advancing Taliban. This timely intervention saved many lives as well as alerting the vanguard and inflicting losses on the enemy. By pinning the enemy down for two hours, Esdale's squad allowed the company to move out of the killing area after which he called in close air support and attack helicopters, which completed the destruction of the enemy force. With that accomplished, Esdale and his ANA squad withdrew in good order.

Thus, in two significant engagements in a twenty-four-hour period, Sergeant Esdale demonstrated the highest levels of valour and leadership with such courageous actions and disregard for his own safety that he inspired the ANA soldiers. This was typical of his service in Helmand which was rewarded with a Mention in Despatches.

Captain Graham Rainey, commanding a mentoring team with an ANA company, set up a new patrol base in Musa Qaleh district shortly after the Battlegroup arrived. This was to be a 'satellite station' to the north of Musa Qaleh, an integral part of Major Kenny's protective ring concept. As the 'satellite station' was established in territory that the Taliban considered to be theirs, they vented considerable frustration on it and its occupants, assailing it with small arms, machine gun and mortar fire at every opportunity. However, as the base represented a further extension of the writ of the Afghan government, it was defended with even greater determination, with Captain Rainey playing a major part in that defence – and in taking the fight to the enemy.

The PB garrison included Afghan National Police as well as ANA soldiers and a measure of Rainey's success was that he was able to weld the garrison's disparate elements into an effective force. He achieved this through strength of character and complete dedication to his task while his remarkable leadership was demonstrated through his leading more than a hundred foot patrols into the Green Zone and the urban desert area around his base. Many of those patrols were carried out in temperatures soaring into the high 40s. Rainey's commitment to his task was inspirational for the men he was mentoring and he showed humility in his dealings with indigenous soldiers and police officers, thereby gaining their trust since they appreciated that he respected their culture, beliefs and traditions. As a result, the garrison was able to dominate the area north of the base and no ground was ceded to the Taliban in spite of their worst efforts.

On 22 May, Captain Rainey's OMLT and ANA soldiers set out on an intelligence-gathering mission to the north of Musa Qaleh while, to the south of the town, a Battlegroup operation was in progress. When the patrol had reached the 85 Northing, Rainey realized that something in the atmosphere had changed. His soldier's instinct was backed by electronic surveillance which confirmed that a Taliban attack was imminent. While Captain Rainey was advising the ANA commander to withdraw, since no Battlegroup support would be available, heavy enemy fire from PKM machine guns and AK47s was put down on the platoon's position. At this the ANA commander froze and the interpreter fled.

Rainey reacted by organizing the ANA into a baseline to provide fire, extracting the OMLT and positioning them where they could give support with effective fire. He then gripped the ANA platoon commander and led a move from the patrol's exposed position to the comparative safety of a nearby compound. This was carried out under constant enemy fire. Then, without warning, a single enemy sniper engaged them from the east; but Rainey retaliated against both threats, inspiring the ANA soldiers to follow his lead. After this he adjusted light mortar fire on to the Taliban positions which allowed him to break off the contact and withdraw the patrol.

Next day, Rainey's OMLT and ANA troops were moving westward to Musa Qaleh wadi when they came under a sudden attack from Taliban using RPGs, mortars and small arms. The immediate effect was to paralyze the ANA soldiers but Rainey stepped in, identified the enemy locations and led an assault, pausing briefly to motivate the ANA and organize the OMLT. His speedy reaction wrested the initiative from the Taliban and his effective fire killed at least two enemy fighters and injured others. He then led a pursuit to clear enemy forces from the compounds but the ANA had lost their momentum. Moreover, they had a Taliban prisoner in one compound whom they were abusing physically by kicking and beating him. The OMLT soldiers tried to stop this abuse but, in the prevailing tense situation, the ANA turned against their mentors. Only the speedy arrival and diplomatic intervention of Captain Rainey prevented this situation from becoming much worse.

This altercation occurred against the background of unremitting enemy fire. Unfazed by an enemy round passing within an inch of his face, Rainey withdrew the pinned-down cover group and, at the same time, instructed his OMLT members to treat the prisoner's injuries, which were splinted and bandaged. Then, aware of the threat from the flanks, he co-ordinated the Quick Reaction Force (QRF) from his PB and organized the withdrawal of the ANA from the Taliban's killing zone. The prisoner was sent off with the QRF while Rainey gathered both the ANA and OMLT, ensured that all were present and withdrew them safely out of the ambush. Once returned to the PB, his first concern was for the wellbeing of the prisoner.

That only enemy personnel were killed was due solely to Captain Rainey's distinguished command, leadership and tactical skill. He earned extraordinary respect with the ANA as well as with his own team and his physical courage was superb while his moral courage and fighting spirit enhanced security north of Musa Qaleh. Standing well over six feet tall, Rainey is an imposing individual who inspired confidence in those under his command. In the operational honours and awards list of 6 March 2009, Captain Rainey was awarded the Military Cross.

On the last day of May, OMLT 1 was training and preparing ANA personnel for deployment to Musa Qaleh, for which purpose the team was operating temporarily from Camp Shorabak. Ranger John Haveron, aged twenty, was a member of the OMLT, which had deployed to Sangin early in the tour. That day Haveron was detailed to drive a Snatch vehicle, a lightly–armoured Land Rover, from Shorabak to Camp Bastion as part of a routine convoy. Haveron's was the lead vehicle and it was followed by soft-skinned troop carrying vehicles (TCVs); the threat level on the route was considered to be low. Such proved to be the case on the outward, and uneventful, journey to Bastion but the reverse was to be the case on the return trip.

As the convoy drove back from Bastion to Shorabak there was no indication of anything untoward. However, Haveron's suspicions were aroused by a blue Toyota approaching the convoy. Although such vehicles are in regular use with coalition forces and, therefore, might not be considered unusual, Haveron felt that there was something not quite right about this Toyota and flashed his vehicle's headlights at it in the recognized signal for an oncoming vehicle to pull over or stop. In this case, the Toyota driver did not respond and Haveron considered him, accurately, to be a threat.

In this situation, Ranger Haveron had few options. Decelerating would have caused the convoy to slow down and might have had devastating results through bunching the vehicles. Therefore, he accelerated aggressively, thus warning the other drivers in the convoy of immediate danger. It also panicked the driver of the Toyota, who was a suicide bomber. As Haveron's Snatch raced by his vehicle the Toyota driver detonated his device, but Haveron had prevented him from doing so when his action would have been most effective, i.e., alongside a soft-skinned TCV. In fact, the Snatch had shielded the following soft-skinned vehicle from the blast but sustained such damage that it was brought to an immediate standstill. Straightaway, Haveron left his seat and raced around the vehicle to rescue his trapped commander, in spite of intense heat from the explosion. Showing no concern for his own safety, he returned to assist in rescuing the top cover sentry. At any time his vehicle might have suffered a further explosion from either fuel or ammunition that would have killed or seriously injured both men.

Ranger Haveron's acute perception and anticipation – another classic example of a professional soldier's instinct – in what had hitherto been a quiet area saved many lives while, in rescuing his commander and top cover sentry, he also demonstrated intelligence, composure and raw courage. Normally a member of a six-man mentor team deployed alongside an Afghan army company in an isolated PB, he saw many serious engagements during which he demonstrated outstanding courage and initiative in spite of his youth and relative inexperience. His actions on the road from Bastion to Shorabak that day were typical of his behaviour throughout the tour.

In the back of Haveron's Land Rover that day was WO1 Andrew Taylor, of 16th Close Support Medical Regiment, RAMC, and a medical mentor to the ANA. His usual role, as an operating department practitioner, would generally see him working in a rear echelon in reasonably normal clinical conditions, but there was no normal rear echelon in Helmand and Warrant Officer Taylor became used to the many complex and disturbing events that war of this nature can bring.

When the blast from the suicide bomber's vehicle caught the Land Rover it blew the top-cover sentry, Private Thompson, into the rear of the vehicle and onto WO1 Taylor; flames from the explosion accompanied the stricken soldier. As soon as he gathered his wits, Taylor pulled the wounded soldier from the blazing Land Rover, saw that the vehicle commander was still in the front and went to assist in his rescue. He then attended Private Thompson who had sustained burns to his hands and neck, as well as suffering shock. Having treated Thompson and made him ready for evacuation, he checked the condition of everyone involved in the incident. Later, at Camp Shorabak, he was assessed himself: his right eardrum was perforated, he had suffered hearing loss and there was blood behind both ears.

That same day, Corporal Christopher Kennedy was a member of a six-man Royal Irish mentor team in the Kajaki region, a dangerous area disputed by ISAF and the Taliban and where resupply was carried out by helicopter. Kennedy, a section commander mentor in an ANA platoon working alongside X Company of 2nd

Parachute Regiment (Battlegroup North), had been detailed to search several compounds in the northern area, all of which were in sight of the enemy's forward line. The patrol was aware that they could come under attack from determined enemy forces as this was an area of high threat where there had already been accurate enemy fire, including mortars, rifles and RPGs.

Kennedy's section was to blow its way into several compounds in Shomali Gulbah village, none of which had been searched before. The task was all but complete when Kennedy's section was assigned another compound to search. Without warning, at 6.33pm, the section came under accurate, heavy and sustained fire from two nearby villages, Bagai Kheyl and Makikheyl. This fusillade, which was coming from a number of positions, included rifle fire that was followed quickly by RPG fire. Grenades from the RPGs were landing in and around Kennedy's section. One detonated no more than five metres from Kennedy and the ANA section commander. Both were bowled over by the blast but Kennedy was quick to recover and get back on his feet.

As the RPG rounds detonated amongst the section, one ANA soldier was injured by a grenade fragment. Such was his injury and the severity of incoming fire that he could not move. However, Corporal Kennedy made his way to the casualty to administer first aid and try to move him to a safer location in spite of being under constant enemy fire. At the same time, the ANA commander had also been pinned down by the ferocity of the attack and, suffering from shock, could not command his section effectively. Whilst aiding the wounded soldier, Kennedy realized that the other ANA soldiers were in marked disorder and so began issuing fire control orders. He remained calm, although he was under extreme pressure from the enemy attack and, over a fifteen-minute period, gave accurate and timely situational reports so that all friendly forces were aware of the enemy's positions. All the while he was treating the casualty, controlling the section and liaising with the other mentors and his calmness allowed others to call in accurate mortar fire on the enemy positions, which led to their rout. Not until the Taliban fire had been suppressed could the section receive any further support.

Corporal Kennedy appreciated fully his role as a mentor and thus, in the prevailing circumstances, took the initiative to assume control of the section under heavy fire. His rescue of the wounded Afghan soldier was carried out at great personal risk while his overall conduct was an example of selflessness, dedication to those under his command and highly professional soldiering.

In late-May there were two reminders, if any were needed, of the lethality of IEDs and the ruthlessness of the Taliban. As work progressed on the new patrol base, Attal, and the ANA company and its mentors patrolled to interdict any Taliban incursions towards Gereshk, a loud explosion was heard one exceptionally warm morning. The sentry in the 'super sangar' reported a rising plume of dark smoke and its location,

Imjin Company pose before a Boeing CH-47 Chinook of the RAF's No. 1310 Flight, 904 Expeditionary Air Wing at Camp Bastion. The Company was to provide force protection at the base but its role was broadened as the tour progressed.

These poppies provide a livelihood for many farmers in the Green Zone along the Helmand river. A Royal Irish patrol moves through a poppy field in the early days of HERRICK VIII. In the background may be seen a compound, typical of the local countryside.

Afghan soldiers in one of their Ford Ranger vehicles, a pick-up with no protection against explosive devices or enemy bullets. Many Afghan soldiers display a fatalistic attitude to safety and do not wear body armour or combat helmets.

The greatest danger on HERRICK VIII came from IEDs. On 6 April 2008, Major Simon Shirley, OC A Company/ OMLT 1, was injured seriously when his Wimik was blown up by an IED. Only the quick reaction of a medic, Lance Corporal Al Sutherland, saved his life.

The Wimik is based on a stripped-down Land Rover, fitted with a stout roll-over cage and a weapons mount installation kit (WMIK), including a Browning .50-inch heavy machine gun and a 7.62mm GPMG. This Wimik is festooned with camouflage netting and is also fitted with ballistic matting, which gives a little protection against small arms fire. As Major Dave Middleton commented, these cannot be driven with impunity but they do have their uses as patrol vehicles.

IEDs ranged from anti-personnel devices with small explosive charges that could maim or kill a man to those that could disable a heavy armoured vehicle. This could have destroyed a Wimik or caused severe damage to a heavier vehicle.

25/07/2008 09:12

The Afghan National Army has no shortage of machine guns with which to defend its patrol bases. These soldiers, on sentry duty, have a choice of at least four heavy or medium machine guns including a *Dushka* 12.7mm weapon.

Look at this one. A Royal Irish soldier – note the beard growth – tries out a Dushka for size. This photograph provides a good scale for this 12.7mm (.50-inch) Soviet weapon, originally designed as an anti-aircraft machine gun.

West and East in harmony. A Battlegroup soldier from an OMLT with his SA80 is backed up by an Afghan soldier with two RPGs. Although wearing a helmet, the ANA soldier has no body armour.

Through the poppy fields of the Green Zone. A patrol wends its careful way through a field of poppies, while one of their number watches for enemy activity.

Afghan youth, in common with youth everywhere, are interested in sport and these two boys are happy to be presented with a football from the Royal Irish.

Patrols also operate in urban or semi-urban areas. This built-up area has a reasonable road along which the patrol can have the support of the Wimik in the background.

The presence of children behaving normally suggests that there are no Taliban in the area but this can never be a guarantee that an area is safe and it certainly does not guarantee that there are no IEDs about.

Imjin Company on patrol. As the tour progressed, Imjin Company's duties were extended beyond the initial role of force protection. One platoon from Imjin Company deployed from FOB Keenan on OMLT duties and another from FOB Robinson. This patrol is from FOB Keenan.

Much resupply to isolated patrol bases was undertaken by helicopters, usually the Chinook HC2/2As of the RAF's No. 1310 Flight. As this Chinook approaches the HLS, an Apache AH1 of the Army Air Corps provides cover against an enemy attack on the bulky transport helicopter.

'Brownout'. As the Chinook lands on an improvized HLS, its twin rotors create a huge cloud of dust that can blot out the immediate area. These clouds are known as 'brownouts'.

Some downtime at Sangin for Ranger Company and a dip in the Sangin canal that flows through their base.

Danish soldiers from Battlegroup Centre provided support for the Royal Irish Battlegroup in the Gereshk valley. The commander of this Leopard II main battle tank of the Jutland Dragoons ensures that the photographer will know that the tank is Danish. In spite of their size and excellent armour, Leopards have been crippled by IEDs and crew members have been killed or injured.

A Wimik of the Royal Irish Battlegroup shows off its two machine guns for the camera while its ownership is made clear by the shamrock on the panel just behind the driver.

Proof of the damage IEDs can inflict. This Warrior has had its running gear destroyed by the explosion of an IED. An ANA soldier surveys the damage.

Another visitor was actor and TV presenter Ross Kemp who was filming a series on Afghanistan, which included an episode featuring the Royal Irish OMLT in Musa Qaleh.

On patrol Lieutenant Steve Swan meets and greets two smiling Afghan children. In the background an ANA soldier watches on.

Operation OQAB STERGA, transporting a third turbine to the Kajaki dam, was the largest operation undertaken by ISAF and the ANA during the tour. Above, a transporter in the convoy is throwing up a dustcloud that almost hides following vehicles on the road to Kajaki. Each tractor unit carried a machine gunner in the cab while the final section of the rout was secured by Royal Irish and ANA soldiers. Among the many assets deployed were armoured fighting vehicles (AFVs) and Apache AH1 helicopters as seen in the lower photograph.

Trust. On a joint patrol of ANA and Royal Irish soldiers, the crouching ANA soldier is guarding the back of the Royal Irish soldier who is checking the ground beyond the archway.

Ranger Justin Cupples, of Ranger Company, the only Royal Irish soldier to be killed in action during HERRICK VIII. Ranger Cupples, born in the United States and a veteran of the US Navy, was killed by an IED in Sangin on 4 September 2008. Known as 'Cups' to his comrades, he was commemorated by his ANA comrades in the name of PB Pylae – 'cups' in Pashtu.

We will remember. The Royal Irish wreath commemorating the Regiment's dead of HERRICK IV and HERRICK VIII at the memorial in Camp Shorabak.

The burden of Command. Colonel Ed Freely stands before the memorial to the dead of Task Force Helmand.

Welcome home. The people of Shropshire turned out in large numbers to welcome 1st Royal Irish back to Tern Hill, their duty in Afghanistan done.

which was checked by the watchkeeper in the command vehicle. A quick check of the operations map indicated that no patrol should have been in the area of the explosion; this was confirmed by radio messages to patrols in the field. Nonetheless, the QRF was deployed to investigate and an explanation was soon forthcoming: a wandering herd of camels had been in the vicinity and one beast had triggered the IED, which was close to a settlement west of the Green Zone and might therefore have claimed the life of a villager.

Further evidence of the Taliban attitude to local people was revealed as the investigation continued and soldiers with mine detectors discovered a radio-controlled device for a pressure-pad IED. The IED was dug in at a track junction in the middle of a village. Children had been playing blithely in the vicinity and might have become victims of the bomb. It was discovered that, two nights before, a group of Taliban had come into the village and, using a loudhailer, threatened to kill anyone who left his or her compound. With the villagers thus intimidated, the insurgents then planted a number of devices to kill ISAF personnel or local villagers. Who became a victim did not seem to matter to the Taliban.

In the searches and patrols that followed, observant soldiers spotted the telltale signs of hidden IEDs. Earth had been disturbed and replaced carefully but some traces remained visible and mine and metal detectors confirmed the presence of concealed IEDs. The Commanding Officer and Lance Corporal Stewart probed the sandy soil in two places and discovered IEDs. Both were marked with mine tape and the EOD team was summoned. One was a pressure-pad IED while the other was a fiendish combination of a car's fuel tank packed with homemade explosives dug in on top of five mortar rounds.

By the end of May, the Royal Irish Battlegroup was established firmly in Helmand and its soldiers were becoming attuned to the pulse of life in their operational areas whether in the OMLTs, with Ranger Company in Sangin, or with Imjin Company at Camp Bastion. Those in the OMLTS were also very much aware of the strengths and weaknesses of their Afghan counterparts and the scale of the task they had to accomplish. Corporal Alan Hendron, with almost twelve years in the Regiment, had deployed with OMLT 3 to a PB at Kajaki. This isolated location, intended to protect the great dam on the Helmand river that produced the province's electricity, had been attacked before by the Taliban. At Kajaki there was a platoon of ANA whom Hendron considered to be 'up for a fight and knew when we were going to be hit', such was their knowledge of the local situation. With a company of Royal Marines also based at Kajaki, there were joint operations using Marines, ANA and Royal Irish. The Marines 'weren't scared to put us and ANA out in front which showed trust in our ability and the potential of the ANA'. This was a clear indication of the potential of the ANA and showed that, with good leadership, they could achieve high standards as operationally effective soldiers. Not all their leadership was good, however, as was demonstrated on those occasions when a few ANA officers or NCOs lost their nerve. Some of this may be attributed to the fact that they were receiving their 'battlefield inoculation' on a live battlefield rather than a controlled exercise situation. However, the recruitment of officers probably also contributed to the problem, as men were often commissioned because they were well educated, or because of tribal connections: leadership skills were not high on the attributes required of a potential officer.

At Sangin, Ranger Company had settled in well, and the relatively calm period at the beginning of the tour helped them prepare for the high operational tempo that was ahead by giving them some time to get to know the region and its people. Meanwhile, Imjin Company had demonstrated its professionalism to such an extent that a platoon had been formed from its soldiers to mentor ANA personnel. This platoon was deployed to FOB Keenan in the upper Gereshk valley and when Lieutenant Colonel Andrew Cullen and WO1 Patton, CO and RSM of 2nd Royal Irish, visited their soldiers in Afghanistan at the beginning of June, they were able to see not only the excellent work being carried out by Major Hudson's men at Bastion, but also the mentoring undertaken by the platoon at FOB Keenan. Ed Freely confessed to watching the visitors' discomfort in the heat and taking it as 'reassuring evidence that we have all acclimatised to the severe heat and weight of our equipment' after more than two months in Helmand. The Imjin Company IRT had been called out eight times in one month to emergencies across Helmand, ranging from an Afghan child injured in a traffic collision to an ISAF soldier who had been wounded in an engagement with Taliban.

There could be little doubt that the Battlegroup had made a good start on Operation HERRICK VIII. And there was a deep-rooted determination that that would be built upon in the months ahead.

Notes
1. Wimik is a stripped-down Land Rover fitted with a Weapons Mount Installation Kit (WMIK) of a rollover cage, a GPMG and a .50-inch Browning machine gun.
2. He was also Commander Task Force Helmand and Commander British Forces (COMBRITFOR).

Chapter Four

Ranger Company at Sangin

Ranger Company had moved to join Battlegroup North – Lieutenant Colonel Joe O'Sullivan's 2 Para Battlegroup – as soon as the Royal Irish arrived in Afghanistan. Based in the Sangin area, arguably the most dangerous in the country, the company group was to discharge its role with distinction. Commanding Ranger Company was Major Graham Shannon, a native of County Tyrone, who was commissioned in the Royal Irish in 1998. His story of the intervening ten years emphasizes the operational maturity of 1st Battalion the Royal Irish Regiment as a whole.

Second Lieutenant Shannon joined the Battalion as it was undertaking an Operation BANNER tour in support of the Royal Ulster Constabulary GC in Northern Ireland. The Battalion was based in Dungannon, covering East Tyrone, and, twenty minutes after arriving in Dungannon, he was on his first patrol. Serving in Northern Ireland was, in his opinion, 'a great grounding; you got to know your men and how to plan an op, even if in a minor way'. Between then and Sangin, he had also served with the American 101st Airborne Division, 'The Screaming Eagles', in Baghdad, for which he was awarded the US Bronze Star.

For Operation HERRICK VIII, the Ranger Company Group was built around HQ and two platoons of Shannon's C Company, with a rifle platoon from B Company, a Fire Support Group from D Company and individual soldiers from A and HQ Companies, thus making the company group representative of the entire battalion. (At one stage of the tour, Ranger Company's three platoon commanders were from the Republic of Ireland: Lieutenant Paddy Bury from Wicklow, Second Lieutenant Peter Gavin from Mayo and Second Lieutenant Pete Franks from Kildare.) Also included in the Group were a Royal Artillery Fire Support Team (FST), Sappers from the Royal Engineers, 'Redcaps' from the Royal Military Police, personnel from the Royal Logistic Corps, Royal Electrical and Mechanical Engineers, Royal Army Medical Corps, Royal Army Veterinary Corps and 2 Para; in addition there was a single Welsh Guardsman, a reservist, while men of the United States Marine Corps were to be found in the Operations Room. Later in the tour, a company of US Marines, Echo Company of 2/7 Battalion, would also operate in the area; the Marine

Company's role was the mentoring of Afghan National Police in the area. In all, there were about 180 in the Ranger Company Group, which administered over 300 personnel in total. Ranger Company worked well and carried out many joint operations with OMLT 1, the ANA Kandak, ANP and the National Directorate of Security.

Ranger Company's advance elements arrived in Sangin on 28 March and soon experienced the Taliban's malevolent intent. On the night of the 29th a rocket attack was launched on the base but caused no casualties. On 2 April Ranger Company assumed responsibility for the Sangin AO from Bravo Company, 40 Commando, following what Major Shannon described as 'an excellent handover'.

Lieutenant Paddy Bury described the arrival at Sangin District Centre

We touch down. Within seconds the helicopter has disgorged our supplies and us and is soaring back into the bright blue sky. As the dust clears the Irishmen of Ranger Company, 1st Battalion, The Royal Irish Regiment, get their first views of their home for the next six months. We have landed in a converted Afghan compound, a ramshackle fortress of ancient Afghan buildings and modern military engineering. As we move off the massive dirt helipad we have to cross the Sangin canal. This fast flowing, green blue river, eight metres wide, runs right through our base, known as Sangin DC (District Centre), cutting it in half. We cross the footbridges quickly, eyes on the torrent below that will only increase as the mountain snows melt in the summer.

Observation over a wide area is provided by the fire support tower, which is directly in front of the new arrivals, and resembles a four-storey-high medieval castle, built of concrete and rock, with sandbags piled upon sandbags on the roof. Off to one side are the thick mud walls and low ceiling of the accommodation block that will house most of them for the next six months, their rest taken on cramped camp beds. There are also a field kitchen, makeshift solar showers and wooden latrines, surrounded by thick Hesco bastion walls. Those walls provide a concrete and iron protective barrier with each piece of Hesco 'three times as thick and tall as the concrete barriers that divide the motorways back home'.

Hesco is critical in keeping the garrison safe. Some twelve feet in height, a Hesco wall encloses the complete camp, rather as an earth and wood wall protected a Roman legion's overnight camp. The Hesco collapsible containers are easily moved and can be filled with whatever is available at any site, including sand and rubble; they are the modern equivalent of the gabions of an earlier age. Looming over the wall are the sangars, towers from which sentinels can observe the surrounding terrain. Paradoxically, the term *sangar* is originally Persian, meaning barricade, and was adopted by the British and Indian Armies to describe small fortified posts, usually built of local stone, in the North West Frontier and Afghanistan. The word has been familiar to generations of British soldiers; in Afghanistan it came home. Some sangars are more important than others, such as that over the camp's main entrance. Through that gate, local people entered to meet the governor, or to seek first aid or compensation. All this traffic made the sangar and the entrance busy and stressful, but the added threat of suicide bombers, either on foot or in a vehicle, ratcheted up the tension. For those on stag, or duty, in the other sangars, their time on watch was about staying alert and alive in the enervating heat. At all times, they had to keep their eyes peeled, looking for 'dickers',[1] a word that has travelled from Northern Ireland to Afghanistan and now refers to Taliban scouts using mobile phones to pass information to their mortar and rocket teams lying in wait somewhere not far away.

On the other side of the river lie the quarters of the Afghan National Army. Paddy Bury considers these soldiers, from other provinces of Afghanistan, to be brave men.

> They are generally a likeable lot, hardened and experienced soldiers. They provide protection to the governor who lives in our base, man many of the vehicle checkpoints in Sangin town, and come on patrol with us when we move out into the green zone. They are integral to our mission of ensuring a security zone around Sangin.

And what of the town itself? A busy market town of 14,000 people, most inhabitants are Pashtun. War has visited it many times and it carries the scars of wrecked buildings, like rotten teeth, that provide silent evidence to both the Soviet war of the eighties and of much more recent battles between British soldiers and the Taliban in 2006, in which men from 1st Royal Irish fought. West of Sangin flows the Helmand river on its southward journey; this has long been the lifeblood of the area. Through a system of irrigation canals the river provides water that allows the neighbouring land to be cultivated out to a mile from the bank of the waterway. That cultivation creates a green 'tangle of man–high crop fields, irrigation ditches, small canals and trees'. Although beautiful, this area is also very dangerous. This is the Green Zone.

> Impassable by vehicle, heavy going on foot, the Green Zone is where much of our contact with the Taliban occurs. With local knowledge of the ground, prepared firing positions and covered escape routes, the Taliban feel superior here. It is perfect ambush country, yet we must dominate it to ensure the security of Sangin town. And so, every day we leave our safer, dusty base and venture out into the damp, hostile greenness.

From its HQ at Sangin, Ranger Company maintained outposts, or patrol bases, from which to dominate its operational area. These included bases codenamed Derry,

Enniskillen, Armagh and Boyne; the last two named are the same base, the name having been changed from Boyne to Armagh. It was at a *shura* outside PB Derry that the village headman commented to Major Shannon that 'Afghanistan is the most dangerous country in the world, Helmand is the most dangerous province in Afghanistan and Sangin is the most dangerous town, and you are sitting here talking to me. Why?' However, the patrol bases proved their value on many occasions and gave assurance to locals, such as that headman, that stability could be achieved, given the right security conditions. The presence of the PBs thwarted many Taliban operations and, although the bases were in fixed locations, their existence was not always known immediately to the Taliban. When an attack was made on PB Enniskillen, the attackers did not know that PB Derry had been established and the reaction from there came as a considerable shock to them.

PB Armagh, formerly Boyne, had been a Taliban safe house but became a thorn in their side when Ranger Company took over. Until then, the base, in an area of fruit orchards, had seen the greatest concentration of violence in Battlegroup North's operational area. With the arrival of Ranger Company, the level of information from local people 'went through the roof' as they saw the opportunity to remove the Taliban from the area. PB Armagh cut the enemy's lines of communication and gained a huge amount of information for coalition forces, all of which helped to weaken further the Taliban threat. Before the end of the tour, PB Armagh was closed, having served its purpose well, and was replaced by PB Pylae, named by the Afghans in honour of Ranger Company's – and the Battlegroup's – sole Royal Irish fatality, Ranger Justin Cupples, known as 'Cups' to his comrades, both Irish and Afghan. The name *Pylae* is Pashtu for 'Cups'.

On Major Shannon's first visit to PB Pylae, his first to 7 Platoon after the death of Justin Cupples, the base came under furious assault from Taliban who attacked with rockets, RPGs, machine guns and rifles. The base sangar was hit but 'each time the Taliban pulled a trigger he lost somebody'. Such was the deterrent that the base provided.

There was a flurry of Taliban activity in the first weeks of Ranger Company's time in Sangin with IEDs claiming the lives of Afghan policemen while another wounded Major Simon Shirley, commander of OMLT 1. During an advance to contact, there was an attempted suicide attack against the company; this was foiled by 9 Platoon who also fought off the planned ambush that was intended to follow the attack. Presumably panicked by 9 Platoon, the suicide bomber had detonated his device too early and, although members of the patrol were blown off their feet, there were no injuries. In addition, the FOB came under mortar and rocket attack on several occasions and there was also the tragic incident in which a number of Afghan policemen were injured seriously by the detonation of an RPG round in the DC, which killed two of their colleagues. This was the occasion on which Lance Corporal

Al Sutherland of OMLT 1 did so much to help the injured. Ranger Company's CSM Frankie O'Connor and the Medical Officer, Captain Mike Stacey, had rehearsed a mass casualty (MASCAL) plan which was implemented immediately, thereby saving the lives of six of the eight policemen who had been caught in the blast.

Commanding 7 Platoon was Lieutenant Paddy Bury. Although the platoon usually operated with about twenty-eight men, it had thirty-one at its peak, with attached personnel including a lance bombardier of the Royal Artillery 'who was a great guy' and Corporal Kayley Hournegould, Royal Army Medical Corps, who 'fitted in well with the boys and was treated exactly the same'. Medical support was not only excellent but also provided a great boost to morale; Captain Mike Stacey 'was amazing' and had 'saved a couple of Ranger Platoon in 2006'. JTAC – Joint Tactical Air Controller – was provided by a two-man team of Corporals Getty, Royal Irish, and Bishop, 2 Para. Initially, the platoon sergeant was Sergeant Trevor 'Speedy' Coult MC, a Belfast man who had been decorated in Iraq in 2005, but, about a month into the tour, he was succeeded by Sergeant PJ Brangan from County Kildare. Overall, 7 Platoon was a very good, well-led platoon with excellent junior NCOs and included in its ranks up to five veterans of Ranger Platoon, one of the three Royal Irish platoons to deploy on Operation HERRICK IV with 3 Para in 2006; these veterans kept the younger rangers in line, provided sound guidance and advice and never lost sight of the risks.

Ranger Company's area of operations was a rectangle measuring two by one-and-a-half kilometres and it took about a month before things began to liven up fully, apart from those several incidents in the first weeks. Otherwise, with the poppy harvest underway, there was little Taliban activity, thereby giving an opportunity for the soldiers to get to know the inhabitants.

Ranger Wesley Clyde, from Ballymoney, recalled meeting local people while on patrol. The children were friendly although some older people were hostile, while others were friendly and some remained silent. Rangers learnt basic orders and greetings in Pashtu to be able to communicate on a basic level with local people, greeting them as they met them in the streets. Although most communication was through interpreters, none of whom were military men, three of Ranger Company had undergone a short Pashtu course. These were Rangers Justin Cupples, Peter Maher and Maurice Reidy who were joined by Private 'Andy' McNabb of 2 Para, who had completed a nine-month course in Pashtu before deploying to Afghanistan. Major Shannon noted that

> Their ability to communicate with the local people quickly broke down barriers and earned the locals' respect and confidence. In doing this, many Afghans put their trust in the job that Ranger Company soldiers were doing, risking their lives to inform on Taliban activity. By simply speaking their language soldiers

like Ranger Justin Cupples, who died in the most contested area of Sangin, helped gather information on threats that helped to save the lives of many other soldiers and civilians throughout the tour. It is testament to what he and the other soldiers accomplished that a Joint Patrol Base was established by Ranger Company in the final days of their tour in the heart of this area. It was named Patrol Base Pylae, Pylae being the Pashto for Justin's nickname 'Cups'. Ranger Company surged into this area, clearing many IEDs, disrupting the Taliban's hold over the people and the Patrol Base will help bring enduring stability to a highly dangerous area.

The patrolling Rangers were surprised to hear some youngsters shout 'Up the 'Ra!' as patrols passed. Nonetheless, the youngsters reacted well to the Irishmen and especially loved receiving pens, stationery and chocolate. They were 'mad about chocolate'. However, by the end of the tour, Taliban violence had 'separated us from the people'.
    Ranger Clyde also recalled his first contact at a location codenamed Wombat Wood.

We knew it was coming through radio intercepts and our interpreters, and it was almost a relief when it happened. We were there for five days. We carried out section patrols in and around the local area to maintain a presence and there were also patrols in greater than section strength with attachments from the RAMC, JTAC…[as well as] 2 Para personnel.

There was never any doubt that Sangin was anything other than 'a dangerous place' but the training had fitted Ranger Company's men for high-intensity operations; low intensity operations were more complex. Paddy Bury considered that they 'were well prepared. We could have had a longer preparation time but overall the training was good'. In addition to the danger from the Taliban, there was also the problem posed by local conditions as the summer saw temperatures climb ever higher. Carrying a load of some 30 to 40 kilos, on average, it was impossible to run more than fifty metres and patrols were carried out very slowly. With the mercury hitting 52 C, it was like 'cooking your head inside a pressure cooker' and, on one occasion, three men were affected by heat in thirty minutes; they had travelled only 400 metres. Combined with the constant threats of ambush and IEDs, it is hardly surprising that patrols were exhausting experiences but, in spite of such exhaustion, it was often difficult to sleep at night; in the Hesco houses a temperature of 39 Celsius at 2.00am in mid-July was not conducive to restful slumber. However, except for about two weeks, it was not too humid, although that is a comparative assessment: one Ranger commented that you just learned to live with the sweat.
    Those who served in the desert in the Second World War had to endure strict water rationing but this was not the case in Afghanistan where water was in good supply.

There were even fridges in some patrol bases and cans of Pepsi were bought in the bazaar for storing in them. On patrol, each man could carry about four to six litres of water in a Camelbak, a very useful inclusion in the soldiers' kit. Those going out on patrol also hydrated before leaving the PB, usually drinking about two litres of water. In the intense heat endured by the men of Ranger Company, the ready availability of water was critical and a tremendous boost to morale. In contrast to the heat, dust did not create a great problem: rifles and other weapons were protected well, kept clean, and oiled so that dust did not penetrate the working parts. There were occasional dust storms but these brought the bonus of knowing that the Taliban were not about; they did not operate in such conditions since their targets would be all but invisible.

The Taliban used fairly simple but effective tactics, including ambushes combined with IEDs. Those who had served on HERRICK IV identified this as a major change as there had been no serious IED threat in 2006. Much effort was dedicated to reducing that threat and patrols used mine detectors to search for devices while keeping a keen lookout for command wires leading to buried mines. The Taliban also used radio–controlled IEDs but these were easier to combat with electronic counter measures that had been refined over the years of Operation BANNER in Northern Ireland. However, the danger remained and Sangin was the most dangerous area of all for IEDs with three times as many devices as the next greatest threat area. Thus 7 Platoon's search team of Corporal Corbett, Ranger Turner and Ranger Millar acted as the point team on patrol, sweeping the ground for any telltale signs of an IED. Before quitting base on patrol, Millar established the practice of kissing his legs and saying 'you're coming back with me', but he never left anything to chance when out on the ground. Luck played no part in the battle against IEDs. As far as the Royal Irish were concerned, they made their own luck through their professionalism and attention to detail.

The potent threat from IEDs meant that it could take up to an hour for a patrol to cover 500 metres, with this time extending to two hours if an IED was detected. Even when a patrol stopped the threat was still present: one Ranger commented that 'We never sat down without looking for IEDs, command wires et cetera'. In spite of being quite good at hiding their IEDs the Taliban often made the tactical error of burying them in the same holes. Some locals would give the Taliban reports on patrol activity while others helped Ranger Company with local information; paradoxically the same people might provide information to both Taliban and Royal Irish. One man told soldiers that he was fed up seeing people being killed and thus was prepared to assist the coalition troops if this helped bring the killing to an end.

As well as the point team with their mine detectors, the other patrol members scanned the ground for any sign of a command wire or a pressure pad while drones, or unmanned aerial vehicles (UAVs), were also used for this task, giving additional assurance to those below. Gunners from 32nd Regiment, Royal Artillery, operated

Desert Hawk, a small UAV with a wingspan of little over four feet and a weight of about three kilos, to give support. In the inimitable way of soldiers, Desert Hawk became known as Desert Chicken but its presence above them was a morale-booster. If all else failed and an IED exploded, some protection was offered by the Osprey body armour which includes collar and arm protectors designed specifically to meet the roadside IED threat encountered in Iraq. These offer good protection to the wearer's neck, face and upper arm. In addition, soldiers were issued with ballistic eye protection, looking rather like fashionable sunglasses and known as ballistic shades. The latter are good and protect the eyes but have the drawback, as any wearer of spectacles can testify, of causing irritation when worn in very hot conditions.

The arrival of Ranger Company in Sangin coincided with the poppy harvest. By the middle of April, the pink and white opium poppies growing in the nearby fields were being harvested for sale to the opium factories. With the harvest complete, fast-growing maize was planted which, in less than a month, would grow to the height of a man before it, too, was ready for the harvester. In the spring, as the snows on the high mountains melted, streams and rivers rose and life-giving water brought growth to both poppy and wheat and gave a living to the people of the area and from farther afield. Not surprisingly, the local landscape changed as the weeks of spring passed by, a change that was obvious to the men who patrolled the area on a daily basis.

Let us have a look at a typical patrol carried out by 7 Platoon during its tour. Once again the words are those of the platoon commander, Paddy Bury.

> While the wind whistles around base we prepare to leave. The sandstorm is reaching its crescendo as, goggles down, we venture out into the haze. Our mission is simple: to go deep into the Green Zone and establish the platoon in a patrol base for forty-eight hours. From here we will be able to interact with the locals, hopefully glean some intelligence, and provide a security footprint in an area we need to protect. It will be the first time a patrol has stayed this long in the Green Zone and 7 Platoon's progress will be monitored closely by those in command.

This was one of those occasions when a sandstorm was a welcome friend. The clouds of sand and dust screened the platoon's movement effectively, allowing Bury and his men to reach the target area without the Taliban even knowing that they had left their base. Eventually the storm died down, allowing the patrol to identify a suitable building to use as their temporary base. Lieutenant Bury spotted a large concrete compound with clear commanding views of the surrounding poppy fields and sent his interpreter to speak to the occupants. A cash offer for use of his compound was agreed upon by the old man who lived there and he and his family seemed happy to leave; they were squatters and not the owners of the compound. The Royal Irish moved in, locking shut behind them the large blue steel gate of the compound.

An examination of the compound suggested that, previously, it had had wealthy owners whose occupations were probably illicit. Within the walls were small rooms, closed with metal doors like those of a safe while, through barred windows, televisions and sofas were visible. Fortunately, the squatter had also handed over the keys to those rooms, which would provide some protection should the Taliban try to mortar 7 Platoon. At the back of the compound there was an old Soviet well that allowed the patrol to filter their own water and a concrete roof supported the sentries who fanned out quickly to provide observation.

While 7 Platoon was deploying and making itself comfortable, a Ranger alerted the platoon commander to a gathering of locals who had arrived at the gate. Lieutenant Bury went out with the interpreter and a protection party to be greeted by some thirty local males who wanted to talk. They were clad in a variety of dish-dashas and turbans but the village elders were identified easily by their white turbans and white beards. Although friendly, they said that they wanted the soldiers to leave.

'The Taliban will come and they will attack you from our compounds, so we must leave if you do not.'

'Why?' I ask.

'Because if we stay the Taliban will force us inside and attack you, and you might fire back and we will be caught in the middle.'

'And if you leave?'

'The Taliban won't come; all will be quiet because they know the compounds are empty and therefore you can bomb them if they attack you.' I realise I am in a Catch 22 of Hellerian proportions.

Of course, we don't want the locals to leave and I explain that we are here to provide security for them, to keep the Taliban away and to stop them intimidating and taxing the village. They are concerned and say they will leave tomorrow if we do not. We pass an uneventful night on an Afghan rug.

The following morning the villagers were in the fields, harvesting the poppies as 7 Platoon patrolled around the compound and waited for the arrival of the Company Sergeant Major. The CSM arrived with rations and with what was termed consent winning activity (CWA) material. Such material is a pivotal element in winning hearts and minds and its positive effect was immediately identifiable. When the elders returned with their request for 7 Platoon to leave, Bury explained to them that the base set up by his platoon would be the first of many such small bases in the area. The elders listened attentively and were receptive to the explanation. They became even more receptive when the CWA material was handed out; this included bags of tomato seed, tea, prayer mats, various tools and wind-up radios; the last items, especially, were always popular. The platoon took care to appease the elders and the mullah. The end result? That evening no one left the village.

During the night the stillness was broken by a tuneless chorus of barking dogs which alerted 7 Platoon to the presence of someone close to the base. One Ranger spotted three males but the intruders raced off into the darkness of the night. Perhaps they were Taliban scouts.

We leave the next evening and the locals are understandably relieved when we go, but we have achieved a lot. With subsequent daytime patrols in the area and another forty-eight-hour patrol completed, a tangible difference can be felt in the village. We recognise locals and they do us. Intelligence has been gathered and, later, some of this definitively saves our lives.

Also in Ranger Company was 8 Platoon, the other C Company platoon, which, initially, was commanded by Lieutenant Peter Gavin with Sergeant Stephen McConnell as his platoon sergeant. At the end of the harvest season, the Taliban targeted a PB in a hotspot near the town centre. This was PB Templer, named for Field Marshal Sir Gerald Templer, one of the most distinguished Irish generals of the twentieth century; commissioned in the Royal Irish Fusiliers he had also been Colonel of that Regiment. The Taliban attack was determined and vicious and was no shoot-and-scoot effort. It lasted for sixty hours during which 8 Platoon defeated a series of enemy assaults. During the battle for PB Templer, Corporal Peter Devlin and Lance Bombardier Gwyn Martin provided excellent and accurate fire support for the platoon, with Devlin controlling mortar fire and Martin artillery. The defeat of the Taliban on this occasion had a long-lasting effect as it enabled talks to be held with local people, many of whom provided valuable information on the attackers.

When Lieutenant Gavin left, Sergeant Stephen McConnell, a Ballymoney man, assumed command of 8 Platoon which he led with distinction for the remainder of the tour; this was half its time in Sangin. McConnell looked back on that experience as the highlight of his Army career and commented that he 'would go back tomorrow'. Although a platoon is commanded normally by a lieutenant, with a sergeant as his second-in-command, it may be commanded by a sergeant and those NCOs who find themselves as platoon commanders regard it as one of the best jobs in the Army. For Stephen McConnell it was just that, especially as he commanded a platoon on active service.

Sergeant McConnell emphasized the danger from IEDs and of having to patrol with the constant threat of such deadly devices in the area dubbed 'IED alley'. He was full of praise for the Explosive Ordnance Disposal (EOD) team from the US Marine Corps that was attached to Ranger Company whom he described as 'very good, no nonsense [soldiers, who were] highly professional'. In an area where there was always a need to be aware of IEDs, it was good to have these excellent EOD personnel at hand. Ranger Company's commander, Graham Shannon, also underlined the quality of the Marine Corps EOD men. Their team leader, Master Sergeant Chavez, reached 'a century of IEDs' destroyed while Ranger Company was in Sangin. Although caught in blasts four or five times, Chavez continued at his task and was known to work at making IEDs safe while Taliban bullets whizzed around his head and tore up the ground around him. The constant pressure that was felt by those clearing IEDs seemed not to affect Chavez. Some indication of that constant pressure can be gained from the fact that, close to one bridge crossing point in the Company area, an estimated ninety IEDs had been laid by the Taliban.

Not every IED was discovered or neutralized before it exploded and attacks on Ranger Company by IEDs included one in which there were four casualties in a Wimik, and another in which a Sapper was blown twenty feet over a wall into an orchard. In the latter case, an extended line of soldiers went out to rescue the casualty whose back had been broken. Yet another IED exploded between Ranger Joevsa Boginisoko, one of the Battalion's Fijian soldiers, and Sergeant Coult MC. Both suffered temporary deafness as a result of the explosion.

Nor were the EOD team members the only US Marine Corps personnel to gain Sergeant McConnell's admiration. US Marine scout/snipers also worked with Ranger Company and with McConnell's 8 Platoon. They, too, 'were very good' and had excellent equipment, including a .50 calibre sniper's rifle and the benefit of a laptop computer to use in calculating the many variables a sniper must assess to achieve accuracy. Scout/snipers are usually to be found in the reconnaissance platoon of a headquarters company but may be interspersed in squadrons and troops, as was the case in Sangin. By comparison with the professionalism of their scout/snipers, the Marine Corps' riflemen appeared slack. The relationship that built up between the Royal Irish and the Marine scout/snipers was excellent, with each developing respect for the other. In fact, the Marine scout/snipers even adopted the Royal Irish shamrock emblems, stitching these to their uniforms. Not one Marine wearing a shamrock badge was injured during Ranger Company's time in Sangin.

On patrol, Sergeant McConnell was always aware of the need for adaptability, flexibility and forward thinking to deal effectively with contacts with Taliban fighters. These were often furious and protracted engagements that, on two occasions, McConnell brought to an end by ordering his men to fix bayonets and charge. The sight and sound of a group of screaming Irishmen with vicious bayonets on the ends of their rifles proved too much for Taliban stomachs on both occasions and the enemy broke. On other occasions, smoke grenades were fired to allow a patrol to move out of a Taliban killing zone. (The grenades were fired from launchers underslung from their rifles; known as UGLs, underslung grenade launchers, these are Heckler & Koch AG-36 40mm grenade launchers, with ladder sights, that can fire a grenade out to a range of 350 metres; one rifle per fire team is UGL-equipped.) One member of Ranger Company said simply that, overall, there were too many contacts to count.

One of the occasions on which Sergeant McConnell led a bayonet charge was on 6 July when 8 Platoon was carrying out a framework patrol into the Green Zone south of Sangin DC to clear a route used for casualty evacuation and to search for enemy weapon hides. The Taliban had shown their intention to contest the control of the area and, recently, had made a number of attacks on ISAF patrols. Movement was difficult in the area with its patchwork of fields, the irrigation ditches, compounds and lines of trees, and the baking heat of the afternoon simply added to the difficulties. Nonetheless, Sergeant McConnell edged his platoon forward towards a Taliban stronghold and a key line of communication.

As they advanced, McConnell made sure that the section conducting the route clearance, which was flanked by his own group, was also protected in depth by the group led by Corporal Walker, the acting platoon sergeant; this group was to the west of the main body. When the patrol had covered 1,400 metres, Sergeant McConnell halted the route clearance team and redeployed Walker's group 200 metres west of the main body. Having ensured that flank protection was in place, the main body resumed its advance. Then 8 Platoon came under intensive fire from several locations, one of which Corporal Walker identified quickly and ordered a hail of 51mm mortars to be rained into the enemy's depth, thereby disrupting his withdrawal. At the same time a sniper engaged an enemy fighter armed with an RPG launcher.

When the Taliban ambush was sprung, Sergeant McConnell and his group were in an open field and caught in the enemy's heavy bombardment of RPG rounds and machine-gun fire. He realized quickly that 8 Platoon was under attack from a larger force than usual and that they might be surrounded. This required immediate and decisive action – the implementation of Sergeant McConnell's watchwords of adaptability, flexibility and forward thinking. He had already formulated a plan in his mind: he ordered the route clearance section to put down suppressing fire to the east and Walker's group to do likewise to the west and south.

Bayonet fixed, McConnell led the third section in a charge across the open field towards the main Taliban positions. Already he had identified two machine-gun posts from which the enemy were engaging his position with heavy fire. After crossing the open ground he used a compound wall as cover before, single-handedly, tackling and destroying both positions with grenades and rifle fire. While fighting through the difficult complex of compounds and irrigation ditches, Sergeant McConnell stopped briefly to confirm the locations of his soldiers after which Corporal Walker was able to join his Sergeant in the assault. Both sections then fought through to the far side of the ambush.

In the course of this action, Sergeant McConnell's section came under fire from behind but he had members of the section engage the enemy firing point to keep the Taliban's heads down while he and Corporal Walker continued the assault. A post-action assessment indicated that the Taliban had engaged 8 Platoon from at least eight well-concealed positions with a force of no less than fifteen men. From the observations of 8 Platoon's soldiers, and later intelligence reporting, it was believed that there had been at least six Taliban casualties. But there might have been innocent civilian casualties as follow-up searches found that the enemy had been firing from compounds occupied by civilians. These local people had not run away as was the usual practice, having been locked inside by the Taliban. This led to the belief that the enemy may well have wanted Ranger Company to call in artillery fire so that there would be civilian casualties and a propaganda coup for the Taliban. However, Sergeant McConnell's decision to launch an immediate assault without waiting for in-direct fire saved many civilian lives.

While showing total disregard for his personal safety, Stephen McConnell had displayed both decisive leadership and outstanding bravery, as well as adaptability, flexibility and forward thinking. His tactical deployment of his sections had deceived the enemy who had failed to identify and engage the other elements of 8 Platoon while his assault was so fast that he closed with the Taliban before they could close their trap. This threw the enemy into considerable confusion and, undoubtedly, saved 8 Platoon from suffering heavy casualties. Although this was a violent action that inflicted significant casualties on the enemy, it was balanced by 8 Platoon's ability to ensure the minimum of collateral damage, which saved many civilian lives. His 'decisive leadership and outstanding bravery' earned Sergeant McConnell the Military Cross.

To the east of the Green Zone is the bazaar, Sangin's market, a scene of activity and commerce that, for a mile, straddles Route 611. This broad road, constructed of stone and covered in dust, has the doubtful reputation of being the most dangerous road in the world. On a daily basis, ANA soldiers patrol Route 611 to look for and clear any IEDs that may have been laid during the night. Needless to say, there are frequent finds of deadly devices.

The bazaar is nothing more than an arcade of open-fronted buildings, in various states of repair, that display their goods to those passing along Route 611. Here are to be found DIY stalls, fruit and vegetable stalls, butchers' stalls, bakers' stalls and other food suppliers. There are also motorcycle repair shops catering for the many Afghans whose favoured mode of transport is a motorbike. None of these establishments has any doors or windows. Generally, local people are friendly, but their attitude changes if the Taliban are in town when they become taciturn since to be seen talking to the infidel ISAF soldiers can result in brutal reprisals. This might mean the loss of a hand or, at worst, beheading. In spite of this inherent threat, the locals, including the stallholders, felt safe when ISAF soldiers patrolled through their area and there were frequent invitations to share a 'chai', or tea, if time could be spared.

Afghan National Police (ANP) checkpoints on Route 611, both north and south of the bazaar, controlled local traffic. In the past these had been targeted by Taliban, who entered the area at night, warned locals to stay indoors, and booby-trapped the police sangars with the inevitable horrific results. In the aftermath of such attacks, there was always a palpable air of tension in the bazaar and everyone became more cautious.

> The twisting maze of high alley walls, dirt tracks, rubble and buildings is perfect territory for a homemade bomb to be placed. Taliban on motorbikes favour the 'shoot and scoot' whereby they drive up to us, fire off a few rounds and run off. Added to this is the threat of the suicide bombers who look to target us. In the cramped conditions of the bazaar, they are ready to spring out on us from anywhere and detonate. We use flares to keep suspect individuals at a safe distance, and explain through our ANA and interpreters to the locals the need to keep back. It is a fine balance between being friendly and protecting ourselves, but something that the Irishmen of Ranger Company … understand the importance of acutely.
>
> Only a few days ago, as we patrolled through the green zone, collecting medical information from the locals so that we could fix water pumps and assess the medical infrastructure, a suicide bomber detonated himself in our midst. The first 7 Platoon knew of it was the bang and huge plume of black smoke and dust that rose into the air, accompanied by a flying leg. We dived into an irrigation ditch as suspects on a motorbike skidded to a halt and ran off to our front. We took incoming fire from our flank as 9 Platoon were engaging Taliban with Rocket Propelled Grenades on the other flank. Then it comes over the radio net, like a huge weight being lifted from our collective shoulders, that there are no friendly casualties.

Following this, 9 Platoon stormed the Taliban compound by explosive entry, the sappers placing a charge against the thick baked-mud wall to create a 'mousehole' through which the leading section made their assault. The section attacked in 'red', tossing in stun grenades before they passed through the breach. However, there were no Taliban. The enemy had fled, dumping the impedimenta of battle at their sandalled heels. Paddy Bury's 7 Platoon then moved through 9 Platoon to search other compounds. They entered in 'green', without firing. Soon Bury and his men were talking to friendly locals while, overhead, fast jets circled, as did attack helicopters, scanning the ground beneath for signs of the fleeing Taliban.

> My platoon brings a local elder back to my boss, where he is offered compensation for the damage done to the buildings. He is very pro-ISAF and understands that we have caused the damage due to the Taliban presence.

Then it was time to move off back to base, having restocked water supplies. But the threat remained high and everyone was on full alert as the sun beat down on his or her backs.

our feet sting as we trudge homeward, through waist-deep irrigation ditches and the beautiful, white, pink and purple poppy fields, flanked by cone-shaped trees. Sometimes this place feels like Tuscany. After ten hours on the ground, we are all safe inside the DC's walls.

Patrols were not the sole activity undertaken by Ranger Company as there were also planned offensive strikes on Taliban strongholds. Among these was a Battlegroup North air assault, Operation GHARTSE TALANDA, into Sar Puzeh in the upper Sangin valley, which was launched on 24 June at the end of the harvest season. Intelligence indicated that Sapwan Qala village was the Taliban command and control centre for the upper Sangin valley. The aim of the operation was to eject Taliban fighters from the northern Sangin area, where they had been increasing their presence after achieving local success in the area, in which lay their key lines of communication and their narcotic facilities. Operation GHARTSE TALANDA, which was to restore NATO's initiative, was a helicopter-borne assault by a reinforced company into the built-up area of Sapwan Qala. It was known that the local Taliban were numerous, as well as being experienced and dedicated fighters, and that a large enemy force was present. The operation was intended to reconnoitre Route 611 and determine the locations of enemy forces.

Chinook helicopters lifted the attackers, including 7 Platoon, and put them down amid the Taliban in darkness, in what Paddy Bury remembered as 'a defining moment of the tour for me'. Alongside 7 Platoon were two platoons from 2 Para and a platoon of ANA with Royal Irish mentors. The landing took place at about 4.00am and was followed by some thirteen hours of 'very hairy' fighting. From the start the fighting was fierce as the landing zone was 'hot', the Taliban contesting the ground immediately. Some of the 'heat' came from Soviet 12.7mm machine guns, known as Dushkas, which were being used in their original anti-aircraft role as well as against the men on the ground. However, the Dushka teams did not last long as they were engaged by Apache attack helicopters that silenced them quickly. Other weapons used against the Chinooks included Chinese rockets that looked like fireworks; these, too, received the attention of the Apaches. Although Apaches usually would arrive later in an action, having been called in, on this occasion they were present from the beginning, to protect the lumbering Chinooks and help suppress enemy fire. They gave excellent support throughout the engagement.

The battle that ensued 'was crazy all day from daylight'. However, in such circumstances, training kicks in and the Rangers were unfazed by the firefight although Sergeant Trevor Coult, a veteran of Iraq where he had earned the MC and of HERRICK IV, described it as the heaviest fighting he had seen. In addition to the Army Air Corps Apaches, air support was provided by the US Air Force with two F-15 Eagle fighter-bombers, a B-2 Spirit stealth bomber and A-10 Thunderbolt II attack aircraft striking at the Taliban. Fire support came from 105s of 7th (Parachute) Regiment Royal Horse Artillery, firing from FOB Inkerman. Their shooting was accurate and welcome with the response to requests for fire always speedy. There were two fatalities among the Paras with WO2 Michael Williams, from Cardiff, of 2 Para killed, as well as Private Joe Whittaker, of Stratford upon Avon, a TA soldier from 4 Para. In all, the operation lasted twenty-four hours and was a major test of 7 Platoon's training and preparation but they had shown themselves to be well prepared – air assault is, after all, the role of 1st Royal Irish – and acquitted themselves with considerable distinction. The successful mission was a major setback for the Taliban. The actions of Corporal Matthew McCord, of 7 Platoon, which earned him a Mention in Despatches, illustrate clearly the nature of the battle at Sapwan Qala.

As Corporal McCord and his section landed, they came under heavy enemy fire and 7 Platoon had to deal with a severe casualty who was shot whilst moving to secure a position. Although recovered to safety, the wounded man subsequently died. Several hours after landing, while McCord and his section were still pinned down by intensive enemy fire, they were ordered to assist in securing a helicopter landing site (HLS) to bring in urgent re-supplies of ammunition and water and evacuate the dead soldier. As McCord and his section, with the platoon commander, moved off, they soon realized that their route to the HLS was covered by accurate enemy fire. Having fought for several hours in intense heat, the exhausted soldiers appraised the situation. An alternative route to the south was considered too dangerous as there was a heavy volume of enemy fire from that direction. Finally, it was decided that the safest option was straight up an embankment, although McCord knew that an enemy sharpshooter had that embankment in his sights.

When the Chinook was but moments from the HLS, McCord 'shook his men into action, fired them up and decisively led his section forwards up the steep embankment'. They were advancing on the designated HLS in full view of the sniper and, as they did so, they faced an increasing rate of enemy fire. Dust plumes from bullet strikes rose all around them but McCord pushed on, encouraging his men through the hail of enemy fire. Finally, they were in fire positions from which they could suppress the foe.

The Chinook aborted its initial intended landing due to the great weight of enemy fire around the HLS. Throughout the hour that followed, Matthew McCord directed and controlled his section's fire to suppress the enemy until the helicopter could land, knowing that if he faltered the vital re-supply would not take place. When McCord and his men had turned the firefight sufficiently, the helicopter came in to attempt another landing. The aircrew touched down although enemy fire continued – and some rounds damaged the Chinook's avionics system – and the ammunition and water were unloaded quickly while the body of the dead para was taken aboard for evacuation to Camp Bastion.

Matthew McCord had shown remarkable bravery and leadership, inspiring his soldiers to keep their nerve over a lengthy and lethal period and, through his courage and determination, ensuring the resupply of troops who had been in action for eleven hours. This was combat leadership of the highest order in the finest traditions of the Regiment.

Second Lieutenant Pete Franks, commanding 9 Platoon in Ranger Company, recalled a memorable August day in Sangin when Paddy Bury's 7 Platoon went out to talk with villagers about possible development projects in their area.

> While the sections were in their cordon surrounding the shura, an IED explosion [nearby] rocked a section…Luckily, none of the men were even scratched by the blast which left a crater three-feet wide and two-feet deep. After receiving some hot intelligence from the locals, 7 and 8 Platoons, together with the OC, returned the following day to uncover more IEDs. What ensued was a true testament to the progress being made in Sangin. Numerous locals approached the callsign giving the exact locations of all the IEDs in the area, including a booby-trapped motorbike in a nearby mosque. In total, six devices were discovered and destroyed by the American disposal team – a bad day for the Taliban. Their day got even worse when they decided to vent their frustrations by attacking 8 Platoon who had set up a cordon. In true 8 Platoon fashion, they returned an immense weight of fire forcing the Taliban attackers to run for cover. The resulting firefight lasted minutes before the Taliban were forced to flee, realising they [had bitten] off more than they could chew.

The IED that exploded during the shura was a daisy chain and it was fortunate that the entire chain did not detonate as both the medic and platoon sergeant were seated over the buried shells at the two extremities of the device.

Pete Franks also noted that the food in Sangin had begun to improve by this time 'with rare delicacies including home-made spam and canned cheese pizzas appearing on the menu'. Chips also materialized but had the drawback, albeit acceptable, that one Ranger had to spend an afternoon peeling and chipping potatoes so that he and his comrades could enjoy them. It was 'a small price to pay for a Company of happy and well fed soldiers'.

Morale was high in Ranger Company, its soldiers knowing that they were doing a dangerous job and doing it well. Ranger Shane Conboy, from Mohill in County Leitrim, had been in the Royal Irish for two and a half years when he deployed to Afghanistan. However, for the first six weeks of HERRICK VIII, Ranger Conboy was on a medics' course and found the separation from his comrades an unsettling experience. 'It was horrible. I was turning on the news morning and evening wanting to know how the boys were doing.' When he finally rejoined he found that 'morale was generally good', even though there was no time to rest. Even during downtime, soldiers were on the alert and, perhaps, standing by as a part of a Quick Reaction Force (QRF) or performing guard duties.

A major factor in maintaining morale was mail. According to Conboy 'The worst two words you could hear were "no mail".' However, there was good contact with home through welfare phone cards, which allowed a thirty-minute call per week free of charge, and there were also e-mail facilities, although those based in Sangin lost this facility for about six weeks. That other factor in maintaining a soldier's morale, keeping his stomach full, was achieved generally through ration packs which, although sustaining, were not inspiring; 'We had fresh food twice; the choppers were bringing in more essential material'.

As Ranger Company extended the writ of the Afghan government in Sangin, one task that fell to 7 Platoon, along with troops of the ANA, was the clearance of the apparently hostile village of Naji Nisamadeen, some 700 metres from their base. In spite of being so close, the village had been the setting for two IED attacks on ISAF troops and hence the decision to clear it. The operation began in the small hours of the morning.

> It's 2 am, and beneath a bright moon that illuminates the alleyways of the bazaar, the men of Ranger Company are preparing to enter the night. With hushed voices radios are checked, equipment tested and weapons made ready. We move out at H Hour. Laden with kit and ladders it requires special effort not to make noise.

Under cover of darkness the Rangers passed through the deserted bazaar quickly and then along Route 611. Can there be any doubt that this is the world's most dangerous road? Before long, 7 Platoon arrived at the location where its cordon was to be established and, assisted by ANA soldiers, began entering and searching a series of empty compounds. Nothing was found in the first compound and the Rangers spread out on to the compound roof to obtain good observation of their immediate surroundings.

Leaving two thirds of the platoon at this location, under command of his platoon sergeant, Lieutenant Bury moved with one section to a large building dominating the area. The gate was padlocked but the Sappers broke the lock quickly, allowing the Rangers to move inside, into a series of darkened corridors and opened doors leading to ransacked rooms. Room by room, and with great caution, the Rangers checked by the light of torches that followed rifles into every darkened cranny. When 'Compound clear' came over the radio, the section climbed onto the roof as the sun began its daily journey across the heavens.

With daylight, the Rangers were better able to assess their surroundings and realized that, by Afghan standards, the building they now occupied was palatial, with two floors, ten rooms, piped water and electricity. All this suggested that this had been the home of a prosperous drug dealer or smuggler. That led to an even more thorough search which soon yielded a significant find: two mobile phone boxes. This was evidence that Taliban 'dickers' had used the building to pass on information on ISAF troop movements to others, or to call in mortar fire. Before long, the search uncovered a Pakistani ID card belonging to a man of fighting age. The presence of such young Pakistani men in Helmand, while not unusual, also indicated the nature of the Taliban forces with whom Ranger Company were engaged in the Sangin area.

Another find was a large bag of powder with some needles. The powder was greenish-brown and the kilo or so of heroin was held up in a soldier's hand. Since most of them had never seen raw heroin before, the Rangers were interested, as was Lieutenant Bury who, also, had never seen the drug in this state. There was a discussion about the value of the haul as it was scattered over the porch and to the winds before the soldiers went back up to the roof.

By that stage the other platoon was also in position. With the village sealed off effectively, the ANA began a sweep, carrying out 'soft knocks' with soldiers rapping on the villagers' doors, explaining who they were, what was happening and asking if they could have a look around each dwelling. With the villagers' consent, the ANA had searched the entire village in a matter of hours, which was much quicker than the Rangers could have managed alone.

> With the village checked and cleared, and with the sun starting to cook our heads inside our helmets, the Company begins to fold back into base. We have moved right through what had been a 'no go' village and found it relatively benign. Now, hopefully, we can start to improve their security and eventually encourage development that will benefit their daily lives.

Perhaps it was repayment for their presence, but, a few days later, information was received about a possible IED buried in an alley in the area.

> We approach with caution and can just make out the ground sign that indicates [that] a lethal trap awaits. Whilst we cordon and clear the compounds nearby, a specialist explosives team helicopters in. They confirm this is a complex device that would have killed a lot of us. Soon they have skilfully destroyed it with a controlled explosion. Nothing could highlight to us more that having the locals on side is key to staying alive in Sangin.

At 7.10 am on 4 September, 7 Platoon was on foot patrol in Sangin town when its members were caught in an IED blast. Ranger Wesley Clyde had walked over the site of the device before it exploded, mortally wounding his comrade, Ranger Justin Cupples. Ranger Shane Conboy was caught by some of the force of the blast and landed in the crater left by the explosion but he had been shielded from the worst effects by the Afghan interpreter who suffered serious injuries including the loss of fingers, part of his nose, lacerations to an arm and metal fragments in his left leg. Conboy described the shock wave that went through his body as 'like being hit by a bus' while he also suffered a temporary loss of sight as his eyes 'went red'. He regained his feet, although he believed that it may have taken him three minutes to do so, and went to help Justin and the interpreter but 'Justin was beyond help'. Corporal Kayley Hournegould, the other medic, with some of the other members of the patrol, had already gone to Justin Cupples' assistance. In spite of her immediate assistance, Justin Cupples was pronounced dead fifteen minutes later. His body was repatriated quickly to the hospital at Camp Bastion where Father Ian Stevenson, the Roman Catholic chaplain, administered absolution and anointed his remains.

Ranger Cupples had been born in the United States on 29 July 1979 and had served with the US Navy during Operation IRAQI FREEDOM in 2003. His family had lived in Miami before moving to County Cavan in the Irish Republic, where Justin met his wife Vilma, a Lithuanian. He began training in ITC (Infantry Training Centre) Catterick in February 2007 and joined the Battalion in September 2007. Posted to 7 Platoon C Company, he fitted in immediately.

Ranger Cupples' death 'brought everyone down for a couple of days, especially so close to the end of the tour'. Shane Conboy carried out only two more patrols after that during which he recalled that 'We'd be sitting laughing and joking and then, all of a sudden [silence] and we'd feel guilty'. The death had a general effect on Ranger Company – Graham Shannon noted that they all 'tasted the raw emotion of loss as one of their own became part of this statistic' (the thirteen dead of Battlegroup North) – but especially in 7 Platoon, of which Justin Cupples had been a popular member.

When the last man of Ranger Company left Sangin on 2 October and W Company of 45 Commando took over the area of operations, there had been marked changes in Sangin. Progress was obvious and W Company had a solid foundation on which to build. Closer cooperation had been achieved between NATO troops, the ANA and the Afghan police through the creation of a joint headquarters. This had improved considerably the level of security in the area, which had allowed the building of schools, mosques and a recreational ground while the main road had also been resurfaced. The town's bazaar was flourishing and the police were better trained. 'More importantly,' as Graham Shannon noted, 'the capability of the Sangin District

Government has developed beyond that expected at the start of the tour, with community based projects flowing into the outlying areas. There are huge changes for the good between the Sangin of March and October 2008.' Major Shannon's contribution to those changes has since been recognized with the award of the Queen's Commendation for Valuable Services.

Note
1. Derived from the Irish Gaelic *dearc*, an eye, 'dicker' comes through *dearcaí*, a watchman or guard. It was from the original Gaelic *dearc* that the American slang word 'dick' meaning detective originated. The expression 'keep dick', meaning to look out, was familiar to the author as a schoolboy as it was sometimes used when a game of street football was being played and someone was assigned to 'keep dick' for the 'peelers'. Likewise, it was used at school when some doubtful activity was underway and early warning of the approach of a teacher was necessary. In the nineteenth century, the word 'dick' was also a slang term for a policeman in parts of Ireland.

Chapter Five

A Long Hot Summer

As the Battlegroup consolidated after Operation OQAB STERGA, and the temperature pushed further up the thermometer, the performance of the OMLTs and the ANA was reviewed and analysed and post-operational reports drafted. The new patrol base, Attal, suffered its first attack, a small arms fusillade followed by mortars, and support was provided for the occupants. Elsewhere, Taliban attacks on two positions at Sangin were fought off after a lengthy action in which one Afghan soldier lost his life. He was not the sole ANA casualty of the day: another had been injured critically in a traffic incident in Gereshk and died of his injuries. Both bodies were recovered to Camp Bastion where Captain (now Major) Michael Potter, the Adjutant, and his staff arranged a dignified ramp ceremony as the remains of the two soldiers were carried onboard an aircraft for the flight to Kabul.

> The ANA attended in numbers, standing to attention, to pay their respects to the two dead soldiers as comrades in the bearer parties carried the coffins onto a Hercules aircraft. As the plane took off in the balmy night air towards Kabul both ANA and R Irish stood solemnly, saluting in silence.

Plans for the Commanding Officer, the Operations Officer and the RSM to fly to Kajaki to visit Captain Beattie and his team came to naught on three successive days due to the unavailability of support helicopters. Such was the shortage of helicopters that the use of these workhorses, so critical to the movement of troops, was restricted. With increased numbers of soldiers on the ground there is an increasing demand for more helicopters. The RAF will deploy Merlins to Afghanistan in the near future as the Merlin fleet increases; additional Chinooks are also to be deployed as the fleet is augmented. Interestingly, the Merlin fleet is being increased with a number of machines bought back from the Danish government and converted to British requirements as medium-lift helicopters. A number of Chinooks that had been in storage for several years because of problems with specialized avionics are being returned to standard specification to help meet the demand imposed by operations.

OMLT 3, based on D (Support) Company and commanded by Major Vance Crow, deployed initially to Camp Shorabak where its members carried out conversion training of the ANA from the AK47 to the M16. There was also minor tactical training at platoon level, plus some other low-level training in other skills. WO2 Billy Roy found that the first company of ANA under training were quick to learn as they had good officers and some very strong NCOs, but not all companies were of this standard. Since the ultimate aim of the Battlegroup was to train the Afghan National Army to a level at which it could operate on its own, it made sense to use the first company to assist in training the others, a strategy that proved successful.

Interpreters assisted the training programme, relaying the instructions of the Royal Irish to the Afghan soldiers. Some interpreters were very good but, again, the standard was not consistent. However, WO2 Roy recalled one exceptional interpreter who was 'worth his weight in gold'. Maktar was an ethnic Hazara who possessed not only very good language skills but was also military minded, an invaluable asset in his role. The ANA soldiers also liked him and when OMLT 3 moved to Sangin, he demonstrated his military knowledge by identifying a suicide bomber and his facilitator who were both arrested. Maktar also got to know several locals while the ANA company commander was very good at making contact with local people. One problem with those local inhabitants who were willing to pass on information was that some had an axe to grind with their neighbours, a seemingly universal problem. None of the interpreters were military personnel and, as already noted, they varied in standard with some, it was said, not even being able to understand the dialects of their own countrymen. On the other hand, some were extremely comfortable with military terminology and provided a very good link between ANA and OMLT personnel. The interpreters also earned the admiration of the Royal Irish soldiers, since they were all under threat of death from the Taliban.

The first ANA company to pass through OMLT 3's hands was able to go unmentored and serve as an exemplar for those that followed. Billy Roy noted that this company 'made big strides' and the company commander was a man who would go down to the mosque and 'have strong words with the locals'.

OMLT 3 redeployed to Sangin with Kandak 3 by road convoy, arriving on 19 April after an exhausting journey of almost thirty hours. Since Kandak 3 had been based at Sangin during two previous tours of duty, they knew the layout of the area and the foe they faced. OMLT 3 had also benefitted from a strong advance party overlapping with OMLT 1 in Sangin. Captain Markis Duggan, a Dubliner, was OMLT 3's Operations Officer and second in command. He had been up on a recce when Major Shirley was casevaced and remained in place, assisting OMLT 1 and preparing the ground for the arrival of the D Company OMLT. Whilst in Shorabak, Major Crow had time to conduct a study of Sangin, its Patrol Bases and the problems it faced. Lengthy discussions were held with Lieutenant Colonel Freely, who negotiated with

General Mohaiyodin on improving the situation. At this time, plans were afoot to move the Battlegroup HQ of 2 Para from Camp Bastion to Sangin District Centre. All this meant that, before any changes took place to the laydown of the ANA and OMLT, it made sense to have Lieutenant Colonel Joe O'Sullivan on side since, as BG North commander, he was the ground holding commander.

Billy Roy noted that 'we had a honeymoon period … during the poppy harvest and had good contacts with locals but this changed once things went noisy and they would then run away from you'. Thus the threat of retaliation from the Taliban for any local who was even suspected of aiding ISAF troops was very real.

Roy was another who expressed a willingness to go back to Afghanistan although he qualified that by adding that it would depend on his role: 'I was lucky enough to go out into PBs and would like to do that again'. As a mentor team commander he had extensive experience of PB Attal in the upper Gereshk valley. Built in the summer following the major operation to clear a Taliban force from the valley, the patrol base was intended to consolidate that gain for NATO. At first it was garrisoned by a company of ANA soldiers, about a hundred men, with seven Royal Irish included in a NATO complement of thirteen; later, the original ANA troops were replaced by a reduced complement of Afghan soldiers from the Counter Narcotics (CN) Kandak, which was also part of 3/205 Brigade. The other NATO troops included a Fire Support Team of Royal Artillery – a captain and two bombardiers who were 'good guys'. In addition, there were three US Army personnel – initially a captain and two SNCOs but later two captains and one SNCO. The FST could bring down artillery fire in two minutes. Artillery available to the team included GMLRS (Guided Multi Launch Rocket System) which was excellent and was used on one occasion to take out a Taliban trench system. Fifteen Taliban perished in that bombardment which followed the blowing up of a NATO vehicle by an IED. Air support was also on call, through a Danish JTAC who gave the PB garrison times when aircraft would be available. The aircraft came from several air forces, including the RAF, USAF, Royal Netherlands and French; aircraft were also on call from the US Navy, flying from an aircraft carrier on station in the Indian Ocean. These were all very good and 'quick off the mark' while there were no worries about bombing accuracy; the planes usually dropped 1,000lb 'iron' bombs, although 500lb laser-guided Paveway[1] bombs were also in their inventory. Apache helicopters were not normally on call but deployed to cover casualty evacuations, which were usually by helicopter. The ANA soldiers found the air support an invaluable boost to their morale and it stiffened the willingness to fight of the CN Kandak men, who, although not attuned to firefights, were buoyed by the presence of fast aircraft.

The ANA company sent out fighting patrols every other day. These pushed about 1.5 kilometres into the Green Zone but it soon became clear that they were expected. To increase security, mobile phones were taken from the ANA soldiers before any operations as it was suspected that some individuals had been using their mobiles to call in Taliban mortar fire. Patrols in the Green Zone could call on fire support from PB Attal while there was occasional support from the Danish Battlegroup with their Leopard II tanks and armoured personnel carriers. However, the Leopards were quite vulnerable on the western side and could approach only through the desert and the IED belt; the death of a Danish driver, when his Leopard struck a mine, emphasized the danger. As with all tanks, Leopard II's main armament has a limited range and can fire effectively only over 4,000 metres; the tanks' armament was no substitute for conventional artillery which, in the form of a British gun troop of 105s, was located at FOB Armadillo, run by the Danes. The latter had mortar-locating radar and, on detecting mortars being fired, would contact PB Attal immediately so that counterfire could be put down.

OMLT 3's commander, Major Vance Crow, considered the ANA soldiers 'very well placed to deal with the present asymmetrical threat in Afghanistan'. His assessment was based on a number of factors, not least the Kandak's ability to develop human intelligence (HUMINT); they had good sources in the area soon after their arrival. Moreover, they 'seemed to have a superior eye for the enemy when on the ground, spotting them more quickly than UK forces' and they were also better at searches. Furthermore, Kandak 3 had a very capable commanding officer, Colonel Rassaul, who had considerable presence and was an excellent leader. Rassaul also had a clear understanding of counter-insurgency (COIN) operations 'including the need to isolate the insurgent from the local population and the importance of intelligence'. By developing the recognition of the first of these factors within the Kandak as a whole, OMLT 3 was able to bring about an impressive improvement in the area. By the time OMLT 3 left Sangin, Kandak 3 had produced a multi-faceted action plan that helped turn numerous areas that had been held by the Taliban into pro-ISAF areas that were 'no go' for the Taliban. Major Crow outlined how this was achieved:

> The first step … was to increase our patrolling profile. After much consultation we managed to get the 3rd Kandak to agree on the principle that if our boots were not on a piece of ground then we could not claim to be dominating that area. The Kandak soon realised that they needed to carry out joint high frequency low density patrolling in order to dominate an area and create an atmosphere of uncertainty for the insurgents … The next step was to win the locals over. This was done at every level and at all our outstations. Slowly we introduced weekly medical clinics for the local people surrounding our outstations. As these became more popular, the 3rd Kandak started to hold Shuras with increasing numbers of local elders. Eventually some of our outstations were running schools and medical clinics for women. Quite an achievement in areas that were, only four months before, pro-Taliban.

As the summer heat increased it created a problem for the European soldiers but, as we have seen, there were plentiful supplies of water and soldiers could carry a generous personal supply in a Camelbak (the back plate of the Osprey body armour has attachments for a Camelbak). Even so, there were still occasional dehydration problems as could be seen when drips were being used to rehydrate during patrol debriefs. Quads, those buzzing little four-wheeled vehicles with motorcycle engines, were used to resupply patrols with water and ammunition, the fresh stocks being carried in a small trailer. In such heat, the weight of kit, including that vital Camelbak, was also a problem and the quads were used to carry heavy weapons and, from time to time, for casualty evacuation using a specially adapted stretcher. For the latter, casevac points were reconnoitred along the Green Zone and the Medical Emergency Response Team (MERT) could be on the ground in thirty minutes. The only occasion on which the response was longer than that was the first time the team was called out for a PB Attal casualty when it took an hour. This, recalled Billy Roy, was because 'there were too many in the chain; it was always sharper later. This was a great morale point'.

Water discipline with the ANA soldiers presented a problem as they needed water to meet Islamic religious requirements on washing. They could not use the wipes that British soldiers used before eating but had to wash their hands in water. This increased the amount of water needed at the PBs and added another headache to those already facing the Quartermaster's team.

Further north up the Helmand valley, but also in the Sangin-based OMLT, was Corporal Scott Elder who demonstrated marked leadership skills and great courage while mentoring ANA soldiers in a PB. During June, Corporal Elder played a notable part in several brutal firefights, the first of which occurred on the first day of the month.

That day the PB was hit by a Taliban onslaught that included RPG fire. Grenades exploded inside the compound but Elder, his fellow Royal Irish and the ANA soldiers reacted immediately and took post at their assigned stand-to positions which, for Corporal Elder, was a roof-mounted GPMG. On reaching the GPMG Elder realized that its protective wall of sandbags offered him no shelter at all, as it was on the wrong side for this attack and enemy fire was coming in from a distance of under 150 metres. Elder was not alone in finding his protection facing the wrong way but, while others leapt from the roof to take cover from small arms and RPG fire, Elder and his Number 2 remained with their weapon. Although exposed to heavy enemy fire, he retaliated with the GPMG, putting down suppressive fire on the attackers. This courageous example proved an inspiration as some ANA soldiers also returned to the roof to bring into action a Dushka near his position. Throughout the engagement, Corporal Elder encouraged his Afghan colleagues to maintain their battle stations, using his characteristic humour to achieve this. His leadership ensured such an effective defence that the Taliban attack was rebuffed and the enemy retreated, taking their casualties with them.

Exactly a week later, a British platoon on patrol close to the PB was ambushed by Taliban and pinned down by intensive small-arms and RPG fire. Once again, Corporal Elder reacted immediately. He raced to his rooftop GPMG position, identified the enemy positions and opened fire with his GPMG. All the while he was under small-arms fire from the enemy but seemed impervious to this and his retaliatory fire dissuaded the Taliban from continuing their attack. This engagement ended with the patrol being able to take the fight to the Taliban who broke off the engagement. There were no losses in the friendly forces either in or outside the PB.

Shortly after this a new patrol base, PB Nabi, was being constructed when, on 22 June, it came under attack without warning. Once again Corporal Elder was present, having been working with Afghan soldiers at the construction of the PB. Almost immediately, a round from a recoilless rifle struck a partially completed defensive sangar and was followed by a hail of small-arms and RPG fire from all directions. Rather than taking cover, Elder raced through the storm of bullets to the damaged sangar and made his way through the chaotic aftermath of the strike to find the .50-inch Browning heavy machine gun. Discovering that the weapon was undamaged, he encouraged an Afghan soldier to act as his Number 2 and they brought the Browning into action, returning fire on the attackers. This drew the bulk of the Taliban's fire on to his position, but his action inspired the other ANA troops to take up their action stations and return fire. Throughout this engagement, Elder remained at his post and encouraged the Afghan soldiers to bring their weapons to bear on the attacking Taliban, his instinctive reactions, courage and personal leadership, ensuring that the base repelled the Taliban attack and was able to mount a successful counter-attack.

Thus Corporal Elder, on three discrete occasions, influenced the outcome of an action. This he achieved through solid leadership, effective gunnery and rallying others to turn the tide of these actions. In so doing, he saved many lives and preserved the integrity of patrol bases while his courage and leadership contributed to the aims of the campaign by helping to establish and maintain the ANA's presence in Sangin. PB Nabi was one of the new bases that gave depth to the OMLT/ANA laydown and did much to disrupt the Taliban and wrest the initiative away from the insurgents.

On 8 June, the day that Corporal Elder helped fight off the attack on the patrol near his PB, a six-man Royal Irish mentor team was operating with its ANA company close to the bazaar area in Gereshk, an area heavily trafficked by pedestrians. One team was conducting a vehicle checkpoint (VCP) near the bazaar when a radio message warned that a suicide bomb attack might be imminent. This served to increase the tension in an already very tense situation.

Within minutes, a car was spotted as it accelerated towards the VCP, driving through the lead section of ANA and racing towards the soldiers manning the VCP.

Although several members of the patrol raised their weapons to fire at the car, one man, Lance Bombardier Paul Gray, of N Battery (The Eagle Troop) Royal Horse Artillery, grabbed a mini-flare, which he fired at the car. The flare hit the windscreen and bounced off but caused the driver to stop. Quick thinking on Gray's part and an appropriate response had ensured that civilian lives were not put at risk by gunfire in such a crowded area. In such cases, soldiers are authorized to try to stop the vehicle either by firing a flare in front of it or, if that fails, by firing into the engine block; should the driver continue then shots may be fired through the windscreen.

A day earlier, on the 7th, a patrol from Musa Qaleh, operating to the east of the town, was caught in an IED blast. Nine Afghan soldiers were killed in action, the largest single loss sustained by the Afghan National Army thus far in Helmand. Since Islamic culture requires that the dead be buried as soon as possible, Battlegroup HQ made every effort to have the bodies brought from Musa Qaleh to Shorabak where Royal Irish soldiers joined their ANA colleagues of 3/205 Brigade HQ to say farewell to their deceased comrades at a ramp ceremony.

During this period in early June, Lance Corporal Richard McKee was in a team mentoring an ANA platoon attached to D Company, Argyll and Sutherland Highlanders (5 Scots). The ANA platoon was taking part in a Battlegroup operation to take and clear Qaryeh-Ye-Kats-Sharbat, a village in the disputed territory north of Musa Qaleh. At a forming up point (FUP) north-east of the village, the ANA were detailed to act as the scout force for the company group. Previous operations had met significant enemy forces in the village and intelligence indicated that Taliban fighters were present that day, 12 June.

Early that morning, the OMLT commander divided his six-man team and the twenty-man ANA platoon into two equal squads with McKee's team mentoring ten Afghan soldiers. ANA elements were to spearhead the company advance on both sides of the wadi to Qaryeh-Ye-Kats-Sharbat, a tactical bound ahead of the main body of the company. South of the village, another company was already in action against the enemy as the OMLT and ANA left their FUP. It was soon clear that the ANA soldiers would need much encouragement from their mentors to begin the advance. Realizing this, Lance Corporal McKee took the initiative immediately by leading the ANA forward with no regard for his own safety. Thus he spearheaded a company group assault into the village where, as his squad approached, they came under small-arms and RPG fire from no fewer than four enemy positions. In the face of this opposition, McKee showed tremendous composure, encouraging the Afghan soldiers to move forward and not seek shelter from the enemy fire. At the same time, he was engaging the enemy himself.

With his commander busy elsewhere, McKee made a quick appreciation of the tactical situation and pushed the ANA through the final hundred metres of open ground to the comparative safety of the village's compounds. By then he had been advancing with them for over ninety minutes in temperatures of up to 46 degrees, but he understood the need to maintain the advance, which he decided to continue. Therefore, he ordered and led the ANA in fighting through the village, clearing compounds on the Musa Qaleh wadi's southern side as they advanced, to ensure a clear route for the company into the village and their objectives on the far side.

While this task was underway, McKee and his ANA soldiers came under effective fire from enemy fighters who were under cover in a compound. With another team in contact, McKee pressed on with his squad, ignoring accurate fire from further enemy positions and also indirect fire. Continuing to disregard the threat, and with considerable élan, McKee led both OMLT and ANA to reach their limit of exploitation and, in so doing, captured a Taliban fighter alive, a rare achievement. His decision to clear forward allowed the company group to move through with the ANA to seize their objectives in the Green Zone and to the west of the village.

Lance Corporal McKee displayed leadership well above that expected of his rank and experience, and superb valour that inspired the ANA to fight by his side against a dedicated and fanatical foe. It was McKee's inspired and decisive actions on 12 June that allowed the company to execute its mission: without his gallantry and drive, the company attack might well not have happened. His actions were rewarded with a Mention in Despatches.

As a result of an imminent Taliban threat in June, the Combat Support (CS) Kandak of 3/205 Brigade ANA was ordered, at short notice, to deploy eighty men from Gereshk to Lashkar Gah for the defence of the provincial capital. Sergeant Kevin Morris, of 3rd Regiment RHA, was second-in-command of the mentor team that accompanied this deployment.

As the troops were travelling to Lashkar Gah on 13 June, one of the ANA's Ford Rangers was blown up in an explosion that, at first, was believed to have resulted from a Taliban ambush. Three ANA soldiers escaped from the Ranger with their uniforms ablaze. The flames were extinguished by their comrades but Sergeant Morris ran forward immediately with a first aid kit to attend to the casualties, who were about fifty metres from the blazing vehicle. Morris directed both the casualties and the uninjured soldiers, assisting them to seek the cover of a gravel mound as ammunition in the stricken vehicle was beginning to heat up, 'cook' and explode. Such was the heat that RPG rounds and small-arms ammunition began detonating and flying off in all directions with fragments showering in airburst effect over Morris and the casualties. It was established later that the initial explosion had been caused by an RPG round which had detonated spontaneously in the rear of the vehicle.

Regardless of the great danger posed by the exploding ammunition, Morris remained calm and administered first aid to four ANA soldiers, one of whom had a serious head injury while the others had major burns. This immediate intervention was crucial in ensuring the survival of the casualties until professional medical assistance arrived. During all this time, Sergeant Morris behaved with admirable bravery and calmness although faced with a real and unpredictable danger from exploding ammunition and the threat of attack by the enemy.

A week later, at 8.26am on 20 June, a suicide attack in the bazaar at Gereshk killed one US soldier, an interpreter and six local civilians; two US Marines and nine civilians were injured. Sergeant Morris deployed to the bazaar with ANA soldiers and brought two casualties back to the joint District Co-ordination Centre (JDCC), in the safety of which he assessed their injuries. The first was a six-year-old boy who had suffered two major injuries, one to his head and the other to his abdomen. The second casualty, a young man in his twenties, had splinter injuries to his arm and leg plus numerous other lacerations. Sergeant Morris administered first aid calmly and organized soldiers around him to assist. His efforts kept the boy alive until he was taken into proper medical care at which point Morris returned to the attack scene to help recover the bodies of the two dead US soldiers.

In an incredibly tense atmosphere, and with rumours of a follow-up attack, Morris appreciated the impact of two disfigured bodies on the younger members of the patrol and, selflessly, went to remove the scattered remains which littered the bazaar, road and stalls. He collected all the body parts with respect and efficiency and tactfully ensured that the younger soldiers were kept away from the grimmest sights.

These actions were typical of a man who, on several occasions, displayed extreme bravery in the face of very real danger and whose example to his ANA colleagues was supreme. By taking on truly horrific tasks, thereby saving others from being exposed to very disturbing scenes, he showed astonishing selflessness.

The junior member of a six-man Royal Irish OMLT working with an ANA company in the Kajaki operations area, Ranger Alan Owens left his base on 17 June on a domination patrol to the north of Shabaz Kheyl and Kanzi. Ranger Owens was mentoring an eight-man ANA section with X Company of 2 Para.

In the course of the patrol, X Company's commander detailed the ANA platoon to clear and dominate open ground north west of Kanzi, an area that was but 300 metres from known enemy positions in the villages of Bagai Kheyl and Makikheyl. On three earlier occasions the platoon had seen action in this area. Owens' section was the lead section of the company and, at 7.25pm, as he approached a mud–walled compound, his men came under sudden, accurate and deadly fire from RPGs and automatic rifles. With bullets whistling about their heads, the section took cover quickly in the compound where, once firm, they returned fire. Owens radioed the initial contact report before joining the ANA troops in putting down suppressive fire on their attackers. He also began organizing the ANA's fire positions and their resupply so that they would prevail in the firefight. While he was doing so, heavy accurate fire from four different locations was being laid down on the ANA soldiers who were terrified. Lethal fire from other Taliban locations had also pinned down the supporting ANA sections.

Ranger Owens could have taken cover and waited for fire support from the remainder of X Company but, instead, for the duration of the hour-long contact, he attended to the ANA section and moved constantly between their positions to encourage them and harden their resolve. During all this time, he instilled fire discipline, ensured that ammunition was not wasted and kept the ANA soldiers in cover when they were not firing. All this he did in full view of the enemy, thus placing himself in great danger to ensure that the ANA remained effective. He continued transmitting accurate reports, with detailed grid references for the enemy positions, and co-ordinated and adjusted fire with mortars, artillery and aircraft. When he spotted a threat from a flank, he issued quick fire control orders for two anti-bunker missiles to be fired at the enemy and, as light faded, made certain that his ANA section would maintain its discipline by assigning arcs of fire to its members and ensuring that each soldier knew exactly where the Taliban were located. This almost led to his death or serious injury as supporting ANA sections behind his positions saw his movements in the diminishing light, thought he was Taliban and fired at him.

As the contact was drawing to a close, Owens, on the orders of X Company's commander, organized a night withdrawal which was executed under fire with artillery support. When they reached relative safety he accounted for his men and continued with the patrol. Knowing that the Taliban fire had been indiscriminate and suspecting that a neighbouring village might have suffered casualties, he led the ANA into the village to check for any injured before returning to the PB. There had been no casualties but the villagers expressed gratitude for his concern which gave them reassurance.

Although Ranger Owens' task was to mentor ANA soldiers, his actions demonstrated leadership and maturity well in excess of what might be expected of a soldier of his rank and experience. By his presence he had strengthened the resolve of the ANA, especially as night came down. In the face of the enemy he displayed great personal courage in individual actions and showed that he had a clear grasp of the key principle of counterinsurgency. He also showed empathy with the local population through his checking for casualties; this was something no amount of fighting could ever have created. Ranger Owens' courage and leadership brought him the Military Cross in the March 2009 awards list.

We have already noted the speedy actions of WO1 Andrew Taylor, of 16th Close Support Medical Regiment, RAMC, on 31 May when the Land Rover in which he was travelling was blown up by a suicide bomber. Less than a week after that incident, Taylor was in Musa Qaleh when an ANA soldier was brought in with very severe injuries from an IED explosion. There were also seven ANA dead, whose bodies had all been torn apart in the blast.

WO1 Taylor assisted with the treatment of the wounded man in the Regimental Aid Post (RAP) before volunteering to prepare the body parts of the dead soldiers for return to their families. While this highly unpleasant task was underway another ANA soldier recognized one of the dead as his brother. In a state of considerable distress, the unfortunate man shot himself in the stomach. Taylor went to his aid immediately, made a call for oxygen and then cut off the man's clothes so that he could apply direct pressure to the wound. Calling for assistance to maintain that pressure, Taylor then tried to ensure an open airway before transferring the casualty to the RAP.

Once again, this warrant officer had shown great presence in difficult conditions as well as selfless commitment. He would continue to do so.

During the first week of June the Battlegroup Tactical HQ visited Gereshk to study the east bank of the Helmand river in the Gereshk valley, where it could be seen that the security situation was changing, with an already obvious increase in commerce in the town; the bazaar was now thriving. That improvement in the area's commercial life could also be seen in the Green Zone just north of Gereshk where the local farming community was working at the wheat harvest and bringing their harvest and other produce to market. Such positive signs were among a number of indicators that the security offered by the ANA and its ISAF allies was a welcome factor for local people while 'The Taliban are more often rejected reflecting a growth in local confidence'.

Tac HQ also patrolled to the PB known as the 'Witch's Hat' where Captain Shoukru and his mentor team with their ANA counterparts had developed friendly relations with the inhabitants of the surrounding villages. That they had created such a positive and productive relationship in the area meant that the incidence of Taliban attacks had decreased markedly while Taliban activity, generally, was also much reduced. Westward across the valley was a different story as the Taliban remained determined to eliminate PB Attal which menaced their domination of the area around Shurakay village. However, the Battlegroup was doing its utmost to present and establish the ANA as the face of the Afghan government. This had long been an area of Taliban influence and wresting control from them required a psychological struggle as well as the physical battle.

For their part, the Taliban were launching attacks on PB Attal that showed their level of determination; but the Royal Irish and the ANA troops had interdicted many attacks and controlled the key ground, thereby forcing the enemy to change their tactics. At the same time, OMLT 4 and the ANA were 'cultivating the people in the valley to wean them away from the Taliban'. It promised to be a long struggle but the men in PB Attal were on their mettle and determined not to let the enemy win. It is worth remembering that the patrol base had been built after a major operation to push back the enemy front line. After its initial garrison of a composite ANA company, known as Attal Company, and a mentoring team of twenty, including a Gunner FST, had been reduced, there was a respite of about a week before the Taliban began attacking the post. Sadly, this reduction in strength and the deployment of the less effective CN Kandak at PB Attal also ceded some of the initiative to the Taliban. Nonetheless, the base was a real deterrent to the enemy and with artillery support on call through the FST, as well as air support, that deterrent was credible and obvious to local farmers and villagers as well as the Taliban.

Captain Jonathan Huxley served at PB Attal in its early days and was impressed by the skill of the FST. Infantry are usually slightly cynical about their Gunner colleagues with soubriquets such as 'long-range snipers', 'drop shots' and 'all over the shop' (a reference to the Royal Artillery's motto *Ubique*, Everywhere) among those that are printable. However, the speed of response to calls for fire support and the accuracy of that support opened many eyes. (Guided MLRS could only be used if a ten-figure grid reference for the target was provided.) As Jonathan Huxley commented, most infantrymen saw Gunners tagging along on exercises and passing on messages over their radios but never saw the effect of those messages. That changed in Helmand. Huxley, who had served in the RAF Regiment for eight years before transferring to the Royal Irish, commented also on the air support. This was always good but could not be used unless a qualified forward air controller (FAC) was available on the ground. Airmen also had to be very careful when dropping bombs to ensure that they did not cause casualties amongst civilians. On many occasions, the risk of creating civilian casualties was so great that the aircraft would be asked to perform a show of force, a low pass over the enemy positions that was often enough to frighten the Taliban into withdrawing. There were also occasions when the range of languages in the NATO forces could present a problem. One such occurred with the presence of a Czech Air Force FAC and a Dublin signaller on the ground. A report relayed from the ANA suggested that fifteen 'jeeps' had arrived in the enemy positions. This was the type of target that justified calling in fast air support as fifteen jeeps – now a generic descriptor for almost any 4 x 4 vehicle – could have brought as many as six or eight men apiece. A RAF Harrier arrived overhead but the pilot reported that he could not see the target although, in the area where the jeeps were reported to be, he could see a flock of sheep. It transpired that the ANA soldiers, for some unknown reason, had counted the sheep and reported their appearance. As the message passed along its route, 'sheep', or possibly 'sheeps', became 'jeeps'. Fortunately, no strike was launched on the sheep which were destined to become mutton in more conventional fashion.

While all this activity was underway, the Battlegroup received a visit from HRH The Duke of York, Colonel in Chief of the Royal Irish Regiment. Prince Andrew, who was interested both in the way in which the Regiment was deployed with the ANA and the nature of the conflict in Helmand, met and talked at length with members of both 1st and 2nd Royal Irish, asking them about their experiences and what they had done. In the course of his visit, the Duke of York also met General Mohaiyodin from whom he received a gift of an Afghan carpet from the General's home province of Ghor.

In Chapter Four we saw that Operation GHARTSE TALANDA, was launched in late-June to eject Taliban from the northern Sangin area where they had been increasing their presence. The helicopter-borne assault into Sapwan Qala was undertaken by a reinforced company which included ANA and OMLT, among whom was Ranger Sitiveni Bolei, one of a number of Fijian soldiers in 1st Royal Irish.

In the course of the operation, Ranger Bolei, with five other OMLT members and an ANA platoon, had the task of clearing compounds, searching local people and conducting key leader engagements. This task was especially dangerous in an area where the Taliban were making increasing use of IEDs and suicide bombers.

Bolei's team deployed by helicopter on 24 June and by the time they debussed the LZ was under heavy small-arms fire from Taliban. British casualties had been sustained and Bolei's platoon commander was ordered to advance to cover the northern flank of the assaulting company, which was to push westward to Sapwan Qala. However, the mentors did not know that the Afghan platoon commander, who was immobilized with fear, had refused to leave the LZ with the rest of the ANA soldiers. As his team moved to cover the company flank, Ranger Bolei realized that their position would become impossible and that the ANA platoon might be outflanked and captured by the Taliban. On his own initiative, and without thought for his own safety, Bolei left his position, which was secure, and raced back over forty metres of open desert to the disheartened and exposed Afghan soldiers. All the while he was under heavy small-arms and RPG fire from the enemy. When he reached the ANA soldiers, Bolei was able to restore their confidence and take back the tactical initiative. He did so by moving from soldier to soldier, still under enemy fire, and encouraging them to move forward to the mentor team. Once there, the platoon secured the company flank and a dangerous situation had been averted.

There followed a lengthy battle, in temperatures over 45 degrees, during which all radio communications broke down. After almost eight hours, the ANA soldiers and mentors were pinned down by accurate Taliban sniper fire and split between two locations. In this chaotic situation, the Taliban attempted to outflank Ranger Bolei's position. As this was happening, Bolei volunteered to act as liaison between the group's two positions. Moving between them, he became, once again, a focus for enemy attention, drawing much fire. Nonetheless, he continued with his task, ignoring the fire, and acted as the sole communications channel between the two elements. As he moved he fired at the enemy positions to suppress their fire. Finally, radio communications were restored and the situation was stabilized with ANA and British soldiers safe from being overrun by the Taliban.

By his gallant actions and leadership, well above that expected of a soldier of his rank, Ranger Bolei secured the vulnerable flank, ensuring the success of the opening phase of the operation and saving the lives of his fellow soldiers, both British and

Afghan. His great courage, physical strength and determination inspired his comrades throughout a determined and vicious enemy onslaught. Ranger Bolei recieved a Joint Commanders' Commendation.

In early-spring 2008, in the contested town of Sangin, Taliban forces increased pressure on ISAF and ANA bases with attacks concentrated on the small patrols projected from PBs Waterloo and Viking, two isolated bases in the southern Sangin area; the latter was unmentored. This tactic seemed to stem from an enemy realization that they had little chance of overrunning a PB. As a result of this aggression, patrols from Waterloo and Viking suffered daily attacks through ambushes and IEDs, in which both ANA troops and their British mentors sustained several casualties.

When Colour Sergeant John Mason's Officer Commanding, Captain Chris Wright, was evacuated as a casualty, he was given the tasks of mentoring both PBs Waterloo and Viking, a role to which he proved well suited. Accepting the additional responsibilities, Colour Sergeant Mason demonstrated resolute leadership and discharged his duties fearlessly, guiding the ANA in aggressive daytime and nocturnal patrols to seize the initiative from the Taliban. Because of this, and under his leadership, the Taliban suffered numerous losses while over fifteen IEDs were disabled; Mason himself discovered a significant number of these. With Sangin's southern flank secure for the time being, Mason's six-man mentor team, with a platoon of twenty ANA soldiers, deployed on Operation GHARTSE TALANDA, the heliborne assault on Sapwan Qala on 24 June.

Unfortunately, both the ANA platoon commander and his sergeant became immobilized by shock as they debussed from the helicopter and witnessed the ferocious enemy reaction which had already taken one life. With the pair paralyzed by their fears, their soldiers were, to all intents, leaderless. Mason reacted quickly to restore the morale of the terrified and directionless Afghan soldiers. Moving constantly amongst them, in spite of effective enemy fire, his personal example rallied them and encouraged them to advance over 3.5 kilometres through eleven hours of contact with a numerically strong and determined enemy in stifling heat.

When, at one point in the battle, the forward elements of Mason's patrol were ambushed, he reacted by leading an attack through the Taliban positions. Realizing that several ANA soldiers had not advanced, and thereby risked being isolated and overrun, he ignored his own safety and dashed back through the ambush position to gather up and rally his ANA men. Although exposed to heavy fire throughout this period, he led or, in some cases, dragged the Afghan soldiers forward to continue the fight.

All twenty of Colour Sergeant Mason's Afghan soldiers and his five mentor comrades, returned to Sangin unscathed, thanks to his inspiring leadership from the front, his courage and his selfless actions. Stepping up to an unfamiliar level of command responsibility, he overcame a brutal enemy attack while his deeds contributed to the success of Operation GHARTSE TALANDA through which ISAF regained the initiative in the upper Sangin valley. His subsequent Mention in Despatches was richly deserved.

Lance Corporal Cecil Carter, of the Adjutant General's Corps and attached to The Highlanders (4 Scots), was a company clerk who was with an OMLT resupply convoy as it came back from a provisional PB in the Marjah area, which has probably the greatest concentration of opium farms in southern Helmand. Criss-crossed by irrigation ditches, the area is difficult to patrol as the waterways make it exceptionally hard to vary patrol routes, thereby allowing both Taliban and local criminals to set ambushes.

On 30 June, as the resupply convoy, of six vehicles including two stripped-down Land Rovers, two Ford Rangers and two seven-ton lorries, was returning from Marjah, it had to stop at a defile entrance so that, as with every such vulnerable point, it could be checked for IEDs or mines. However, when a number of vehicles had passed through, Taliban forces attacked. Rifle fire, at a considerable rate, was supplemented by RPGs from two different positions. No ambush position was more than 200 metres from the rear of the convoy. Carter, the top cover gunner in the last vehicle, opened fire with his machine gun, an immediate reaction that probably saved several ANA soldiers who were able quickly to debus from their soft-skinned Ford Rangers and take cover behind an embankment. However, their doing so meant that their vehicles blocked the defile, isolating Carter's Land Rover at the tail of the convoy. Thus the vehicle was not only in a vulnerable position but also made a choice target for the enemy.

Carter had little more protection in his Land Rover than the ANA had had in their Rangers. Other than some ballistic matting, his vehicle was unprotected but he continued engaging enemy positions with his machine gun. This allowed both the mentors and ANA to deploy into positions from which they could return fire, as Carter had distracted the enemy from pouring fire on the sheltering soldiers. Before long, however, the Taliban had found their range and bullets were striking Carter's Land Rover, from which he continued to fire as the commander made a plan and radioed a contact report. Calmly and deliberately, Lance Corporal Carter fired aimed bursts at identified positions, although he had to change ammunition belts several times. All the while he was still under fire, his vehicle taking strikes, and he remained isolated.

As the other mentors and ANA got into position and began firing, the situation stabilized, taking some of the pressure off Carter. However, he remained in place to identify the enemy positions for the ANA and give them fire control orders. Then, without warning, the convoy was also engaged by Taliban to their front and the ANA switched their attention to deal with the fresh threat. This left Carter isolated again and under fire from around the compass with rounds striking his vehicle.

Nonetheless, he did not desist, engaging the enemy with sufficient suppressive fire to allow the commander to make a new plan to move the convoy forward and get the ANA out of contact.

Lance Corporal Carter's behaviour throughout the engagement was exemplary and was instrumental in effecting the safe extraction of the convoy from the ambush without loss of life. For a junior clerk to act in such a way was remarkable, showing great professionalism and courage and the standards of a veteran infantry NCO. His actions on the road from Marjah brought him a Mention in Despatches.

By this time the Battlegroup was deployed more broadly across the province than was any other unit of Task Force Helmand. To the north, there were Battlegroup elements in Kajaki, Musa Qaleh and Sangin while, to the south, they were in Lashkar Gah and Garmsir, with other elements in Gereshk and Shorabak in the centre. Garmsir had also been the scene for much fighting for the US Marine Corps' 24th Expeditionary Unit in a struggle that was much more along conventional warfighting lines than elsewhere. Enemy fighters had taken the field in substantial groups, with many of them having but recently crossed the border from Pakistan; among them were Arabs and Chechens as well as Baluchs and Punjabis. However, the Marines and Task Force Helmand had fought hard to clear Garmsir town of Taliban and their efforts had enjoyed considerable success with refugees returning home and the bazaar open again for business. Sergeant Russell and Corporal McCready of the Royal Irish had both 'managed to get involved and contribute to a significant degree'.

At a high-level security conference in Lashkar Gah in mid-June, attended by Governor Gulab Mangal, his deputy, the head of the National Directorate of Security and the provincial police chief, as well as Lieutenant Colonel Freely and General Mohaiyodin, the last-named had been charged with redeploying a Kandak of his brigade.

In Gereshk, on 19 June, General Mohaiyodin had a pleasant official duty: he was to hand over to district education officials the keys of two new school buses that were a present from the United States. Ed Freely noted that this handover marked 'the increased security levels that have enabled schools to open again since being forbidden by the Taliban'. Even so, the visit of the brigade commander and his mentor was marked by a suicide bomb in the town and a single gunman firing at the military vehicles. Neither incident marred the handover ceremony. Peace was restored quickly by troops who reacted with professionalism.

Another significant pointer to changing attitudes in Helmand was related by General Mohaiyodin to Freely. There were many Pashtun volunteers from the province coming forward for the ANA, something that would hitherto have been impossible due to the level of Taliban domination. This was certainly a tribute to the increased professionalism of the ANA and the degree of assurance they had instilled in local people. A further tribute came from an unexpected source. General

Mohaiyodin received a phone call from a Taliban fighter who explained that he respected the ANA and really did not want to fight them but was 'under a serious obligation' so to do. Yet again, this was a conversation that no one would have expected to happen earlier in the year.

However, that the situation in Helmand was still fragile was emphasized in the last week of June when a young girl was killed during an engagement between ISAF troops and Taliban. Although not involved in the incident, there were repercussions for Captain Shoukru's mentor team as a crowd of angry locals gathered outside their patrol base. The British were to blame for the child's death, was the crowd's cry, and they wanted revenge. This led to one of the few breakdowns between the Royal Irish and their ANA colleagues as ANA troops in the PB turned on the OMLT members. Over several hours, Shoukru's team used all their diplomatic skills to try to resolve the problem and calm the crowd. However, it was a situation that was heaven-sent for the Taliban who exploited it ruthlessly to place gunmen in the crowd. When firing broke out, two of the enemy were identified positively by the Royal Irish who returned fire and killed the pair. The crowd then dispersed and, in the confusion that followed, Captain Shoukru led his men out of the PB in a fighting withdrawal to FOB Gibraltar, about a mile to the north. As the section moved they were engaged by Taliban with both direct and indirect fire but completed their journey with no casualties. Fortunately, peace and order was soon restored, allowing the Royal Irish team to resume their duties but it had been a sharp reminder of the inherent Afghan distrust of foreigners and could have had even more tragic results.

As June came to an end, the Battlegroup's tour had run half its course. After a relatively quiet start, it had developed into a hectic and violent experience and more along the same lines could be expected as the Taliban fought to maintain control over what they considered their areas. The end of June saw the rotation of Kandaks. Kandak 1 relieved Kandak 2 in Musa Qaleh. Kandak 2 returned to Shorabak to take some leave and begin conversion to M16 weapons under their OMLT 2 mentors. OMLT 1 had by now received their successor to Major Simon Shirley, who was undergoing a programme of surgery to rebuild his arm. Major David Middleton, the new OC A Company, had been in theatre approximately three weeks before taking his OMLT and Kandak 1 up to Musa Qaleh. He had had time to liaise with David Kenny, who had achieved much in Musa Qaleh – but Middleton and his boys were to be severely tested too, as the Taliban developed plans to unseat the 'turncoat' Governor, Mullah Salam, and the combined forces of the Afghans and ISAF. Although Middleton had not done the training in Kenya, he was prepared well for his task; he had seen operational service in Iraq in 2003, as well as Kosovo in 1999, Sierra Leone in 2000 and in Northern Ireland.

While the fighting during July was a constant grind with enemy aggression encountered on a daily basis, there was a pronounced spike of enemy activity in the middle of the month. An example of that spike occurred on 14 July when two patrols in the Green Zone north of Musa Qaleh met planned Taliban ambushes.

The Taliban had not given up their aspiration of regaining Musa Qaleh and intelligence during July indicated that they remained determined to do so. As a result, Satellite Station North, the northern security outpost for Musa Qaleh, became the focus of frequent heavy fighting. A six-man team from OMLT 1 had moved into the post alongside an ANA company at the end of June, relieving OMLT 2. They were soon embroiled in sharply contested engagements with the Taliban. Major Middleton noted that

> Musa Qaleh presents a unique challenge as an operating zone in Afghanistan. Whilst other areas, such as Sangin or Gereshk, boast significant NATO ground holding force elements, in Musa Qaleh it is the Afghan National Army who primarily hold the line and generate the operating space for reconstruction and development activities. This operating area is immature; the town returned to government control in December 2007, before that being heralded in Helmand Province as the Taliban capital of the north. In addition, Musa Qaleh occupies a special place in the minds of Royal Irish soldiers; it was here after all that much of the Battalion's contribution to the 3 PARA Battlegroup in 2006 spent their time. Rgr Anare Draiva was killed in action here and LCpl Paul Muirhead mortally wounded; many more bear the physical and mental scares of that fight.

With Satellite Station North only a hundred metres from the southern edge of Taliban territory, almost every patrol included an engagement with the enemy. In their determination to see off the coalition forces, the Taliban employed small arms, RPGs, machine guns, mortars and, of course, IEDs. On 14 July, the mentor team commander, Captain William Meddings, a Royal Anglian Regiment officer attached to the Battlegroup, led a patrol of six British and twenty ANA soldiers into the Green Zone. In conditions of visibility limited by the high growth in the area, the patrol pushed north, aware that they were on ground where they had often come under attack before. Their objective was to identify enemy locations in Towghi Keli. At the outskirts of the village they stopped to look for possible enemy positions.

They were unaware totally that they had stopped in the killing zone of a prepared ambush which opened with the detonation of a 'daisy-chain' IED, eight linked devices that tore up the ground in a ripple of deafening explosions. One British soldier suffered severe injuries from one of the blasts, which was followed immediately by a storm of small-arms fire. A quick assessment told Meddings that the wounded man needed immediate treatment if he was to have any chance of survival. Thus he organized defensive positions, regrouping his men to give suppressive fire and provide time for the team medics to treat the casualty.

The situation was confused further by another ambush on a supporting patrol, some 300 metres away, which struck that patrol from two directions. In spite of all this, Meddings remained calm as he commanded his patrol, organized the casualty's protection and called in the assistance needed to evacuate the wounded man. Having identified the Musa Qaleh wadi as the best point from which to evacuate the casualty, he led his patrol through swampy ground and thick growth for several hundred metres to rendezvous with the Quick Reaction Force. En route, he took his turn at carrying the stretcher. Having handed over the casualty to the QRF, he organized his men for a counter-attack on the Taliban positions and continued the battle for several hours before withdrawing to base.

On this July day, Meddings had ensured that a badly-wounded soldier survived by organizing his rapid evacuation. Such decisive and courageous actions as he had demonstrated that day were typical of his leadership at Satellite Station North throughout July and August.

Sergeant Hughie Benson commanded the supporting patrol that day and his leadership and personal courage proved exceptional, inspiring all the members of the ANA company as well as his OMLT members. Those qualities of courage and leadership were typical of this son of the Regiment; his father was serving as the Quartermaster and three members of the Benson family were in Helmand.

When Captain Meddings' patrol came under attack, Sergeant Benson moved to assist but his patrol was ambushed also. In spite of fierce enemy fire, Benson led his patrol from the front, fighting through to link up with the other patrol and assist in evacuating the casualty. In total, this engagement lasted for four hours while the evacuation was being carried out after which Benson led his patrol in a series of counter-attacks that defeated the Taliban.

A few days later a battalion-scale operation was launched to eject Taliban from the area north of Musa Qaleh and Sergeant Benson's team of OMLT and ANA were once again engaged. They had also been involved in several other actions since Towghi Keli. At Shawaruz, Benson's men were pinned down by heavy and accurate machine-gun and RPG fire. Yet again, Benson took the fight to the enemy, calling in supporting mortar fire and leading his team in a series of sharp attacks that pushed the enemy some two kilometres northwards during more than three hours of sustained combat during which several Taliban were killed. When one of his Afghan soldiers was wounded badly and fell in open ground, Benson ordered covering fire while he rescued the wounded man and took him to an exchange point from where he could be evacuated. Having done so, he returned to the fighting where he organized defensive positions at the end of this lengthy but very effective action.

Such sustained outstanding courage and inspirational leadership typified Benson's command of Afghan and British soldiers. All his patrols were conducted in a daily high tempo, intensely threatening, brutally harsh environment and we will see yet another example of his exemplary soldiering in Chapter Six.

Another who was involved in the action at Towghi Keli was Ranger Gavin Fox, a member of the OMLT Battlegroup Intelligence Cell and its photographer. Ranger Fox deployed to varying locations as required and, during July, was at Satellite Station North where he was frequently in the centre of heavy fighting as the Taliban maintained the pressure that they hoped would regain Musa Qaleh.

On 14 July Ranger Fox was part of Captain Meddings' patrol of six British and twenty ANA soldiers which was caught in the IED blast at the village. As a trained team medic, Ranger Fox was the first to reach the wounded soldier, who lay in six inches of mud and stagnant water, bleeding heavily from amputated lower limbs. Although the ambush continued around him, Fox showed no concern for his own safety as he treated the wounded soldier in an effort to stabilize his condition and allow his evacuation. Working with great speed, Fox applied dressings and tourniquets and administered pain relief. His speedy reactions proved critical in saving his comrade's life.

Having given this immediate treatment, Fox then participated in the evacuation. The injured man had to be carried fifty metres along the bed of a canal before being lifted over the canal bank into a nearby field. All of this had to be done under enemy fire. To ensure that the casualty remained stable, Fox supervised this difficult move. Then, realizing that the ANA soldiers' response to the enemy fire was becoming inadequate, he organized them as stretcher bearers, thereby allowing the British soldiers to put down effective suppressing fire so that the wounded man might be carried farther. At this point, the casualty evacuation party was able to break contact with the enemy after which Ranger Fox organized another changeover of personnel with the British soldiers taking over the stretcher. He monitored the condition of the injured man until the emergency rendezvous was reached and the casualty was handed over to the Quick Reaction Force for evacuation. Ranger Fox then rejoined his team which was launching a counter-attack into the Green Zone to drive out the enemy.

The professionalism, coolness and courage of Ranger Fox were critical in allowing a badly-injured soldier to be extracted from the battlefield. Time was critical in saving the soldier's life and without the speedy reaction of Ranger Fox the casualty would have died. His determination and courage were demonstrated further by his immediate return to action in an area that the enemy had dominated and the full part that he played in the subsequent defeat of the enemy.

Anyone who watched Sky TV's series 'Return to Afghanistan', in which actor Ross Kemp made a return visit to Helmand in 2008 – he had previously presented a series featuring the Royal Anglian Regiment – will know that one programme concentrated on Dave Middleton's OMLT 1 in Musa Qaleh. Viewers could not but be impressed by Major Middleton's professionalism and his calm approach to command, especially when his patrol was pinned down by Taliban fire for several hours. To Kemp's query, when the presenter realized that the soldiers were running short of ammunition, Middleton commented that he needed only one soldier to fire occasional bursts at the Taliban to keep them pinned down. His coolness reflected his confidence in his soldiers, both Royal Irish and ANA, while he knew that support in the form of artillery fire and NATO aircraft was at his call. Paradoxically, Musa Qaleh had been having a quiet week until Kemp and his team arrived but, as soon as they ventured out on patrol, the Taliban gave vent to their anger prompting the Commanding Officer to ponder if the Taliban did not 'also object to Eastenders?'

The members of Imjin Company who had deployed on mentoring duties to FOB Keenan became part of a composite company under command of the Argyll and Sutherland Highlanders (5 Scots) in the Danish Battlegroup Centre. In addition to Royal Irish personnel, the company also included soldiers of both the Royal Highland Fusiliers (2 Scots) and Argylls, plus ANA. In the first two weeks of July, two of the TA soldiers, Corporal William Lynn and Lance Corporal Lee Averill, demonstrated the professionalism that had led to their platoon being assigned to the mentoring role.

When the platoon arrived at Keenan the ANA soldiers there were from the CS Kandak, and were members of the Afghan artillery with limited infantry skills. After a month, on 1 July, the CS Kandak soldiers were rotated and relieved by members of the CN Kandak. By the time the CS Kandak soldiers were relieved, their infantry skills had increased markedly, largely due to the efforts of Corporal Lynn.

A daily patrolling routine had been established at Keenan with patrols usually at platoon-plus strength, with each patrol including a section of 2nd Royal Irish, two ANA sections and a small HQ with an SNCO from the ANA and a Royal Highland Fusiliers' mortar fire controller (MFC). One such patrol left Keenan on the morning of 3 July with Corporal Lynn commanding the Royal Irish section. This 'reassurance' patrol into an area of the Green Zone north-east of the base was aimed at establishing and increasing confidence in the coalition forces amongst the local population; it was also the first occasion on which 2nd Royal Irish soldiers patrolled with personnel of the CN Kandak whose quality was thus unknown to them.

By early July the harvest season was over and the Green Zone had changed its face, now presenting wide open spaces of fields under the plough, ragged tree lines and the irrigation ditches that broke up the landscape. In the area where the patrol was operating, there were clusters of compounds, some occupied, some not, that ranged from individual family homes to compounds around fields. It was an area where, hitherto, there had been little enemy activity.

Lynn's patrol was to loop around the base, covering about seven kilometres and, while reassuring the local population, it was also intended to gauge the attitude of that population towards ISAF while allowing the CN Kandak troops to get to know the area. Along its route the patrol visited a number of local families whose reaction to the troops was positive. After some two hours, as the patrol moved northwards, a civilian contractor's helicopter, carrying out resupply to the FOBs, flew over and the platoon commander radioed the Operations Room to inform them of the helicopter's approach to FOB Keenan. As he did so, there was a burst of machine-gun fire from the north-east and the patrol went to ground but it soon became clear that the helicopter had been the target. Since ICAT, the contractor, helicopters usually operated in pairs, it seemed that the second helicopter would also be shot at.

To counter this threat, Lieutenant Byrne, the platoon commander, deployed his patrol to draw enemy fire away from the incoming helicopter. He did so by turning his platoon around to face the enemy firing positions and advanced in a two-up formation with Corporal Lynn's section on the right and the second ANA section to the rear. As Byrne's men moved east-west, across the northern face of Keenan, and about a kilometre and a half out from their base, the second helicopter came under enemy fire. Several rounds struck the machine's fuselage. Byrne increased the speed of his advance and Lynn led his section through the waist-deep water of one of the irrigation ditches while the Operations Room at Keenan called down mortar fire with the intention of covering with smoke the departure of the helicopters from Keenan.

As the patrol advanced, the HQ element and the leading ANA section were engaged by accurate small arms and RPG fire from an enemy position some hundred metres to their front. While they returned the fire, Corporal Lynn led his section in an advance towards the Taliban position and, such was the momentum of that advance, that the enemy abandoned their position and ceased firing at the helicopter and the HQ element.

Corporal Lynn led his section from the front and was not discomfited by the sudden change from a routine patrol in a perceived quiet area to an advance to contact. By making good use of the ground and inspiring his soldiers he distracted the enemy from their intention and allowed the helicopter to get away safely. He also showed considerable skill in commanding and controlling his young and comparatively inexperienced TA soldiers. He was rewarded with a Joint Commanders' Commendation as was his comrade, Lance Corporal Lee Averill for his actions six days later.

Lance Corporal Averill was commanding a section in a similar-sized patrol on 9 July, which was also operating to the north of FOB Keenan and included two ANA sections as well as the 2nd Royal Irish section. Aware from a handheld radio scanner that a Taliban ambush was planned, the platoon commander – Lieutenant Byrne again – appraised Averill of this information immediately; he passed it to his men. On Byrne's order, Averill began moving his section towards a tree line to his front to cover the HQ element and the lead ANA section. As the section began its move, Averill spotted a local civilian whose close attention to the section made him suspect that the man was a 'dicker'. He challenged the man before firing a warning shot at which the Taliban moved from hiding into ambush positions.

The ANA soldiers identified the enemy fighters and their line of travel and the patrol HQ then moved forward. However, as Lance Corporal Averill and his section continued to the line of trees, they came under heavy fire. Averill reacted immediately by bringing return fire to bear on the enemy with all the weapons at his command, GPMG, UGLs and a 66mm rocket. With the enemy thus fixed in their positions the HQ element with the lead ANA section pushed forward and disrupted effectively the Taliban ambush before it had been set up properly. Under this pressure, the Taliban fell back into alternative positions but, once again, Averill brought such intensive fire down on them that they were unable to move and indirect fire was then called down to end the engagement.

Lance Corporal Averill, who had been in the rank for less than a year, had not even completed a section commander's battle course but had shown all the skills required of such a commander in the most demanding school of all, combat. Largely due to those skills and his calm control of his section, there were no casualties among his men.

As we have seen, during the summer of 2008, Task Force Helmand fought a difficult operation to dislodge the Taliban from its stronghold in the upper Gereshk valley in which PB Attal was then established to consolidate the gains. It was the task of WO2 Billy Roy, with a seven-man team, to mentor the isolated, composite ANA company at this base, which overlooks the green, populated patchwork of fields abutting the arid, uninhabited desert. When Task Force assets were re-deployed, the Taliban determined to take advantage by ejecting the ANA from the base and made numerous attacks. However, the garrison did not sit inside the compound but carried out numerous patrols and sought to bring some measure of stability to the area.

At dawn on 15 July, WO2 Roy and his team deployed with the ANA company to the village of Shurakay in the Green Zone to promote a medical outreach initiative as part of the stabilization programme. Roy was with the leading elements of the ANA moving through the tight alleys between mud-walled compounds. Movement was restricted further by a latticework of irrigation ditches, which also reduced cover. There was a tense atmosphere as Roy reached the southern edge of Shurakay and, as the patrol rounded a blind corner, he was surprised to see twelve villagers running away across an open field, an indication of the presence of Taliban. Then small-arms fire was opened on the patrol, followed by RPGs. While assessing the situation, WO2 Roy returned fire. With at least four enemy firing points, the ANA faced a danger of being overwhelmed, but Roy assumed command with a firm grip and encouraged the unwilling ANA to re-organize to fight off the waves of attacking Taliban.

Although the enemy were too close to bring accurate indirect fire down on them without endangering Roy's force, he nonetheless adjusted skilfully a barrage creeping in from the enemy's rear which stopped, temporarily, the Taliban attack. In the breathing space thus gained, Roy was able to organize the withdrawal of the ANA company. It was after noon and the soldiers were exhausted both from the battle and the intense heat, of 50 degrees. Roy was then detailed to rendezvous with an IED Demolitions (IEDD) Team and escort them back to the scene of the contact to destroy an IED. On reaching the area, he posted soldiers in a secure cordon around the team but, while they worked at the IED, the enemy attacked again with a determined small-arms onslaught from three sides. Using the cover of close country, the Taliban had approached to within fifty metres.

The fighting that developed was violent and confused. Roy led a charge to repel one surge from a flank but, by then, had expended his ammunition. Spotting a discarded 66mm rocket, he used this to engage the enemy; his charge had rallied the ANA soldiers. However, the cordon had collapsed and, while trying to regroup and reassure the ANA platoons, Roy realized that the ANA company commander, an IEDD Team member and an interpreter were no longer with the main group. His mentor team returned to the fray, where he found all three under cover and disorientated in a compound. Reassuring them, he led them back to rejoin the group before gripping the ANA and directing their fire. He then led the company back towards PB Attal. The Taliban continued to put down harassing fire which caused casualties among the rear elements of the patrol. Roy returned to assist and treat one wounded soldier before removing him from further danger. As the exhausted company group reached PB Attal, night was beginning to fall.

On this day, WO2 Roy's actions were extremely brave and inspirational; but for his bold and decisive intervention the ANA company would have been overrun. For over twelve hours, he had been the effective commander of the company group in a fierce battle and his initiative and leadership were critical to the outcome and, without doubt, saved lives. His remarkable courage and selflessness were rewarded with a Mention in Despatches.

Corporal John Nixon was a member of Billy Roy's mentor team at PB Attal and was with him in that patrol south of Shurakay. At the southern extremity of the patrol's route, a suspect vehicle was spotted; an attempt had been made to conceal it inside a compound. This vehicle, it was believed, might have been that of a prominent IED facilitator and so the patrol approached to investigate. As it did so, it came under fire from four points. Small arms, a heavy machine gun and RPGs were all being used by the enemy, and a brutal firefight developed which was ended when 105mm artillery fire was called down, forcing a Taliban withdrawal. As we have seen, the artillery fire had to be crept in from behind the Taliban who were too close to the coalition troops to engage with indirect fire.

An IED Demolitions team was called to check the car and the compound in which it was housed, and, with the IEDD team commander briefed, the patrol cordoned off the compound, prompting a mass exodus of local people. Electronic intercepts now indicated that a further attack was imminent, an assessment supported by the locals' rapid departure. The fresh attack was launched as the search was underway. Fire was put down on the cordon from three sides and Corporal Nixon organized his platoon to ensure that the southern cordon remained secure. In spite of repeated onslaughts from small arms and RPGs, each enemy attack was broken and the search continued; this lasted for about ninety minutes.

With the search complete, the patrol began its extraction from the Green Zone with Nixon's ANA platoon leading; Nixon took the van himself. The patrol was now at its most vulnerable and the Taliban pushed forward with such enthusiasm that both platoons were soon under fire from many points at less than 100 metres range along their length. Such was the speed of the Taliban attack that the ANA company commander, the interpreter and one of the British IEDD team were cut off from the main body. Losing their commander caused some Afghan troops to panic and this threatened to spread through the ANA ranks. In this rapidly deteriorating situation, with ANA resistance crumbling, Nixon raced back to the beleaguered platoon through intense enemy fire. In spite of the language barrier, he rallied the platoon by his obvious strength of character and personal example, organizing the automatic weapon and RPG gunners to return effective fire that stalled the enemy advance. Nixon's intervention had the immediate effect of stabilizing the platoon, by which time WO2 Roy had found those who had become separated and led them to rejoin their comrades. After this the Taliban attack faltered significantly.

Once again the patrol got underway but, as it was completing the process of extraction, an ANA soldier was wounded in the chest by a single round. The first mentor to reach him was Corporal Nixon who reacted immediately by applying a compression bandage and chest seal to the man's injuries, although the patrol was still under fire. Subsequently, the casualty was moved to PB Attal for evacuation.

Corporal Nixon's actions were carried out in extremely demanding circumstances during an enemy attack that lasted almost six hours. Although, on several occasions during that engagement, the ANA soldiers under his mentorship wavered, they rallied to Nixon's selfless and courageous example and followed his inspiring leadership. Corporal Nixon was Mentioned in Despatches for his courage and leadership.

It will be recalled that OMLT 1 was deployed at first to Sangin before moving to Musa Qaleh. During the OMLT's time in Afghanistan, Captain Tony Dixon commanded a company mentor team which, in July, was based at PB South, Musa Qaleh's southern security outpost. His team and its ANA company were engaged heavily by the Taliban on many occasions as they sought to recapture Musa Qaleh.

On 15 July, Captain Dixon was on night patrol when he and his men became involved in a fast-moving skirmish with motorbike-mounted enemy scouts. Radio intercepts also indicated that a larger group of Taliban planned to ambush his patrol. Although the ANA soldiers, who were disturbed when they heard this, began behaving erratically and attempted to withdraw towards their base in some disorder, Dixon restored the situation quickly and, instead of withdrawing, the patrol established snap ambushes for the Taliban. One Taliban fighter was killed during a brief engagement; it was established later that he was a major intelligence officer in that area. Captain Dixon's actions were instrumental in denying the enemy an opportunity to attack the patrol.

Eleven days later, Dixon took part in a Kandak operation to clear Dagyan where much of the battle revolved around his group. Having advanced south through the front line of the Argyll and Sutherland Highlanders (5 Scots), the Kandak was soon engaged by the enemy with Dixon's group confronted by a defensive system of fortified compounds. These compounds were linked by trenches and bunkers and his group sustained casualties soon after the initial contact; the casualties included the ANA commander who was thus *hors de combat*. Taking control of the situation swiftly, Captain Dixon rallied his men for a series of flanking and frontal assaults. The Kandak attack continued over the following six hours, moving forward over two kilometres through some seventeen defended compounds. At every stage, the ANA had to be urged on to maintain both impetus and initiative whilst Dixon also had to keep control and, at the same time, manage the flow of information necessary to co-ordinate the various forms of fire support. The enemy maintained a constant bombardment of mortar fire and made at least two attempts to counter-attack from the flank. To counter these, Dixon manoeuvred his group to best advantage and led several audacious moves across open ground to create fighting positions. All of these close-quarter assaults were made against a dogged enemy who, although well organized, was forced into retreat after retreat with considerable losses; thirty Taliban were killed and thirteen wounded.

Throughout the month, the excellent relationship Captain Dixon had established with the ANA contributed significantly to several successes, of which these are only two. Dixon's actions in Daygan showed coolness under fire, courage and fortitude while his quick thinking saved the lives of his own soldiers and ensured the enemy's defeat.

Ranger Dominic Flanagan was also a member of OMLT 1, and was with Captain Dixon's company mentor team at PB South. During the night patrol on 15 July, in which a patrol was harassed by motorcycle-mounted Taliban scouts, it was Flanagan who shot and killed the man identified subsequently as a key local Taliban intelligence officer. Without doubt, Flanagan's actions foiled enemy plans for an attack.

On 26 July, Flanagan, a twenty-one-year old with less than three years' service in the Regiment, was involved in the Kandak-scale operation to clear northern Dagyan, during which his team was at the forefront of the six-hour-long battle. In the course of that battle, his team made repeated close-quarter assaults on stubbornly-held enemy positions. Despite a first-rate defensive organization, the enemy was forced to retreat as we have seen, having suffered some thirty dead and thirteen wounded. Ranger Flanagan had demonstrated much courage, professionalism and selflessness on these two occasions but his exemplary behaviour did not end there as will be seen in Chapter Six.

Corporal Robert McClurg, another member of the mentoring team at PB South, also took part in the operation at Dagyan where, for much of the battle, he was in the very centre of the fighting.

As his team commander was engaged heavily in co-ordinating supporting fire, McClurg stepped up to become the primary mentor in the battle and quickly realized that he was faced with a system of fortified positions interlinked with trenches and bunkers. Then his group came under fire and suffered casualties, one of whom was the ANA commander who was out of action. McClurg rallied his force and, for no less than six hours, directed and led a series of frontal and flanking assaults. These took his small force on an advance of more than two kilometres, battling through seventeen fiercely defended compounds. In the course of the battle, they fought off several enemy flanking counter-attacks and endured mortar fire to account for a number of the thirty enemy personnel who were killed; another thirteen were wounded. However, it was McClurg's intervention at a critical time that turned the battle and his command and example so inspired the ANA soldiers that they were confident enough to evict the enemy from their defensive locations. Corporal McClurg was awarded the Conspicuous Gallantry Cross, the citation for which notes that his

> calm, selfless leadership style and great personal courage repeatedly salvaged deteriorating situations, which would have led to the loss of Afghan National Army and UK lives.

Based at PB Attal in the upper Gereshk valley, Ranger Ratu Qalitakivuna was a member of WO2 Billy Roy's eight-man mentoring team with an ANA company that faced considerable regular Taliban aggression and fought a series of bitter engagements with their determined foe.

On 25 July, the ANA company and Ranger Qalitakuvana's team established an ambush with support from the Danish Battle Group. As Taliban forces began withdrawing to a defensive trench system, which had been used regularly to attack ISAF convoys, the ambush was sprung. The ensuing battle was furious, with the enemy fighting determinedly and knocking out of action two Leopard MBTs of the Danish BG; one Danish soldier was killed in the encounter. By the end of the encounter, however, the ANA and the OMLT had killed fifteen Taliban fighters.

Two days later, a joint twelve-man patrol moved north from PB Attal to locate and destroy further Taliban anti-armour IEDs. Before long one IED had been discovered and destroyed and a second located but, with demolition charges being prepared, intense enemy fire, including machine guns and RPGs, was brought down on the patrol from several compounds. Such was the intensity of this fire that the patrol was pinned down and two ANA soldiers, the RPG and PKM gunners, had become casualties with their weapons out of action. In the chaos that followed the initial engagement, the ANA soldiers sought cover and waited for orders from their patrol commander. Realizing that they held the initiative, the Taliban intensified their attack and were engaging the patrol from less than 200 metres with extremely accurate fire from AK47s and RPGs.

Ranger Qalitakivuna, the GPMG gunner, saw that the enemy were closing in on the killing area and, on his own initiative, left cover to assume a better fire position. He made his move in clear view of the enemy to provide better protection for his ANA and British comrades. Ignoring his own safety, he raced across open ground to adopt a position from which he could bring his GPMG to bear on the enemy more effectively. Once in position, he began immediately to put down effective suppressing fire on the Taliban positions and, such was his accuracy, that the enemy fire diminished rapidly. In the lull thus afforded the patrol, quick battle orders were issued that allowed it to start breaking contact and the two ANA casualties were moved to the pre-designated rallying point. Until this move was complete, Qalitakivuna stayed in his position and continued suppressive fire. Only when he was sure that the casualties were safe did he move and, when ordered, conducted an organized withdrawal from the killing area that allowed artillery fire to be adjusted on to the Taliban positions. During his withdrawal, he was engaged by accurate and continuous machine-gun and RPG fire on each occasion that he broke cover. When the Taliban used the cover of the Green Zone to move to engage the patrol in the flank, Qalitakivuna was quick to appreciate the threat and deployed his GPMG to engage the new enemy positions. This allowed the patrol to climb out of the wadi and break contact finally at PB Attal.

While under intense enemy fire, the patrol covered 1,500 metres with two casualties with Qalitakivuna deploying his machine gun on his own initiative to counter the greatest threat. Without doubt, his actions saved lives and he showed great bravery and initiative under extreme stress.

As we have seen, WO2 Billy Roy was commanding the mentor team at PB Attal. Roy is a remarkable soldier with eighteen years' service in the Royal Irish who, during a lengthy interview with the author, spoke of the quality of the men who served at PB Attal with him, including some of the ANA soldiers.

The performance of the blokes as a whole was great. They rose to every challenge and showed great team spirit. It was good from Ranger to Corporal. No worries. I could concentrate on the mentoring job.

What he did not reveal was his own role in that fierce battle at Shurakay, an example of mentoring par excellence which, as we have seeen, has since been recognized with a Mention in Despatches. He had already assessed the fighting qualities of the ANA on the way into Attal when they had come under attack by the Taliban. Their reaction on that occasion had been poor, leading him to comment that they were 'good at planned ops but not so good when hit by the Taliban'. However, he believed that they could raise the level of their soldiering considerably and forming them into platoons by ability helped to achieve that since there were some very good individuals. The best platoon in the company was used as forward troops and its soldiers developed a good conceit of themselves, so that they could also assist in the mentoring task. However, the company's officers were not so good: their leadership was poor and they could not be used to lead troops on patrol. He also noted that, when working with the Counter Narcotics Kandak, the OMLT role was to lead rather than mentor.

The pressure exerted by the Taliban on PB Attal was such that Javelin missiles were fired by the garrison on at least five occasions. Javelin is an American man-portable missile intended, primarily, for use against armour – it might be called the great-grandson of the Second World War bazooka – but it has secondary uses against helicopters or enemy ground positions, such as bunkers or strongly-defended buildings and it was in the latter role that the weapon was used in Attal.

While the PB was an isolated location, with a constant threat of danger, WO2 Roy recalled that morale in the Royal Irish team and amongst the ANA was always high. One factor in this was the food. Although others were critical of the ration packs, one of the mentors at Attal had been a chef before joining the Army and full use was made of his skills and experience during the team's time there; a little imagination can make the contents of the ration packs very appetizing and ovens can be improvized from mud bricks and old ammunition containers. The welfare phone cards also helped with morale and any welfare problems, either at Sangin or at PB Attal, were resolved quickly. Although there was e-mail contact with home at either Camp Bastion or at Shorabak, there was none in the PBs since there was no power; ANA patrol bases had only a small generator to charge batteries for the radios and other vital equipment. The principal problem arising from local conditions was the heat but dust was not a major problem, although there were some dust storms. Occasional eye problems occurred but no worse than might be experienced on exercise in Kenya, or even on Salisbury Plain.

At 3.30pm on 2 August an ANA vehicle in the PB Attal area was destroyed in an explosion, believed to have been either an IED or a mine left from the Soviet era. Two soldiers were injured seriously and were brought back to Attal for evacuation by air to Camp Bastion. In the meantime, the MERT had been alerted and the team was airborne from Bastion in a Chinook. However, a severe sandstorm impeded the helicopter's progress and it took fifty minutes to reach PB Attal. On board the

Chinook, with the Incident Response Team (IRT), was Ranger Finlay of 2 R Irish, who was both a section second in command and a team medic. Finlay was first to debus from the helicopter and, at considerable risk to himself, he secured the two wounded men and then assisted the MERT members in loading them onto the Chinook. Through his speedy action as the helicopter landed, the time on the ground was kept to a minimum which reduced the risk to the machine from both enemy attack and the sandstorm.

When the Chinook lifted off for the return flight to Bastion, Finlay busied himself by assisting the medical team as they treated the casualties and his medical care for the wounded ANA soldier who was closer to him was critical. Ranger Finlay immobilized the man with a spine collar before conducting a full spinal assessment, following which he made a secondary assessment before compiling a full report on the man's injuries. He also marked the casualty to indicate his symptoms and treatment so that he would be ready for an immediate move to the operating theatre in Bastion. Until the Chinook touched down close to the hospital, Finlay maintained his vigil over the casualty. This was but one example of his constant devotion to duty during his six months in Helmand; in that time he was involved in more than twenty responses to contacts and fatal incidents throughout the province in his role as a member of the IRT.

OMLT 3 in Sangin, under Captain Markis Duggan in the absence of Major Crow, enjoyed several successes with Kandak 3. With more information coming in from local people, they worked hard to build up confidence by exploiting that intelligence. This led to several search and arrest operations during which bomb-making equipment and ammunition were uncovered and removed, thereby reducing the threat posed by the Taliban. Of this period, Captain Duggan commented that the OMLT's first few weeks were much busier than expected but the pre-deployment training had ensured that they could endure the tensions and dangers of Sangin to carry out their task with confidence.

Sleep for the first few nights was routinely interrupted by mortar fire to light up the night sky and either illuminate enemy or ... prevent them from carrying on with their tasks. Throughout the incidents it was a confidence boost to see that the kit worked to protect us – we are better equipped than any other Brigade that the British Army has deployed to date, and no doubt the next brigade will be even better equipped. The systems in place to find any gaps in our capabilities and then rapidly plug them means that kit comes to the front line faster than ever before.

Visitors to the Battlegroup in July included a press group from Northern Ireland with UTV represented by reporter Ivan Little and cameraman John Vennard, the Belfast

Telegraph by Lesley-Ann Henry and the Newsletter by Ben Lowry. There had been some other arrivals from home during the month in the shape of the TA volunteers of 204 (North Irish) Field Hospital (V). In fact, hardly had the TA medics taken over the hospital at Camp Bastion than they received patients with the same accents. Six men from Ranger Company had been injured as the result of the detonation of an IED. Three Rangers, Delaney, Herbert and Pepper, were injured by the blast, as was a Royal Engineer and all required hospital treatment. Rangers Delaney and Pepper were treated at Camp Bastion and released but Ranger Herbert had to be evacuated to the UK for treatment. The other injuries occurred as the result of a vehicle crashing during the immediate response to the blast but these were not serious.

Tragically, the Battlegroup suffered a fatal casualty on 28 July when Sergeant Jon Mathews of The Highlanders (4 Scots), attached to the Royal Irish, was shot in the head in Marjah district, not far from Lashkar Gah. His team from OMLT 4 was with an ANA patrol helping to protect Afghan National Police when they were warned by local people that Taliban fighters were nearby. As the patrol went to investigate, they were engaged by the enemy and Sergeant Mathews was hit by accurate small arms fire. Although evacuated to the hospital at Camp Bastion, he died of his injuries in spite of the best efforts of the medical staff.

As July faded into August, the end of HERRICK VIII was looming. But there could be no relaxation in the Battlegroup. The threat was as high as ever and the remaining weeks and months of the tour proved to be every bit as dangerous as those that had gone before. Nonetheless, alongside their ANA colleagues they had extended the writ of the Afghan government and gained the confidence of even more communities who now felt that their army could protect them from the Taliban.

Note

1. Paveway = Precision Avionics Vectoring Equipment. Those who came up with this descriptor seem to have believed that precision and accuracy are synonymous.

Chapter Six

Maintaining the Pressure

With four months behind them, the Royal Irish were completely in tune with the tempo of operations in Helmand, whether in the mentoring teams alongside the ANA, with Ranger Company in Sangin or Imjin Company at Bastion. They knew that the Taliban was resourceful, determined and fanatical, and that he would seize every opportunity to strike at coalition forces with the aim of regaining lost ground, or demonstrating to local people that no long-term protection could be obtained from the foreign troops. A classic example of Taliban zeal came when they moved back into Dagyan only days after the operation to clear the village. Among the several enemy personnel who had been killed in the earlier encounter were some fanatical foreign fighters and intelligence indicated that the Taliban intended to re-occupy their positions in Dagyan as well as avenging the deaths of their fellows.

When reports of Taliban re-occupying positions at Dagyan were received at PB South, a patrol was despatched to investigate on 4 August. Included in that patrol was Ranger Dominic Flanagan who had fought with considerable distinction in the battle to clear the village on 26 July. As this patrol skirted the northern edge of Dagyan, villagers were seen departing hurriedly and it was left empty. This was a combat indicator, a certain sign that enemy fighters were present. Nonetheless, the patrol continued southward into the village where, at 9.50am, it met a well-prepared enemy force. Ranger Flanagan was wounded in the initial exchange of fire, receiving four machine-gun rounds in the chest and shoulder. Although pinned down in open ground by enemy fire, he returned fire and crawled to cover to apply immediate self-aid to curb the bleeding from his wounds. At the same time he recognized that he was cut off from the remainder of his team by the scale and intensity of enemy fire.

Flanagan decided not to use morphine to ease the considerable pain of his wounds but took up a position that would allow him to engage the enemy effectively. Such was the intensity of the Taliban fire that his comrades had to make a long flanking move to recover him, during which time the Taliban tried to move forward to kill or capture him. Ignoring the pain from his wounds, Flanagan played a full part in the action and continued firing at the enemy. It was later learned that five Taliban were killed as the casualty evacuation party moved around to reach him. Flanagan then stood up, walked out of the killing area and took part in the action as the team pulled back. Although artillery support had been provided, and the Gunners were firing 'danger close', and a relieving counter-attack was also launched, contact with the Taliban was not broken until the patrol had fought their way about a kilometre to the north.

Dominic Flanagan showed considerable courage, professionalism and great selflessness throughout this engagement. Although only twenty-one years old, he proved himself an outstanding soldier during the two clashes at Dagyan. A modest and unassuming young man, he returned to duty before the tour had ended, stating that he had already let his comrades down enough. He has received a Mention in Despatches.

Ranger Stephen Manning was also in that patrol to Dagyan on 4 August. At first the patrol skirted the village's northern edge since the ANA's intention was to identify enemy positions. Although villagers were seen to be departing hurriedly, a sure sign of enemy presence, Dagyan appeared deserted. Against this background, the patrol probed into the village to seek out enemy locations. At 9.50am, when the patrol had been underway for four and a half hours, Ranger Manning's team patrolled south through an alleyway with Manning in the lead. Entering a small compound, Manning identified an enemy force in a well-prepared ambush position.

The Taliban opened fire and Manning was fortunate not to be hit by their rounds. He retained his composure and returned fire immediately, killing one enemy and forcing the others into cover before he had to take cover to change his magazine. Fire was taken up by Ranger Flanagan, the second soldier in Manning's team, who engaged another Taliban fighter but was wounded himself as the enemy sprayed the killing area with PKM (*Pulemyot Kalashnikova Modernizirovanniy* – Kalashnikov modernized machine gun) machine-gun fire. Flanagan fell and the Taliban advanced to kill or capture him as he lay pinned down in the open. Manning ignored the intensity of the enemy fire to take part in a flanking attack to recover his comrade.

As he assaulted into the killing area, Ranger Manning was hit repeatedly in the chest by enemy rounds and knocked to the ground by their force. Although winded by the strikes, he had been saved by his body armour and, on recovering his breath, resumed the attack; this was no more than two minutes later. In the face of the assault, a further three enemy were observed falling and the others quit the area speedily. Manning then established a snap ambush position to cover the evacuation of Ranger Flanagan but enemy forces returned in some strength to follow up the evacuation. Thus what had been an ambush became a fighting withdrawal to cover Flanagan's evacuation. This operation took almost an hour to complete, such was the ferocity of enemy fire. At the hub of a valiant team effort was Ranger Manning who alternated fighting with treating and carrying his wounded comrade. Artillery fire was called down but, even with rounds landing 'danger close', the team had withdrawn almost a kilometre northwards before contact with the Taliban was broken at last.

During this action, Ranger Manning showed great courage, coolness and professionalism that inspired his ANA colleagues. His actions ensured that lives were saved, not only that of Ranger Flanagan but of others in the patrol as the fighting withdrawal had to be conducted under the fire of a much larger enemy force with heavy weapons. Manning's behaviour throughout belied his relative youth, rank and experience. He, too, received a Mention in Despatches.

Ranger Robin McDowell, the combat medical technician for his team and its PB, also played a critical part in this encounter at Dagyan and the safe evacuation of Ranger Flanagan. In the initial exchange of fire, when Flanagan was hit and pinned down in open ground by continuing heavy enemy fire, McDowell attempted to move across the open ground to treat and bring him to safety. However, he was ordered to desist as enemy fire was so intensive. Because of that fire, a flanking attack was launched quickly to recover the wounded man and, as the Taliban moved in to kill or capture Flanagan, McDowell took a full part in the attack before turning his attention to his injured comrade, who had been hit four times by PKM fire. A quick assessment told McDowell that the wounds, although serious, were not life-threatening; this allowed his commander to make an objective assessment and opt for a safer casualty evacuation route, rather than the fastest route to the emergency rendezvous, which would have increased markedly the danger to the team. Ranger McDowell continued treating Flanagan in the course of the evacuation while enemy forces followed up and he found himself part of a fighting withdrawal, an extremely arduous operation that took almost an hour to accomplish. Throughout, until the team finally broke contact, he was at the focus of this team effort, both treating his wounded comrade and engaging the enemy.

This behaviour was typical of Ranger McDowell who consistently provided outstanding medical attention to both British and Afghan soldiers throughout Operation HERRICK VIII. He was held in high regard by the ANA soldiers who called him 'Doc' while, on several occasions, the medical chain of command praised, specifically, his actions. That praise referred both to his treatment of casualties and to the professionalism of his handovers, the latter being critical to any successful casualty evacuation from the battlefield. His work with ANA soldiers had the even more important effect of creating an exceptional bond between his team and their Afghan comrades. This relationship proved vital in the period July–September when his mentor team and their ANA comrades were engaged in bitter and prolonged fighting through the villages south of Musa Qaleh. On a daily basis, the team fought against a large, well-trained and determined enemy, including fanatical foreign fighters. Ranger McDowell's contribution to creating an OMLT/ANA team ethos proved vital.

There were many such events where he was at the forefront. Furthermore, his exemplary attitude and manner with ANA soldiers contributed greatly to the success of his team. His approach extended to the manner in which he engaged with civilians, with whom he generated such good will that he was able to obtain local information.

After the first Dagyan operation, Corporal Robert McClurg joined the ANA Surge Company mentor team, based in Musa Qaleh DC, and quickly found himself involved in further Kandak operations, this time to the north of Musa Qaleh. On 3 August his team was advancing through the urban desert as flank protection for a Kandak advance. Mastiff wheeled armoured vehicles supporting the advance were disabled by IEDs, which also provided the signal for the Taliban to put in a flanking assault. Heavy machine-gun fire hit the Kandak in the flank and pinned down Tactical HQ as well as two companies; recoilless rifles and RPGs supplemented the enemy firepower. However, McClurg spotted an opportunity to move east to counter-attack and, pushing north through several scattered compounds, took the fight to the enemy before co-ordinating fire support while leading forward the ANA troops. His quickly planned counter-attack left several Taliban dead, and stopped the enemy assault. It also ensured that the Kandak advance could continue. Following this episode, he organized defensive positions and co-ordinated further supporting fire for the main advance.

A few days afterwards, Corporal McClurg was in another Kandak operation to the south, during which his patrol cleared through Dagyan. On reaching the southern edge of the village, the team came under heavy fire from machine guns and RPGs located farther to the south. Unable to identify the firing point, the ANA soldiers began to panic. However, McClurg steadied them, called in indirect fire to support their move across open ground, and organized volley RPG and 66mm rocket fire to enable them to break in to the compound that was the enemy's firing point. In the face of McClurg's forceful leadership of the ANA assault, the Taliban broke and fled from their positions to be engaged by attack helicopters while making their way to secondary positions. McClurg then organized a hasty defence that allowed the ANA commander to regain control.

Throughout the tour, Corporal McClurg was involved in many similar incidents and, on each occasion, turned around deteriorating situations through his calm and selfless style of leadership, allied with tremendous courage. Without him, these incidents might have resulted in the loss of ANA and British lives. The Conspicuous Gallantry Cross awarded to him in March 2009 was a fitting recognition of his outstanding service.

There had been some changes in the Battlegroup with Major Max Walker departing to the UK on leave after five months in Helmand. Due for promotion to lieutenant colonel, he was succeeded by Major Ivor Gardiner as second-in-command of 1st Royal Irish and Battlegroup Chief of Staff. Captain Graham Rainey had also succeeded Captain Michael Potter as Adjutant; the latter had been promoted major. Lieutenant Colonel Freely returned to Afghanistan, having been on R&R at home, although he had taken time out of his 'rest' period to visit 1st Rifles, who would assume the OMLT Battlegroup role in late-September/early-October as well as visiting Royal Irish casualties at Selly Oak and Headley Court. His short time away had made the 'pace [in Helmand] seem more frenetic' and he noted that

> Sangin appears improved. Musa Qaleh faces a renewed threat. Gereshk seems relatively stable. We have reduced our liability to Lashkar Gah and are committing 4th Kdk/OMLT to Garmsir. The ANA are taking over security for Highway 1. Kandak 2 are preparing for operations. Ranger Flanagan is in remarkably good form recovering from being shot in the shoulder and Ranger Stout is in buoyant spirits having survived an RPG round in the chest. A good advert for Osprey body armour!

In Chapter Five, we saw two examples of Sergeant Hugh Benson's personal courage and leadership. He gave yet another demonstration of these when, on 26 August, he led a patrol to investigate possible Taliban mortar locations north of Musa Qaleh. As the patrol reached the target area it came under heavy enemy fire. At first, Benson chose to assault the enemy before finding that his patrol had been surrounded. He then opted for a fighting withdrawal that was carried out over a three-hour period. This fighting was very fierce as the Taliban tried constantly to outflank the patrol and also brought down heavy fire from RPGs and machine guns. Although the Taliban knew the ground and had more firepower, Sergeant Benson's skilled leadership and excellent use of tactics ensured that his patrol was able to fight its way out of the ambush with no loss of life. Once again his outstanding soldiering skills had saved lives. Sergeant Benson has since been Mentioned in Despatches.

On 31 August 2008, Corporal Alan Cree was second-in-command of a six-man Royal Irish OMLT operating from a satellite Patrol Base south of Musa Qaleh. Cree's team was mentoring an ANA company at the PB and, during the period July–September 2008, was involved in a series of actions south of Musa Qaleh in which they were engaged heavily by large numbers of well-equipped Taliban who had been reinforced by foreign fighters. The latter were especially tenacious.

On 31 August, Cree was with a patrol operating south of a patrol base known as the US PB, located south of Musa Qaleh, that had been adopted only a short time before by OMLT/ANA. The patrol skirmished through Dagyan as it attempted to identify a Taliban defended location. On the southern edge of Dagyan, heavy fire from at least four enemy locations was brought down on the patrol in what was a well-timed attack by the Taliban, since the OMLT and ANA forward elements of the patrol were separated from the main body of ANA troops by a wide expanse of ground that offered no cover.

Since the patrol commander was reporting, Corporal Cree took charge. He recognized immediately the dangers posed by the patrol's being split and, already, the separated ANA troops were not only faltering but beginning to withdraw northward. To prevent their withdrawal, Cree risked crossing the open ground to rally them and, as he did so, he came under enemy machine-gun fire, the rounds kicking up a trail of earth in his wake. Seeking cover, he returned fire before making a second bound to catch up with the separated ANA. His arrival was timely: the Taliban had spotted the weakness in the ANA group and were moving to outflank them. Under sustained and accurate fire from small arms and RPGs, Cree rallied the ANA soldiers and improvised a defensive plan. Although machine-gun rounds and RPG fire continued to strike his positions, Corporal Cree remained steady and, when he sensed an opportunity to seize the initiative, organized the ANA for a charge which he led from the front. This was the decisive factor in rebuffing the Taliban flanking move.

Knowing that the enemy would return to target the weaker element of the patrol, Cree co-ordinated a move back to the open ground before organizing suppressive fire to allow him and his ANA group to rejoin the main body. Having made the link up, Cree was able to take part in an assault to clear through an enemy strongpoint. Following this, he appreciated that further defensive positions would have to be assumed while the patrol commander identified additional enemy locations. Yet again the enemy launched a counter-attack, but Cree's dispositions were well sited and replenished and thus ensured that the Taliban were defeated. Whilst the attack was underway, Corporal Cree showed great courage as he moved back and forth between the defensive positions and encouraged both OMLT and ANA soldiers who were inspired by his seeming disregard of the heavy enemy fire. When the action was over, at least ten Taliban had been killed and several others wounded. This was the Taliban's last engagement in such strength in this area.

Corporal Cree showed exceptional personal courage and great loyalty to his ANA comrades. Throughout his tour, his professionalism, mentoring and support gained him trust, loyalty and respect from the ANA while his actions on 31 August were typical of his leadership and commitment throughout his time in Musa Qaleh. He set an outstanding example of gallantry that day, for which he has since been Mentioned in Despatches.

There was no respite from the IED menace at Musa Qaleh, as Ranger Lee Eager, from west Belfast, recalled. On his first patrol there, he was blown over and deafened when an IED at a track junction was detonated. However, those who had planted the device had been too enthusiastic in their digging and the IED was buried so deeply that its blast went up rather than out. It exploded no more than five metres from Ranger Eager. Every member of the patrol was knocked off his feet and suffered temporary deafness. 'You never knew where IEDs might be,' said Eager, who witnessed another narrow escape when a Royal Artillery TA soldier stood on an IED in the dark. The device detonated but its Taliban maker had used the wrong explosive mix and the Gunner suffered only a blast of 'white powder up his leg'.

Ranger Eager had a further, and very personal, narrow escape during a patrol investigating 'shoot and scoots' at the Musa Qaleh wadi. Four Mastiff armoured personnel carriers drove up the wadi and the Taliban opened up on them. In the ensuing firefight, Ranger Eager 'was kneeling beside my mate when I saw a puff of smoke on the far side of the wadi'. Then he saw what he described as a 'bowling ball' coming straight towards him. Shouting a warning to his comrade, he leapt out of the way but the round hit the wadi's bank, deflected at a high angle and plunged into the field behind, where it exploded in the mud. The 'bowling ball' had been a round from an RPG that very nearly had Lee Eager's name on it. Under cover of the Mastiffs, the patrol made its way out of the area.

An IED had also taken the life of another Battlegroup soldier. Corporal Barry Dempsey, aged 29, was from the Royal Highland Fusiliers (2 Scots) and had come across to the OMLT Battlegroup to reinforce the medical section. He had played a full role as a mentor and was popular with his comrades. He lost his life on 18 August when he set off a pressure pad IED on the shoulder of the Gereshk valley just north of PB Attal. Three other members of his team were injured in the blast and were treated in hospital.

In the second half of August, Kandak 4 and OMLT 4 were established fully in Garmsir, having taken over three patrol bases and a HQ location; patrols to let personnel get to know the area had already been undertaken. On 17 August, at 9.00pm at Camp Shorabak, Major John Laverty, OC of OMLT 2 was told to be ready to deploy as part of a 3/205 Brigade operation to Nad e Ali. His men had four hours to get ready and began a move into the desert at 1.00am. They were to accompany Kandak 2 and elements of the CSS Kandak but were unclear about the ANA's intentions. The Executive Officer of 3/205 Brigade had been giving battle orders to his men, but the Royal Irish had little information about the situation at Nad e Ali. It transpired that the nearby town of Marjah had been taken by the Taliban a week earlier and the ANA were determined to ensure that Nad e Ali did not follow suit. By taking Nad e Ali, which was garrisoned by ANP, the ANA felt that they could influence the situation at Marjah.

OMLT 2 moved west of Nad e Ali and, leaving their vehicles in the desert, moved into the town, which seemed quite prosperous by Helmand standards. The ANA moved into the district centre where the ANP had a station, but the OMLT used a new post, which they expected to occupy for only twenty-four hours. When it became clear that their stay would be longer the vehicles were brought into the town where, at first, 'their time was spent in relatively benign circumstances reassuring the locals and restoring police to their abandoned check points'. ANA patrols were pushing out as far as seven kilometres away, but the OMLT had insufficient resources, including men and vehicles, to support these patrols; there were no quads to carry ammunition and water. On the third day in Nad e Ali, the situation become more difficult as the ANP refused to cooperate with the ANA, prompting the latter to re-locate with the OMLT. Although the Taliban had withdrawn to Marjah, the police were unwilling to join in patrols and follow-up activity and the ANA suspected that the local ANP were Taliban supporters. There followed two days during which the main activity was a visit from a senior government official from Kabul, which indicated that the Afghan government placed importance on the ANA's role in Nad e Ali.

As the OMLT were preparing to leave Nad el Ali, in preparation for the operation to move a third turbine to the Kajaki dam, there came news that Taliban were approaching from the west. To counter this move, the OMLT and ANA troops advanced to contact the enemy and engaged them in a ninety-minute gun battle, the first in this area between Taliban and British troops. At the end of the battle, one ANA soldier had been killed but twenty-seven Taliban had perished. The battle was brought to an end when Apaches strafed the enemy positions. The OMLT interpreter had been shot in the foot but, as he was being carried away, his escort came under fire and the man fled, the adrenalin making him oblivious to his earlier injury.

A fighting patrol to pursue the enemy was ruled out as the OMLT was running low on ammunition and, in any case, needed to get back for the Kajaki operation; it had been eight days in Nad e Ali. John Laverty spent the day trying to convince the ANA that a small force could hold Nad e Ali. Later that night, OMLT 2 and Kandak 2 left for Shorabak, leaving a small ANA garrison in the town. This held until Masonforce arrived later, although the ANA were convinced that their soldiers were in danger and under siege in Nad e Ali. If nothing else, the operation had proved that the ANA could mount brigade operations on its own initiative.

Scarcely had OMLT 2 and Kandak 2 left Nad e Ali than there were reports of large enemy formations besieging the ANA troops in the area, causing General Mohaiyodin to decide that the Kandak should return to meet this threat. This provided a clear example of NATO and Afghan priorities diverging and, with no British presence on the ground at Nad e Ali, it was difficult to know the truth. Moreover, Freely had 'other and conflicting plans for Kandak 2 and did not wish to see them head off again on an unplanned mission chasing a mobile, elusive and possibly ghost enemy'. There was a way to change Mohaiyodin's mind, however, and that was through using UAVs. Driving across to Camp Bastion, the brigade commander and his mentor visited the UAV ground control station where they could see, from real time and recorded film footage, the entire period of the Taliban assault. The live link also showed Mohaiyodin that a coalition convoy was en route to reinforce his 'besieged' men. In truth the entire assault was a figment of someone's imagination and Kandak 2/OMLT 2 were able to turn their attention to the mission planned by Freely, which was one of the most critical yet executed in Helmand. It took this evidence and all of

Getting fit for Helmand. Soldiers of 2nd Royal Irish included this traditional form of working up to operational fitness in their training programme. Major Mark Hudson, who commanded Imjin Company during HERRICK VIII, is on the left in this photograph.

St Patrick's Day 2008. The Saint's Day was celebrated in Tern Hill with a parade at which shamrock was distributed. Wearing desert combats, soldiers of the Battlegroup await the distribution while the Regimental Mascot, Brian Boru, is paraded through the ranks.

And in Helmand the advance party also celebrated the day, although in a more low-key manner.

Afghan sunset. A sangar is silhouetted against the setting sun as a soldier trudges towards the tower with an armoured vehicle in the background. This is the 'super sangar' at PB Attal, which was built partway through the Battlegroup's tour.

A convoy stopped along a road is dwarfed by the scale of the distant mountains. Close to the road may be seen poppies.

In a busy bazaar area, modern and traditional methods of transport mix with Toyota and Ford pick-ups alongside ox carts.

Village elders gather to meet NATO troops. Age is respected in Afghanistan as it is held to bring wisdom and local decisions are made by shuras or meetings of the elders, identified by their white turbans and, often, white beards.

Patrols are planned carefully and the most up-to-date intelligence, from a wide range of sources, is passed to patrol members before venturing out from their bases. These men are receiving such a briefing. Note the water bottles in the hands of several men and also the Hesco wall.

Two Chinooks come in to land at an HLS with underslung loads of equipment and supplies. These machines are worked hard in Afghanistan and are vital to the efforts of Task Force Helmand.

And they're away. A pair of Chinooks take off, their tail ramps lowered and gunners maintaining observation. The Apaches will be hovering overhead.

What's for dinner? Cooking arrangements varied according to the location. These men of Imjin Company are eating in comparative luxury.

Another dining room. Note the Hesco wall to the right and the mud wall to the left. Carpet adds a touch of homeliness to this facility which will not have many visits from food critics.

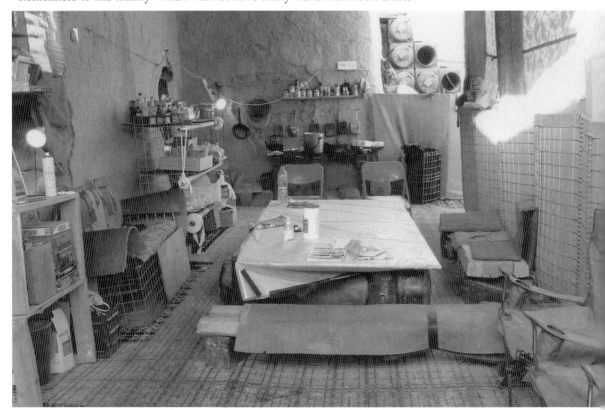

Back in the countryside, another patrol makes its way through fields that offer little cover to the patrolling soldiers.

An OMLT loading up at Camp Shorabak for its move to a FOB. The Pinzgauer is a British vehicle, built in Surrey but developed from an Austrian design and hence the name.

A convoy en route to its destination from Camp Shorabak makes a temporary halt. The crew of the Wimik in the foreground stand guard.

A vital piece of equipment for NATO troops is the mine detector. Such is the threat from IEDs that patrols are accompanied by IED search teams with detectors while all patrol members look out for signs of the possible presence of IEDs, such as disturbed ground.

Resupply for ANA units in their patrol bases was carried out using former Soviet helicopters. This Mil Mi8 Hip is already raising a 'brownout' as it prepares to land. A second Hip is following it in.

Padre Albert Jackson (L) and WO2 Denis McKee check some of the parcels that have arrived for the Battlegroup. Individuals and organizations in Northern Ireland and around the 1st Battalion's base at Tern Hill were exceptionally generous in forwarding comforts to the soldiers. These parcels are being sorted for distribution to the different elements of the Battlegroup.

Partway through the tour the Battlegroup hosted a media group from Northern Ireland. WO2 Denis McKee is on the left with John Vennard (cameraman, *UTV*), Ben Lowry (*The Newsletter*), Ivan Little (*UTV*), Lesley-Ann Henry (*Belfast Telegraph*), Captain Brian Johnston MBE and Ranger Billy Bittles.

HRH Prince Andrew, Duke of York, is Colonel-in-Chief of the Royal Irish and paid a visit to the Regiment in Helmand. With Lieutenant Colonel Freely he met Brigadier General Mohaiyodin, commander of 3/205 Brigade, and discussed the campaign and the part being played by the Battlegroup.

Afghan civilians, including many children, were brought to the Battlegroup bases for medical treatment, including emergencies, some of which were the result of Taliban IEDs. Some also continued to suffer from mines laid by the Red Army which had never been cleared and were not mapped adequately. A young Afghan is being treated by Royal Irish Battlegroup medics in a patrol base.

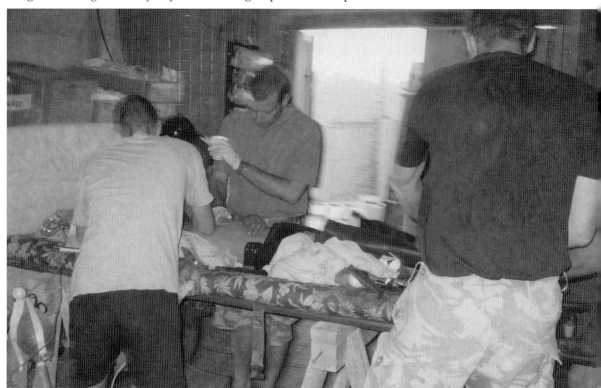

Brigadier General Mohaiyodin with a group of elders who have just received the keys of a new school bus, a gift from the USA.

The remains of an Afghan National Police vehicle that was blown up by a Taliban IED.

Mentoring in action. A Royal Irish soldier gives some guidance to his ANA counterpart. The Afghan soldier has not yet been trained on the American M16 rifle and is still using the Russian AK47 rifle.

In the foreground one of the quads that proved so useful on so many occasions with a Wimik and, hovering in the background, a Westland Sea King HC4 helicopter, part of the Fleet Air Arm's contribution to the Joint Helicopter Force in Afghanistan.

View from a sangar: a fuel lorry enters one of the forward bases. These lorries make the long journey from Pakistan into Helmand and many of their drivers have lost their lives along the way. The very basic nature of the base can be seen from this photograph.

Padre Jackson and Ranger Banter wait patiently for a helicopter to take them to their next destination. By the end of HERRICK VIII, few had been more travelled than this pair.

At Sangin, Ranger Banter and the Padre met Ranger Company. From left: Company Sergeant Major Frankie O'Connor, Lieutenant Paddy Bury, Ranger Banter, Padre Jackson and Major Graham Shannon.

Freely's powers of diplomacy to convince Mohaiyodin of the necessity to have his Kandak 2 at the spearpoint of the forthcoming operation. Shuttle visits to Lashkar Gah and meetings with the Helmand Security Shura were interspersed with planning and preparation for the operation.

Arguably, the most important strategic objective in Helmand is the dam on the Helmand river at Kajaki, part of a hydro–electric scheme that supplies most of the electricity throughout the province; this was the subject of Freely's plan for which he needed OMLT 2. Built in 1953, Kajaki dam is about fifty-five miles north-west of Kandahar and is the main watershed for the Sistan basin, an area encompassing much of south-western Afghanistan and south-eastern Iran, one of the driest regions on the planet. A hundred metres high and 270 metres in length, the dam can store 1.2 cubic kilometres of water. Not only does it provide electricity but it also irrigates almost 2,000 square kilometres of what would otherwise be desert.

American aid provided two 16.5-megawatt generators in a powerhouse at the dam in 1975, when Helmand was sometimes known as 'Little America'. The facility to add a third generator of equal size was built into the design of the powerhouse, which became the target of USAF bombers in October 2001 and suffered damage from the explosions. A subsequent rebuilding programme brought much of the facility back into use and a third generator was planned which, with a new grid of power lines, would allow the generation of 51 megawatts of power, some of which would be supplied to Kandahar province. The third generator, with an 18.5-megawatt capacity, arrived at Kandahar airport in August and plans to move it to Kajaki were then implemented; these plans had been several months in the making. Moving the generator by road was codenamed Operation OQAB TSUKA, Eagle's Summit. Of course, the Taliban, who had tried to capture Kajaki dam in early-2007, could be expected to interdict the convoy and the first element of the OQAB TSUKA plan was to deceive the enemy into believing that the most direct line of approach, west on Highway 1 and then via Route 611, would be taken. This was achieved by deploying Afghan, British and Danish troops along Route 611 to create the impression that they were securing the road for the convoy. In the meantime, the convoy, with its 200-tonne generator cargo, set off north to cross the desert in the direction of the Ghorak pass, along what was dubbed Route Harriet. To continue the deception, a dummy convoy also drove off along the direct route.

Operation OQAB TSUKA was the largest and most complex deliberate operation during HERRICK VIII with an importance at the strategic level since, signalling and reflecting the US President's intent, it could be held up as demonstrable evidence of the international community's commitment to development in Afghanistan. As such, the mission was the ISAF Commander's Main Effort and was to see the weight of all NATO resources, as well as the world's media, in north Helmand. It was highly desirable, therefore, that Afghan security forces were seen to play a key and increasingly prominent role. All was not so straightforward, however. Although, in principle, the ANA were content to play a significant role in the turbine operation, they lacked the enthusiasm of the NATO allies. The ANA knew that the third turbine would not be connected for at least twelve, perhaps fifteen, months and, therefore, it was more symbolic than a tangible immediate improvement. Furthermore, the Afghans had what they considered a much more pressing priority, the rapidly deteriorating security situation to the west of the provincial capital, Lashkar Gah. The ANP had abandoned their posts in three districts (Nad e Ali, Marjah and Nawa) and some had even aligned themselves with anti-government elements. This posed a serious threat to Gulab Mangal, Helmand's governor, and he demanded the attention of both President Karzai and his security forces. This was another example of where Lieutenant Colonel Ed Freely had to try and persuade General Mohaiyodin to align his forces with ISAF's intent against the Afghan general's natural inclination.

In all, some 4,000 ISAF soldiers were deployed to protect the convoy, among them 2,000 British troops; there were 1,000 from other NATO nations and 1,000 Afghans. Among the British troops were Royal Irish soldiers under Major John Laverty, Officer Commanding B Company/OMLT 2. A native of Belfast with twelve years in the Regiment, Major Laverty took over command of the Company/OMLT in July after its return from Musa Qaleh to Shorabak. He was no stranger to active soldiering, having earned much praise for his performance in Operation BASILICA in Sierra Leone in 2000. As with so many in the Royal Irish, however, he is also a modest, unassuming man who gives credit to others rather than himself.

When Major Laverty and his men learned that they were to deploy on a major operation on their return from Nad e Ali, the soldiers 'were up for the push' and preferred this to framework patrolling. Their attitude was 'We've got our war; it might only last three to four days but it's ours'. When first told of the Kajaki operation, Laverty had no background information on the terrain he would be encountering and the possible opposition. However, when he asked for this information, it was not long in forthcoming. Within hours of his request a fast jet flew overhead and within twelve hours he had a complete package, including the aerial reconnaissance photographs taken from the jet. He had all that he needed to make his plan.

B Company's role, with its Afghan counterparts, was to secure the final part of the convoy's route into Kajaki. This was also the most dangerous part of the journey for the convoy which comprised twenty heavy articulated transporters carrying parts of the turbine enclosed in ISO container shells, which had been armoured by REME personnel to protect against small arms fire, IEDs and RPG rounds. There were also 'numerous force protection vehicles', including fifty armoured vehicles, in the more than 100 vehicles of the convoy. To position it to undertake its task, B Company and its equipment was flown by helicopter 'through … spectacular mountain scenery into

Forward Operating Base Zeebrugge'. This move took place over two days but, thereafter, deployment was swift, with the Company taking over compounds before receiving orders to lead the advance with a southward move to begin clearing Kajaki Olya.

At this stage of Operation OQAB TSUKA, B Company was 'at the point of the theatre commander's main effort'. Because of this, John Laverty had access to additional offensive equipment, and to signals intelligence, to assist in his operations. Apache attack helicopters were on call, as was fast air support and artillery, the latter in the form of 105s and GMLRS; an ad hoc troop of two 105s, Opal 50, manned by British and Australian gunners, was helicoptered in to FOB Zeebrugge at Kajaki as part of the preparations for OQAB TSUKA. However, the first phase of B Company's operation was completed quickly with three groups pushing forward against light Taliban resistance. In the Green Zone, Captain Steve Swan led one team while Sergeant Harding's team protected the company flank along the bank of the Helmand river; Captain Richard Henry with WO2 Brennan cleared from compound to compound along Route 611. Those Taliban who did offer resistance brought to bear some mortars and snipers but were overwhelmed by the firepower put down on them from the British artillery. The Royal Irish had cleared the way once again, and at such speed that orders to clear two main enemy objectives the next morning were received; this was two days ahead of the original schedule.

These two objectives were Taliban positions known as Sentry Compound and Big Top. The former, a platoon-sized location on the bank of the Helmand river, was an outpost for Big Top, a Soviet-era system of compounds with interlinking trenches and much reinforced concrete. Big Top, not surprisingly, sat atop a prominence overlooking the road along which the convoy would travel. A series of deliberate attacks was planned and orders were issued at a company Orders Group fifteen minutes after midnight. H-Hour for the attack was set for 6.00am. Sentry Compound would be taken first, allowing full attention to be turned to Big Top with both attacks preceded by air and artillery bombardment.

Intensive fire from artillery and mortars was put down on Sentry Compound while ground attack aircraft also struck at the objective. The bombardment only ceased when rounds were falling 'danger close' to the infantry, whose attack was textbook in its execution. Direct fire support for the assaulting group came from Sergeant Harding's men with machine guns, light mortars and rifles. As they poured fire on the enemy positions, Captain Swan's group attacked from the Green Zone. Sentry Compound fell to the Royal Irish at 7.40am.

Attention from artillery and aircraft was then switched to Big Top in readiness for the main assault. This was a much more difficult proposition with its hardened emplacements and bunkers that protected the enemy from mortar fire and 105 rounds. But there was a heavier weapon in the Gunners' arsenal: Guided MLRS.

Firing from thirty-seven kilometres away, a salvo of GMLRS rounds struck Big Top with absolute accuracy and smashed up many of the positions. In preparation for the infantry assault, Captain Henry's team, Company Tactical HQ and WO2 Brennan's team made their way southward along Route 611 to a forming-up point for the main assault. Alongside Afghan troops, the Royal Irish made their assault. Shocked by the ferocity of the bombardment they had endured, the surviving Taliban provided no real competition for their attackers, although their fanaticism was evident in the initial stiff resistance with which they met the assaulting infantry. But the effectiveness of that assault, combined with the hammering they had already taken, soon took its toll of Taliban morale and the position was secure by 1.21pm. There had been one noteworthy delay in the attack when ANA soldiers stopped to pick melons from a field, prompting the fire support team to radio the gun detachments to 'add five minutes to all timings'.

The mentors from B Company and their ANA Kandak 2 comrades established a new coalition forward line – in military parlance FLOT, or forward line of own troops – which straddled the route and the Green Zone. This line was held for three days and was tested regularly by Taliban attacks using indirect fire, RPGs and small arms; the ANA soldiers performed well in this phase, indicating that their mentoring had been effective. The enemy had recovered his poise but, in spite of his many efforts, made no impression on the new defence line. It was this line that secured the route for the successful move of the convoy into and out from Kajaki. In the final phase, 3 Para moved south to rendezvous with the convoy, which it then supported through the safety zone created by B Company and Kandak 2. It had taken six days in all for the convoy to reach Kajaki, moving at a snail's pace 1 mph with, at times, the Royal Engineers having to rebuild sections of road.

Those three days during which B Company and Kandak 2 held the line created some problems in ensuring resupply as the positions were so far forward. Once again, however, the problems were overcome through the ingenuity of Captain Andrew Nelson, B Company's second-in-command, and the company quartermaster sergeant (CQMS), Colour Sergeant Stewart. They used the cover of last light to bring in stores with the CQMS's party then returning to the FOB under the veil of darkness. Casualty evacuation was also a problem. This had to be carried out in full view of the Taliban, but Company Sergeant Major Faloon used a quad with a stretcher strapped to its trailer to undertake this role; he had few patients and, therefore, little call on his improvized casevac system.

Its holding task complete, Kandak 2 and its mentors were withdrawn from the forward line on 1 September in order to allow the Battlegroup to re-organize for route security on the convoy's final leg to Kajaki dam. There was one further task to undertake at Big Top. Not all the bunkers used by the Taliban had been destroyed in the artillery bombardment and the Engineers demolished fifteen such structures, all with good overhead protection, so that the Taliban would never again be able to use them. Staff Sergeant James McCormick, of 12 Squadron Royal Engineers, attached to B Company/OMLT 2, completed the demolition work as the withdrawal was underway.

Remarkably, Operation OQAB TSUKA was completed with almost no casualties. One Canadian soldier was killed in an IED blast and one transporter driver was trapped under his vehicle. The latter incident happened almost under the eyes of OMLT 2 as the convoy resumed its northward move at 10.00pm on 1 September. It was now dark and, as the vehicles got underway, a heavy equipment transporter developed a problem with its hydraulic system, which failed. The driver left his cab to check the system and jacked up the vehicle so that he could examine underneath one of the wheel arches. However, the jack collapsed and the 35-tonne vehicle fell onto him, crushing him face down. Attempts by others in the convoy to rescue him failed, and it seemed that a specialist-lifting vehicle would be needed to extricate the injured man.

On hearing what had happened, Staff Sergeant McCormick and his troop commander, Captain Wendover, raced to the scene on a quad, where McCormick realized that no one was helping the driver; the convoy party held out no hope of rescuing him until the lifting equipment arrived but, McCormick knew, this would take too long and the trapped man would probably bleed to death in the meantime. He chose to try to dig out the driver. Using his hands at first, McCormick began the lengthy task of digging an eight-feet-long tunnel. After a time, he was able to use his bayonet to speed his progress; he had also discarded both his helmet and body armour, neither of which would have offered him any protection had the lorry collapsed on him. The risk of such a collapse was never far away as the road surface was poor and its camber was adverse; had there been a collapse, McCormick would also have been trapped and crushed.

On reaching the driver, who was screaming with the intensity of his pain, McCormick set to a further digging operation – to allow him space sufficient to turn the driver over and liberate him from the wheel arch's crushing embrace. Once he had done so, he took the driver by the hips and turned him so that he was face up. Although this was agonizing for the casualty, whose hips were crushed, it allowed McCormick to begin the job of extracting him from underneath his vehicle. By now, the Sapper was so exhausted – remember that he had only recently completed the demolition operation at Big Top – that he was unable to do more than hold the driver by his shoulders while others pulled his own feet from below the transporter.

It was at this stage that WO2 Andrew Taylor, of 16th CS Medical Regiment, who had already performed sterling work with casualties, came to McCormick's and the driver's assistance. Although it was pitch dark and the casualty was covered in hydraulic fluid that had leaked from his vehicle, Taylor was able to insert an intravenous drip and remained with the injured man, providing pain relief for his crushed pelvis, until he could be extracted and evacuated. Since he had also entered the crawl space under the huge vehicle, he too risked being crushed, but paid no attention to that risk as he tended his patient. Once again, Andrew Taylor had demonstrated his own considerable courage and the dedicated devotion to duty that is the hallmark of the Royal Army Medical Corps. For 'his bravery and complete disregard for his own safety' on this occasion, Staff Sergeant McCormick was awarded the Queen's Gallantry Medal.

A significant operation had been completed successfully, for a very small casualty toll, the Taliban had suffered heavily and the turbine would eventually add to the positive profile of both the Afghan government and the provincial administration. This had been, in the words of Colonel Freely, 'a triumph for Allied cooperation but more importantly for progress and the people of Afghanistan'. And an important lesson had been delivered to the Taliban: where ISAF wished it, coalition forces could take and hold ground at their own choosing.

John Laverty noted that all his officers and men

found the experience of deliberate warfighting [to be] exhilarating, and as company commander I was astounded at the resources that came with being on the point of COMISAF's [Commander, ISAF] main effort – as much fast air, attack helicopter, 500lb bombs, artillery and mortars as required to do the job.

Back in the UK, there was much media publicity about the operation, although not until it had been completed. In all of that publicity, little was said about the role of the Royal Irish and the ANA, the impression being given that the clearance had been conducted by British and US Special Forces. Even the Army's own magazine, *Soldier*, restricted its mention of the critical role played by B Company to commenting that Major John Laverty 'and 450 troops were based in the upper Helmand river valley for the operation' although it did note that soldiers of the Afghan 3/205 Brigade '[u]nder the mentorship of British soldiers ... fought to secure the settlement and gain support for the operation'.

Praise for those involved came from Governor Gulab Mangal who thanked all the coalition troops involved and made a special mention of the provincial reconstruction team troops and the British people. Incidentally, at this time General Mohaiyodin had left the picture, having suffered a minor heart attack that resulted in his being sent on sick leave to Herat.

Meanwhile, Masonforce had been formed under Colour Sergeant/Acting WO2/Local Captain Mason. This new eight-man OMLT left Camp Shorabak on 30 August to provide support, advice and additional, well-toned, muscle to the 150 CS Kandak troops at Nad e Ali who still felt isolated. Major John Asbee, the new commander of the CSS OMLT, led in his OMLT with a strong combat logistics patrol that brought resupplies for the ANA soldiers but Mason's team was flown in the following night and he was briefed by the local commander, Major Harry Clarke of the Argylls. Clarke's men had been in Nad e Ali for a week although they had expected to spend only a day there. The Argylls

> had been continuously ambushed on patrols that week and they had also taken a large number of casualties; included in this were ANA soldiers. I could see instantly that the ANA were not clearly understood – they needed the 1 R Irish touch and I was certain I could turn around their capabilities in Nad e Ali.

This was not a criticism of the Argylls, but an affirmation of John Mason's faith in his own Regiment's ability to gain the confidence of the ANA; it was after all the role they had trained for whereas the Argylls had been deployed as a ground-holding battalion.

Mason was accurate in his assessment and gained the confidence of the ANA commander – 'a man I grew to have a lot of respect for' – in a short time. At Major Clarke's request, Mason's men patrolled east of Nad e Ali while the Argylls patrolled to the west. In the OMLT/ANA area was the village of Luy Bagh, which the ANA had avoided before. This became the objective for the first patrol which established that the local Taliban were capable of producing IEDs – four were discovered within 200 metres of each other. As the patrol returned to Nad e Ali, they were attacked by Taliban but the fire was desultory. A further patrol led to an engagement on the way in, which ended when air support was called in to deal with the ambush. Nonetheless, Luy Bagh became a hot spot for the OMLT and the ANA. Patrols were also undertaken to other areas but

> The Taliban never let us down … they were always there ready and waiting but so were we. Attacks became more complicated, flanking manoeuvres, IEDs laid where they would initiate ambushes, purpose-built firing positions very well camouflaged, for just a few examples. Thanks to good ANA commanders we were able quickly to counter any enemy action. They took our advice and executed it with confidence, and always knew I would have something extra to bring in the form of air support and mortar fire.

For John Mason this was the highlight of HERRICK VIII, although his original eight-man team, after sixteen consecutive days with fighting each day, was reduced to one effective – three were wounded in an engagement in which two ANA soldiers died and three were wounded; four OMLT soldiers were too badly injured to continue. But, although operating in a remote area, this was an opportunity to see 'how strong we were when face to face with the enemy'. When put to this test, all their skills and abilities worked and, moreover, gave a clear indication of the inherent qualities of the ANA. On Tuesday 16 September, a patrol of Mason's OMLT and ANA troops was engaged at very close range by enemy combatants. Heavy fire was put down on the patrol which returned fire with vigour but also called in air support. This arrived in the form of an Apache AH 1. However, as the Apache flew in to add its fire to the engagement, it became clear to those on the ground that the crew had mistaken their target: the helicopter fired on the OMLT and ANA soldiers. One ANA soldier was killed and five of his comrades were wounded while, of the OMLT personnel, Mason, Lance Corporal Rambottom, Ranger Griffiths and Lance Corporal Gurung, a medic, were all wounded. In the confusion of the battle, a typical example of the fog of war, Paul Rambottom was convinced that he had been hit by splinters from Taliban mortars. Not until he came round from surgery, some two days later, did he learn for certain that he had been a victim of so-called 'friendly' fire.

The Taliban campaign of aggression continued relentlessly. Since March, the strength of 3/205 Brigade had been increasing steadily as recruits passed through training in Kabul and were posted to units in Helmand and elsewhere. (Remember that the KMTC was turning out 1,200 trained soldiers every two weeks.) Whereas General Mohaiyodin's command had numbered fewer than 2,500 when the Royal Irish arrived in Afghanistan, it was now passing 4,000 all ranks. This presented some difficulties for the OMLTs as the Battlegroup was being stretched and Ed Freely had had to call on all his resources, including deploying a platoon of Imjin Company in the mentoring role, as we have noted, at FOB Keenan.

At Sangin on 2 September, Rangers Reidy and McSweeney had been injured in an IED blast with Reidy having to be evacuated to the UK for treatment. Then, on the 4th, came the IED attack that killed Ranger Justin Cupples and injured several others.

Not surprisingly, the Taliban were still hitting hard at coalition forces as they continued trying to destabilize those areas from which they had been expelled. PB Attal, in the Gereshk valley, saw no let-up in Taliban pressure but the enemy received an extremely bloody nose when they engaged a patrol from Attal on 12 September. Such was the rebuff they sustained that they did not appear again in such strength in the Attal area while the Royal Irish were in Helmand.

The 12 September clash began when a patrol of ANA, mentored by a six-man Royal Irish team under Corporal Alwyn Stevens, pushed into the Green Zone north east of their patrol base; this was one of the many patrols intended to dominate the Green Zone. A measure of the success already achieved by PB Attal can be gleaned from the fact that, before long, the patrol was approached by a local civilian who warned them of a strong force of Taliban nearby, and that an ambush was likely. On receiving this information, Corporal Stevens moved ahead of the patrol with six men to secure a compound that would give him observation of the area.

However, as Stevens' group approached the compound, eight Taliban appeared and opened fire, pouring a heavy small arms fusillade at them. Stevens' immediate reaction was instinctive: he charged straight at the enemy, firing his weapon from the hip. This took the Taliban by surprise, as they had believed the initiative lay with them but two of them now lay dead and a third was wounded. The remaining five retreated quickly to take cover in wheat that stood some seven feet high. There they set up a firm base from which they resumed firing at Corporal Stevens' patrol.

With effective small arms fire and RPG rounds coming at him, Stevens no longer held the initiative but he re-organized his five men to overcome the enemy in the firefight, while a second OMLT patrol began flanking to the west in readiness for an assault. Meanwhile, the Gunner FST called up their gun positions to bring in 105 mm fire and an air strike was also called for. Although he was no more than 120 metres from the target for the guns and the aircraft, Stevens chose to stay in his position as the enemy came under bombardment, using controlled fire to prevent their escape as the shells came down.

A second Taliban position, about 100 metres away, had been trying to suppress the coalition troops and, as soon as the strike was over, Stevens led his men in an assault on this location. Again, he led from the front, firing his personal weapon and lobbing grenades, as his team followed him into action. Such was the speed and audacity of his attack that those Taliban who did not fall under his fire made a hasty retreat from their position. But the battle was not yet over. For another three hours it raged as a further ten Taliban positions revealed themselves by engaging one or other of the OMLT patrols. The length of the engagement caused a major problem as ammunition stocks dwindled and the patrols were forced to pull back. However, under heavy fire, Stevens moved his men to a position from which they could apply suppressing fire on the enemy, thereby allowing the other patrol to withdraw. This move was completed successfully but Stevens stayed put as close air support and 105s hit the enemy positions. Even though the fire missions were being conducted 'danger close', Stevens held firm and fired on the enemy until he knew that the other patrol had reached safety. Not until then did he order his men to fall back and join their comrades. His courage was extraordinary and fully merited the award of the UK's second highest gallantry award, the Conspicuous Gallantry Cross.

The Taliban had received a severe drubbing that day, much of the credit for which was due to the calm leadership and marked courage shown by Corporal Stevens whose personal role in the drubbing was significant. As Operation HERRICK VIII drew closer to its end, this was one of many signs of the progress achieved by the Royal Irish Battlegroup. But that September day was also marked by the sad vigil service and ramp ceremony preceding the repatriation of Ranger Justin Cupples' body to RAF Lyneham. It was a moving occasion which brought lumps to the throats of many and tears to the eyes of more than a few.

It was also Ramadan, the ninth and holy month of the Islamic year, during which Muslims fast from sunrise to sunset and are required to meet several other obligations, including prayer, charity and examination of one's spiritual self. Perhaps because of this, the rate of Taliban attacks seemed to reduce from the beginning of September, which coincided with the ninth month of the lunar calendar, suggesting that the Taliban were observing Ramadan to some extent. However, since it was believed that there had been some 250 to 300 Taliban casualties in Helmand over two weeks, this reduction in activity might also have been due to reduced manpower. IEDs remained as great a threat as ever.

In the closing weeks of HERRICK VIII, the Battlegroup were busier than ever as they prepared to hand over to 1st Rifles who would undertake the OMLT role in HERRICK IX. At Battlegroup HQ, Major Ivor Gardiner and his mentor team were working closely with HQ 3/205 Brigade on a planning exercise based 'on a realistic scenario to clear enemy forces from west of Lashkar Gah' and which was intended to enhance the Afghans' knowledge of planning at this level and increase their skills. There were also two teams of American assessors to deal with. These were Validation Training Teams (VTTs), one of which had arrived to assess the standards reached by two of the Kandaks, Kandak 2 in Sangin and Kandak 1 in Musa Qaleh. The role of the second VTT was to examine 'how the British prepare units for the OMLT role'. To do this the team would study the way in which the Royal Irish handed over to 1 Rifles and their conduct of RSOI training for the new OMLT Battlegroup. The same team would also look at how the Rifles had carried out pre-deployment training before arriving in Afghanistan. So the pace of work at Battlegroup HQ was increasing rather than decreasing as the end of the tour approached.

On 20 September the advance party of 1st Royal Irish, under Major Ivor Gardiner, left Camp Shorabak on completion of their tour; they would travel to Cyprus for 'decompression leave' before staging on to the UK and home. That same day, Ranger Jason Cupples was being buried in his wife's homeland of Lithuania. Vilma Cupples' home was in Vilnius where Jason's funeral took place, attended by Major Ricky Kane, OC of the Rear Party, together with a bugler, a piper and a full bearer party from the Battalion. In this way, the Regiment paid its respects to a much admired soldier.

John Laverty's OMLT 2 had returned to Shorabak where they were preparing for the arrival of 1st Rifles. To OMLT 2 would fall the task of training and preparing the Rifles Battlegroup as they arrived in Helmand. This would include the RSOI training. As a result, OMLT 2 was spending considerable time on the ranges and was expending much ammunition. John Asbee's CSS OMLT was also busy with a full programme of combat logistics patrols designed to ensure that every outpost had sufficient supplies to cover the relief in place (RIP) period when soldiers from both the outgoing and incoming battlegroups would be occupying those posts.

As September rolled on, the Quartermaster's Department was working at full capacity to account for, and prepare to hand over, all the equipment needed by 1st Rifles. Rifles personnel were briefed by their outgoing counterparts from the Commanding Officer down, who also introduced them to their ANA partners. Major Laverty's OMLT 2 prepared the new arrivals with realistic induction training and firing exercises while, out in the field, the CSS OMLT was carrying out its last mission. That final combat logistics patrol also brought the Battlegroup's last casualty when an IED blast caught the patrol on its way back to Musa Qaleh. Fortunately, the one casualty, Sergeant Bloor, sustained only 'relatively minor' injuries, from which he was expected to make a speedy recovery.

The Taliban had signed off with that final IED as Lieutenant Colonel Freely took his successor, Lieutenant Colonel Joe Cavanagh, to an OMLT conference attended by the senior NATO officers in Afghanistan: General David McKiernan of the US Army, the Commander of ISAF, and his deputy, Lieutenant General Jonathan Riley of the British Army, both expressed their appreciation of the excellent work carried out by the Royal Irish Battlegroup in HERRICK VIII. Brigadier Mark Carleton-Smith, Commander 16 Air Assault Brigade/Task Force Helmand, during his final visit to the Battlegroup in Shorabak, 'acknowledged the remarkable success of the boys in an immensely difficult role in Helmand'.

On the evening of Friday 26 September, Padre Albert Jackson, the Battlegroup chaplain, conducted a moving field service in which the Battlegroup remembered their dead: Sergeant Jonathan Mathews, Corporal Barry Dempsey and Ranger Justin Cupples, as well as those who had been injured. With hymns and prayers, the assembled soldiers gave praise for the service of those who had died, making the supreme sacrifice in the cause of peace. After the service, General Mohaiyodin, now recovered from his illness, was a guest at supper along with US personnel. In the presence of the US guests the Commander 3/205 Brigade 'expressed effusive gratitude' for the work of the Royal Irish Battlegroup and its contribution to improving the situation in Afghanistan.

Then, on the Saturday, there was a simple ceremony in which the flag of the Royal Irish Regiment was lowered to mark the official handover of the OMLT role to 1st Rifles. The torch had been passed on and the Royal Irish could look forward to going home to their families and friends and to a world without IEDs, RPGs and sniper fire: to peace.

Chapter Seven
The Road We Have Travelled

It was not straight from Helmand to home for the Royal Irish. En route, the Battlegroup's personnel were given a period of decompression leave in Cyprus. Just as a diver will decompress as he heads back to the surface so that he will not suffer the agonies of the 'bends', so soldiers returning from operational duties are given a period in which to unwind from the tension of operations and adjust to the world outside. It is a lesson learned by the US forces in Vietnam, from which young men were flown straight home to the USA and, often, were in their own homes less than two days after leaving a battle zone. Studies indicated that veterans of earlier wars did not suffer the same levels of psychiatric problems as did those of Vietnam and one contributory factor that was identified was the fact that those veterans of the Second World War and of the Korean War had come home the slow way, by ship, and thus had time to adjust to a more normal life. Hence the rationale behind the 'decompression' period in Cyprus, which included lectures on the signs of post-traumatic stress disorder and a chance for soldiers to 'let their hair down'.

Then it was on to the UK and the return to Clive Barracks at Tern Hill. Much emotion was evident as soldiers were reunited with their families but there were also many sad thoughts of those of the Battlegroup who had not survived, and especially Ranger Justin Cupples, for whose wife and parents there would be no joyful reunion. There were sad thoughts also of those who had suffered serious, life-changing injuries, including Ranger Allen who had lost both legs in an IED explosion. Ranger Shane Conboy recalled that, as his aircraft was on its landing approach, he found himself focusing on a car on a road close to the airfield and wondering what the driver had been doing for the past six months. 'The normality is probably the most abnormal thing about being back,' was his thought, but he was glad 'that we had done it.'

Before long, members of the Battlegroup were taking part in a series of homecoming parades. The first was through Market Drayton, close to Tern Hill, where, on 14 October, the town 'received the full Battalion with a tsunami of applause as the boys marched up the High Street led by Brian Boru VIII, the Bugles, Pipes and Drums and the Colour Party'. There followed a service of thanksgiving in St Mary's

Church, which allowed the 1st Battalion to thank both the townspeople and the Royal British Legion for the magnificent support given to the soldiers and their families throughout HERRICK VIII. Two days later, the Battalion were the guests of Shropshire County Council for a memorable service of thanksgiving in Shrewsbury Abbey. Following the service, the Battalion paraded to the Abbey Foregate and, once again, large crowds came out to give the Royal Irish a warm and unforgettable welcome home. Shrewsbury has taken the Royal Irish to its heart, of which there could be no finer proof than the appreciation from the crowds at this parade.

In Northern Ireland, parades had been arranged to welcome the Royal Irish – both 1st and 2nd Battalion soldiers – home. Ballymena had long been the home of the Regiment – the Regimental HQ and Depot had been housed in the town's St Patrick's Barracks which had an almost seventy-year connection with the Regiment and its predecessors. And so it was fitting that Ballymena should host the first of three homecoming parades for the Regiment. This was an evening 'Welcome Home' parade and reception, for which some 5,000 people turned out as soldiers of both 1st and 2nd Royal Irish, with the Colours of both Battalions, paraded through the town accompanied by the Band, Bugles, Pipes and Drums. The musicians' efforts were almost drowned out by the deafening cheers of the spectators. The following day – Saturday 1 November – it was on to Larne, where the Freedom of the Borough was bestowed on the Regiment and the parade was watched by some 6,000 people as it made its way through the town. On this occasion, old soldiers from Regimental Associations also marched, as did representatives of the Cadet forces.

Even with all the warmth and enthusiasm demonstrated in both towns, Ballymena and Larne were but tasters for the Sunday when the Regiment paraded through Belfast. In spite of the efforts of republicans to spoil the day, this was an event worthy of memory as soldiers of 1st and 2nd Royal Irish and the TA medics of 204 (North Irish) Field Hospital, who had deployed for the second half of HERRICK VIII, marched past the City Hall. Some 50,000 people turned out and it was obvious that Belfast had prepared for days beforehand. Flags bearing the Regimental motto 'Faugh A Ballagh!' were on display everywhere along the route and some supporters had even attempted to decorate the Black Mountain, overlooking the city, with the motto but had either run out of material or were stopped in their work: the mountainside bore the legend 'Faugh A Balla ...'

As the soldiers marched through the city centre and past the saluting dais at City Hall, the sound of applause and cheering drowned out even the skirl of the pipes. The band could hardly be heard and soldiers commented later that they felt as if they were eight-feet tall as they were borne along on a wave of emotion. In many ways, the tremendous reception accorded the Royal Irish and the medics of 204 (North Irish) Field Hospital worked as a psychological filter to help them recover from the stresses of Helmand.

A week later, 1st Royal Irish was represented at the Remembrance Sunday ceremony and service in Market Drayton, a particularly poignant occasion, especially as the Battalion was hosting the family of Ranger Justin Cupples. Mrs Vilma Cupples joined Lieutenant Colonel Freely to lay wreaths at the town's cenotaph while, that evening, the Cupples family joined Justin's comrades of Ranger Company to celebrate his life and acknowledge his sacrifice.

And so it was over. HERRICK VIII was behind and it would not be long until the Royal Irish were back to the routine of an air assault battalion in barracks, or TA soldiers in their daily lives. What had they achieved? In the simplest terms, the Afghan National Army's 3/205 Brigade was a much more professional formation than it had been in March, and its boots were now on the ground in more areas of Helmand than had been the case before then. There was much improved security in many of the operational areas in which OMLTs from the Battlegroup had mentored ANA troops, with the Taliban having been pushed back out of areas that they had dominated. The Kajaki dam operation was one obvious example of success but Ed Freely summed up the Battlegroup's achievements when he noted that it

> was remarkably successful in developing the capability and capacity of the ANA, and 1 R Irish left Helmand with the ANA more confident and capable, controlling much more of the Province than before.

Among the weaknesses identified in the ANA by the Battlegroup was the logistical chain, which in no way was comparable to that of the British or other allied armies. Colour Sergeant (now WO2) Darren Clark was with OMLT 1 and responsible for mentoring the ANA on logistical matters. The concept of 'mission command' – whereby a subordinate officer, understanding his commander's intentions and aware of the effect he is intended to have, plans, within his own area of responsibility, how best to achieve those aims – is alien to the ANA. Among other matters, mission command means that a battalion commander should not have to worry about the logistical needs of his soldiers, as that will be taken care of by his quartermaster's (QM's) department. Colour Sergeant Clark soon saw that this did not happen in the ANA and witnessed full colonels carrying out kit inspections on platoons. In fact, the brigade commander himself, General Mohaiyodin, was at the top of the logistical chain and everything passed across his desk. Some of the reasons for this were cultural: as Afghan soldiers were poor men with little education, there was always the temptation to sell off equipment and hence the checks made on equipment issue were very stringent with an array of signatures needed to authorize the issue of items of kit. Individual soldiers usually 'signed' for weapons, ammunition and other major items by thumbprint.

By the end of the tour, Darren Clark could see some improvement in the ANA's logistical capability but considered that it would take some time before it could match western standards. He thought that it might be better if logistical mentors spent more time than the six-month roulement tour with the ANA. As it is, the mentors often do the jobs that the Afghans ought to do, because the latter know that the British will not let them down.

Corporal Chris Rushton, also of OMLT 1, was responsible for mentoring Afghan signallers, as well as driving the OMLT commander. He commented that the ANA signallers were enthusiastic about their role but that they had their own idiosyncratic systems, which worked for them. Their equipment was much older than that issued to NATO troops but there were occasions when, due to atmospheric conditions, the Afghan equipment worked when the more modern British equivalent did not. Improvements were achieved through the establishment of a joint operations room where ANA personnel watched and learned as the Battlegroup staff carried out their duties in the NATO style. Rushton noted that the ANA did learn and, by the time the Royal Irish tour was coming to its end, the improvement could be seen.

WO2 Glenn Mawhinney, of OMLT 3, appreciated the local knowledge of the ANA. Although most soldiers were illiterate and therefore could not read maps, they were so familiar with the ground that this skill would have been redundant for many of them. They could identify individual compounds and name their occupants and were able to glean much information about IEDs and were often keen to deal with IEDs. They worked well with the OMLT soldiers and also with the US Marines, especially when the ANA and OMLT carried out a search operation in Sangin bazaar. Captain Markis Duggan, commanding OMLT 3 when Major Crow was on leave, received information from local people, through the ANA, on Taliban 'hides' for weapons and inaugurated a series of search operations in which US Marines, whose role was to mentor the ANP but who were happy to help the OMLT and ANA, provided a ring of steel, inside which the Afghan soldiers and their mentors carried out the searches, which proved very successful in unearthing many enemy weapons. It was clear to Glenn Mawhinney that such intelligence could not have been gleaned by foreign soldiers and that the role of the ANA was pivotal.

Ranger Dowie, also of D Company/OMLT 3, noted that the ANA 'are very capable soldiers' although they sometimes appeared to be very casual and 'unaware of their surroundings, with their weapon over one shoulder and a cigarette in the corner of their mouths'. Nonetheless, they were 'quite tuned into their environment' and were able to read the body language of the locals and anything out of the ordinary led to 'wordless gripping of weapons with two hands and tactical switch-on'. There were many occasions when the empathy of the ANA with local people saved lives, bringing details of IEDs or ambushes.

Dowie believed that the ANA had made much progress which had been demonstrated whenever there was an engagement with the Taliban when the ANA's enthusiasm often had to be reined in. It is his view that

The ANA … are the future of Afghanistan. The ANA are the people, and hence the key to any counter-insurgency campaign. I know Afghanistan has a very complex tribal system and this overspills into the ANA. The 3rd OMLT have been witness to some very brutal punch ups, but they manage to gel well with the ANA despite these infrequent flares. I genuinely believe that for every British patrol going out on the ground there should be some element of ANA in support.

That view is shared by many: the ANA are the force to bring an end to the Taliban campaign and offer security to the people of a country that has not known real peace for decades.

In the midst of the fighting there were members of the Battlegroup carrying out duties without which operations would have ground to a halt. Those individuals seldom receive the glare of the limelight but deserve credit for their efforts, which all added to the Battlegroup's ability to carry out its task. They included men such as Colour Sergeant Kevin Martin, a soldier with twenty-two years' service in the Royal Irish. A member of the Quartermaster's Department, Colour Sergeant Martin had handled the Battalion's conversion to the new Bowman radio equipment. That bald statement hides the truly hard work put in by Kevin Martin who had to take in to his stores

over five thousand numbered items and associated equipment schedules…, a task completed by Martin without a G1098 storeman. Units awaiting conversion [to Bowman] were advised that they should visit 1 R IRISH to observe [the] 'best practice' accounting procedures that he had established.

That the Battlegroup could deploy with confidence using the new system owed much to Colour Sergeant Martin but, more than that, he also understood the commander's intent and appreciated fully that the ready availability of equipment delivers operational capability. He was one of the key figures in the Battlegroup and made an incalculable contribution to success on Operation HERRICK VIII.

Then there were the five men of the Information Operations Cell, who carried out three main roles: Influence Ops, Media Ops and CIMIC Ops. In the former a Gunner officer collated information on the effects of ANA and OMLT patrols on the Afghan population with the aim of improving those effects; it was this officer who also dealt with psy ops, or 'hearts and minds'. Media Ops was the purview of Captain Brian Johnston MBE, who also carried out his normal duties as RCMO (Regimental Careers Management Officer) for the troops in Helmand and those back in Tern Hill. As Media Ops Officer, Captain Johnston's responsibilities included the collation of blogs for newspapers back home in Ireland and Britain, as well as updating the

Battlegroup's web pages. His was the task of arranging visits and meetings that might provide media opportunities and it was he who looked after a media team from Northern Ireland that included Ivan Little of UTV with cameraman John Vennard, Lesley-Ann Henry of the Belfast Telegraph and Ben Lowry of the Newsletter. Early in the tour, he accompanied a BBC 'Newsnight' team to Musa Qaleh for nine days as they made a documentary on the Royal Irish in Afghanistan. Backing Captain Johnston was Ranger Billy Bittles, a wizard with computers, who kept the IT side working smoothly. Ranger Bittles was on loan from Imjin Company and his expertise with computers was invaluable. A graphic designer by profession, he kept the regimental web page up to date, acted as a photographer and also undertook convoy duties to Camp Shorabak. WO2 Denis McKee, who kept the Mourne Observer supplied with material during his tour, was the CIMIC Ops leader and the Company Sergeant Major for Real Life Support personnel in Camp Shorabak (these included the chefs, among other trades). CIMIC is civil and military cooperation and involves reconstruction and development work in Helmand. In this role WO2 McKee worked with the US forces Logistic Support Team (LST) to find and supply humanitarian aid and medical supplies to the various outstations from which these were then distributed by the ANA. He also dealt with requests for funds for consent winning activities, from digging irrigation ditches through repairing damaged bridges to building or repairing schools or clinics.

The welfare of the soldiers is always a critical part of an operation such as HERRICK VIII and the work of the Welfare Officer back in Tern Hill, as well as those in Helmand, was boosted by the efforts of the chaplain to 1st Royal Irish, the Reverend Albert Jackson. A man with a great sense of humour and a deep commitment to his faith, Albert Jackson did much unsung work for the soldiers of the Battlegroup as well as providing regular non-denominational services at his tented garrison chapel which he christened St Patrick's in the Desert. He was always available to lend an ear to anyone with problems and hopped about by helicopter to visit his parishioners in their many out of the way bases. In Camp Shorabak, he was amazed to see that no welfare arrangements were in place for ANA soldiers. Whenever these men were off duty, they simply lay about the camp as there were no recreational facilities for them. When he mentioned this to Ed Freely the Commanding Officer authorized him to liaise with his Afghan counterparts to provide some facilities for the ANA soldiers.

The ANA does not have chaplains or welfare officers but each Kandak has a mullah, who acts as the religious and cultural officer (RCO). Albert Jackson proposed to the mullahs that they should institute a programme of recreation for their soldiers. To fire their enthusiasm, he suggested that this might start with a film show. This was agreed but then difficulties became apparent. Most western films would offend the sensitivities of a Muslim audience, who would be outraged by the sight of women in swimwear or even ballgowns. So it would be best not to show a Hollywood movie, although there was one possible exception: one of the Rocky films, featuring Sylvester Stallone, included a fight between the eponymous hero of the film and a Russian boxer. This was bound to go down well with the Afghan audience as the Russian is defeated. And so the choice was made. The film was to be shown in an extemporized cinema on a Thursday evening, the day before the Muslim day of rest. The mullahs agreed to this arrangement but later had a rethink. There was a problem with Thursday: this was 'man love night' and it would be tempting fate to allow all these men to sit together in the darkness of the cinema. So another night was chosen and chairs were arranged for those attending. This was the first and last time that chairs were used. Afghans usually sit on the floor and the new arrangement led to many chairs being damaged. Moreover, in spite of the fact that it was not Thursday, there were obvious signs of members of the audience turning their attention away from the screen to fellow members. Nor were these the only problems. When it was decided to show the films in a lecture theatre built by the Americans, an even greater problem surfaced. On the advice of Afghans, the Americans had displayed the legend *Allah uh Akbar* – God is Great – above the screen and flanked it with Afghan national flags. Now the mullahs objected to films appearing on a screen below the declaration of the greatness of God. Eventually, all problems were resolved as far as possible and the film shows became a regular feature of life at Camp Shorabak.

Another suggestion put to the RCOs by Albert Jackson was that they should visit wounded ANA soldiers in hospital. This was met with surprise since the mullahs did not visit the wounded and the question was put to Jackson: 'Why should we visit them? They are ignorant men'. The Chaplain suggested that the ignorance of the soldiers might be abated by visits from the mullahs who could use this time to educate their soldiers. By the end of HERRICK VIII, a number of mullahs were making regular visits to ANA soldiers in hospital. The Senior Chaplain in Afghanistan told Albert Jackson that he had been the first padre to liaise with the mullahs. For his part the Royal Irish Chaplain commented that he had made it clear to the mullahs from the outset that he was not trying to proselytise and that he respected their beliefs, a stance that must have played a major part in his success with them.

On his travels around the Battlegroup's many locations, Albert Jackson was sometimes accompanied by a rather special Ranger. This was Ranger Banter, a teddy bear dressed in a miniature combat shirt and wearing a caubeen with the Regiment's distinctive green hackle. Banter was a mascot that not only symbolized the spirit of the Royal Irish but was also a link in the welfare chain between Helmand and home. On a regular basis, reports of Ranger Banter's travels were sent back to Tern Hill where they were used in the school attended by the children of the 1st Battalion in a project on Afghanistan that developed the children's geography skills and knowledge as well as letting them know where their fathers might be. Banter was to be seen on the flight deck of a Chinook, or manning the rear-ramp-mounted machine gun, or simply accompanying his good friend, Padre Albert Jackson, on a visit to his parishioners. He provided an invaluable fillip to morale in a manner unique to the Royal Irish.

Chapter Eight

Reflections

The debate about the NATO presence in Afghanistan is not one for this book. It has taken place – and will continue – in the media and other public arenas. This book is simply the story of one unit of soldiers, the Royal Irish Battlegroup, who went to Afghanistan to serve their country under the banner of a United Nations' resolution. Any reader who has persevered with the book to this point will agree that the Royal Irish did their job with considerable success and in a style that was all their own. This was true not only of those who patrolled the fields and alleyways but of those whose roles kept them, largely, within headquarters buildings at various levels. These included those men who were mentoring ANA staff officers, quartermasters and signallers and intelligence staff. Among the latter was Sergeant Gavin O'Kelly, a son of the Regiment (the author knew his father as an RSM), who was in the Intelligence Cell at Musa Qaleh and who knew the town and its people as if he had lived there for years. As with so many others of the Royal Irish, Sergeant O'Kelly could talk of Afghans as people he knew and respected and for whom he held out much hope for a better future. Talking to men such as this very perceptive NCO inspires a belief that there will be a positive outcome to ISAF operations in Afghanistan.

On 6 March 2009, the Ministry of Defence announced the operational awards for HERRICK VIII which included three Conspicuous Gallantry Crosses, three Military Crosses, ten Mentions in Despatches, two Queen's Commendations for Valuable Service and seven Joint Commanders' Commendations to members of the Royal Irish. The award of three CGCs – second only to the Victoria Cross – was unique: no other unit had received three CGCs for a single operation. Thus the Royal Irish, who already hold a collective CGC for the steadfast soldiering of the Home Service battalions in Northern Ireland, have added a new chapter to British and Irish military history.

For the Regiment, the awards were a welcome recognition of the work done in Helmand but the respect and confidence of the Afghan National Army, its senior staff and Afghan leaders at national, provincial and local levels were every bit as important – as well as being indicators that Afghans would be able to assume the security role in their own land. Some commentators on the campaign in Afghanistan insist on referring to the three Anglo-Afghan wars as if Operation HERRICK is a twenty-first century reprise of those wars of empire. While Afghans have not forgotten British aggression – General Mohaiyodin reminded Lieutenant Colonel Freely of the campaigns – the majority recognize one essential difference: that the NATO forces are operating alongside Afghan forces with the approval of the Afghan government in a United Nations-backed effort to bring stability to this troubled land. At the time of writing, the new US President, Barack Obama, has signalled that he will adopt an attitude very different to that of his predecessor and is willing to open negotiations with the more moderate elements of the Taliban. While soldiers hold the ground – and they now hold much more than in 2006 – it is up to the politicians to arrive at a resolution that will suit the country; and that now seems much more likely than hitherto.

For the soldiers of the Royal Irish Battlegroup, HERRICK VIII was a memorable six months of their lives. Both Regulars and Reservists had trained for just such an eventuality and their performance in Helmand was a product of that training as well as of their professionalism and dedication. But there is another factor to be considered: the special élan of an Irish regiment. When selecting which of his battalions would form the OMLT Battlegroup, Brigadier Mark Carleton-Smith selected 1st Royal Irish, based on the quality of their junior leaders and the professionalism of the Battalion as a whole. These two qualities are so closely related as to be inseparable.

This account of the Battlegroup's time in Helmand has shown clearly the quality of the junior leaders, the young corporals and lance corporals and, at times, rangers, who met the demands of difficult situations and took command of platoons and even larger groupings, displaying qualities of leadership that were inspiring to those alongside them. Such excellence is founded not only on good solid training but also in the tradition of professionalism that permeates the Royal Irish. That tradition is more than three centuries old and has been sharpened and enhanced in recent years on many operational deployments. There is beating within the heart of the Royal Irish a rhythm that would be recognizable to a soldier of an earlier era: when visiting 1st Royal Irish at Tern Hill Barracks, the author sensed that his father, a Royal Irish Fusilier in the 1920s and 30s, and his comrades, would have felt at home with these latter day Faughs. Speaking to the soldiers of the Royal Irish emphasizes that fact.

Recalling events in Helmand, soldier after soldier, from the most junior Ranger to the Commanding Officer, used one very simple word: trust. Each and every member of the Battlegroup knew that he could trust every one of his comrades. While it may be argued that this is common to all units, there is a particular quality to that sense of trust in the Royal Irish, which is not identifiable immediately to outsiders. Indeed, some outsiders might feel that there is a slack attitude within the Royal Irish when they hear the banter that passes between officers and other ranks. It is that banter – remember Ranger Banter? – that is the abiding hallmark of the Regiment. It is a sense of knowing where everyone fits in this regimental family, of officers and soldiers conducting conversations that might be unthinkable in other units but are everyday in the Royal Irish – and, again, the author comes back to recollections from his father of fusiliers and officers of the Faughs having the same familial respect as is to be found today. This is what makes the Royal Irish unique and it is something that cannot be taught; it can only be absorbed from generation to generation. And it was a quality that was recognized by the men of the Afghan National Army who found that they could relate closely to their comrades of the Royal Irish.

In years to come there will be many gatherings of old comrades at which HERRICK VIII will be discussed. Many of these discussions will be alien to outsiders, if outsiders will not be excluded. Men with grey hair, or almost no hair, will recall the days of their youth when they fought in the harsh climate of Helmand. They will remember the Green Zone, Camp Shorabak, Musa Qaleh, Sangin and the PBs – Attal, Boyne, Pylae. They will remember the Afghan soldiers who fought at their sides. They will remember those who did not come home, especially Ranger Justin Cupples. And there will be laughter, and some carefully concealed tears as well, as specific incidents are brought to mind and memory takes away the sharpest edges. Above all, there will be a feeling that 'well, I'm glad I was there, and I'm glad I was with these guys, the best soldiers in the best Regiment in the Army'.

Faugh A Ballagh!

Operational Honours and Awards

Royal Irish Battlegroup

Conspicuous Gallantry Cross (CGC)

Corporal Robert William Kerr McClurg	Royal Irish Regiment
Acting Sergeant Alwyn Stevens	Royal Irish Regiment
Lance Corporal Jone Bruce Toge	Royal Irish Regiment

Military Cross (MC)

Sergeant Stephen McConnell	Royal Irish Regiment
Ranger Alan William Owens	Royal Irish Regiment
Captain Graham David Bradley Rainey	Royal Irish Regiment

Queen's Gallantry Medal (QGM)

Staff Sergeant James Alexander McCormick	Corps of Royal Engineers

Mention in Despatches (MiD)

Sergeant Hughie Jonathan Benson	Royal Irish Regiment
Corporal Cecil Ian Carter	Adjutant General's Corps (SPS)
Corporal Alan Houston Cree	Royal Irish Regiment
Sergeant Darrell John Esdale	Royal Irish Regiment
Ranger Dominic Raymond Flanagan	Royal Irish Regiment
Ranger Stephen Damian Manning	Royal Irish Regiment
Colour Sergeant John Anthony Mason	Royal Irish Regiment
Corporal Matthew Robert McCord	Royal Irish Regiment
Lance Corporal Richard James McKee	Royal Irish Regiment
Corporal John Nixon	Royal Irish Regiment
Warrant Officer Class 2 William Roy	Royal Irish Regiment

Queen's Commendation for Valuable Service (QCVS)

Major David Brian Kenny	Royal Irish Regiment
Major David Graham Shannon	Royal Irish Regiment

Joint Commanders' Commendation

Lance Corporal Lee Maurice Hugh Averill	Royal Irish Regiment (TA)
Ranger Sitiveni Eleni Bolei	Royal Irish Regiment
Ranger Gary Steven Bradshaw	Royal Irish Regiment
Captain Anthony Charles Dixon	Royal Irish Regiment
Ranger William Clifford Scott Galloway	Royal Irish Regiment
Corporal Christopher Alan Kennedy	Royal Irish Regiment
Corporal William Nigel Lynn	Royal Irish Regiment (TA)

A Journalist's View

Ivan Little of UTV was one of a group of journalists from Northern Ireland to travel to Helmand and visit the Battlegroup. He penned the following comments for this book.

My trip to Afghanistan with the Royal Irish was an unqualified success from a journalistic point of view and a real eye-opener from a personal perspective. Having been to Iraq in 2005 and to Kenya with the Regiment in 2007, I knew what lay ahead but it still didn't stop me feeling nervous about the trip to Helmand. The preparations were limited as we had had short notice that we would be going. Problems with insurance cover were only ironed out by UTV just before we left.

The journey to Afghanistan was arduous and we were delayed for twenty-four hours in our departure. For me, the call to get the helmet and body armour on was not as chilling as it had been on the way to Iraq. I wouldn't say my cameraman John Vennard and I were veterans – far from it – but the first experience is always the worst.

Our transfer to Camp Shorabak was smooth and we were rather buoyed up by the accommodation which awaited us. In Iraq we had some uncomfortable nights in uncomfortable camps but in Shorabak we were billeted with the officers in their prefab and our beds and mossie nets were in place. We were to spend ten nights in the camp and it was an ideal base. We quickly established our contacts with our press team who couldn't have been more helpful in terms of facilities and contact with the newsroom back home.

I telephoned a daily report into UTV and the sister radio station and I also compiled a daily blog to our website. I had not intended to do daily pieces but the news stories certainly cranked up as we arrived. We bumped into the CO, Ed Freely, on arrival in Afghanistan – he was on his way out on R&R – but he agreed to record an interview.

We got the heads up that six Royal Irish soldiers had been injured in an ambush and agreed to hold it until the news had been relayed to their families.

Ed Freely confirmed that another soldier had been badly injured a few days earlier. (This was Ranger Allen who lost both legs.) Over the coming days we were able to film and interview many of the wounded and we had ready and open access to the hospital, which was manned by medics from Northern Ireland, another amazing local angle. Despite the hostile surroundings and the ever present dangers, I found the morale among the troops and the medics remarkable.

We also managed to meet and interview soldiers returning and leaving for the forward operating bases. Their lifestyles, of course, were a million miles removed from the comparative luxuries of Shorabak and Camp Bastion, which we also visited on an almost daily basis, especially as the guard duty fell to 2nd Royal Irish. We managed to get out on patrol with 2nd Royal Irish as well and that was another invaluable experience as it gave us a first hand feel of the remoteness and terrors outside the gates.

On one occasion we met the Afghan Police who told the Royal Irish that the Taliban had been seen in the area the night before. My quick piece to camera recorded that conversation and ended with an unbroadcastable sign off – 'So let's get the f*** out of here!' I thought the cameraman had stopped running.

As I say we found the highest morale everywhere we went. Obviously, when the cameras were out the microphones were on. The soldiers were all on message and they knew what answers were expected of them from their superiors. But late into the night, we mixed freely with the lads and despite their reservations about the war they never relented in their professional and committed approach to what they were doing there.

For me, the level of casualties during our time there was hard to take. I don't think there was a day when 'op minimise' signs were posted around the camp, meaning the end of ordinary communications back home because there had been a fatality. Admittedly, the Royal Irish didn't sustain any fatalities during our time there but one sound will never leave me – the sound of a Royal Irish bugler and piper practising the Last Post just across the way in Bastion in readiness for the repatriation of a soldier's body the next day. The music drifted eerily across the still night air and rammed home the reality of what was actually going on all around us in Helmand.

On our way home from Afghanistan we almost missed our flight from Kandahar but everyone involved pulled out all the stops to ensure we would make it. However, we were not the last to board. We watched in silence as three wounded soldiers were carried on to the Hercules with their nurses caring for them throughout the painful transfer. The plane which took us back to Brize Norton was also part carrier/part hospital and though I had seen that the facilities were available on the flight back from Iraq, they were not used as they were on our return from Helmand. The sight of the soldiers on that lengthy and horrendous flight home was another reminder to me of what war is really all about. But as the soldier sitting beside me said on more than one occasion, 'At least they are still breathing …'

After our return to Belfast, I compiled five reports on our visit to Afghanistan and the response to them from the public was overwhelmingly positive. I also went across to England for the homecomings and covered the medics' return to Belfast … and the larger scale homecoming parade to the city.

Glossary

105	L118 105 mm light gun, used by the Royal Artillery's Commando and Parachute regiments. Has a range of 17.2 kilometres and fires a 15.1 kg round. Its APS (automatic pointing system) allows the gun to be unlimbered and in action in 30 seconds. Can be slung under a Chinook helicopter or towed by vehicle.
AH	Attack helicopter, of which the AgustaWestland Apache AH 1 is the standard British machine.
AK47	Kalashnikov 7.62 mm assault rifle, designed by a Soviet Army officer and used all over the world. It is a favourite weapon with terrorist groups due to its ease of maintenance and robust nature.
ANA	Afghan National Army.
ANP	Afghan National Police.
Apache AH 1	See AH.
B-1B	Originally the North American-Rockwell B-1B Lancer, now the Boeing B-1B, this is a variable-geometry, low-level, supersonic bomber which, in its B-1 guise, was intended to replace the B-52 Stratofortress. However, it was modified to B-1B standard, becoming a transonic, and relatively stealthy, bomber in the process. B-1Bs can drop their bombs from high altitude with great accuracy and are on call to NATO forces in Afghanistan.
B-2	Northrop B-2 Spirit subsonic stealth bomber. With a very low radar 'signature', the B-2 can enter hostile airspace undetected. A small number serve with the USAF and are on call to NATO forces in Afghanistan.
B-52	The Boeing B-52H Stratofortress, the oldest combat aircraft in the USAF's inventory, is an eight-engined strategic bomber, originally intended to deliver America's nuclear deterrent. The first B-52s entered service in 1955 and the type is now the oldest combat aircraft in the world. The B-52H entered service in the 1960s and

those in service are now some forty-five-years-old. With its extremely long range, the B-52 can deliver bombs or missiles from bases far from Afghanistan.

Bowman   The Army's new integrated tactical communications system which includes HF, VHF and UHF radio sets that offer secure communications.

Browning 50   .50-inch/12.7mm heavy machine gun, developed from the Browning .50 MG used in aircraft during the Second World War. Belt-fed, it fires 485–635 rpm and is effective to a range of about 2,000 metres.

C-17   McDonnell-Douglas Boeing strategic freighter aircraft, known as Globemaster III. Douglas produced two other heavy transport aeroplanes under the Globemaster name: the C-74 Globemaster, used in the Berlin airlift; the C-124 Globemaster II which was in service from the Korean War until the early 1970s. USAF Globemaster IIs flew Irish Army peacekeeping troops to the Congo in 1960.

Casevac   Casualty evacuation. The removal, or extraction, of a casualty from a battle zone.

CGC   Conspicuous Gallantry Cross. The UK's second highest award for gallantry in the face of the enemy after the Victoria Cross; instituted in 1993, it replaced the Distinguished Service Order as a gallantry award for officers and the Distinguished Conduct Medal, the Distinguished Service Medal and the Distinguished Flying Medal for other ranks.

Chinook   Boeing CH-47 Chinook twin-rotor, medium-lift helicopter. In service with the Royal Air Force and many other air forces across the world.

Combat Indicators Any changes in the normal patterns of life may indicate the presence of enemy forces. These can include, *inter alia*, the absence of farmers working in fields, the absence of children from a village, the departures of villagers, and an unwillingness of local people to communicate when, normally, they are friendly. More obvious signs include disturbed earth, vehicle tracks where they are not expected in out-of-the-way areas and unusual gatherings of males.

CQMS   Company Quartermaster Sergeant.

ECM   Electronic Counter Measures; equipment that disrupts enemy signals, especially to radio-controlled IEDs.

EOD   Explosive ordnance disposal.

FAC   Forward Air Controller – see JTAC.

Fast Air	Combat jets used to provide support to ground troops. These include RAF Harriers, a variety of USAF and USN types, French Mirages and machines from other NATO air forces.
GMLRS	Guided Multiple Launch Rocket System. Developed by Lockheed Martin, the system uses satellite technology to ensure accuracy and has been used effectively and with total accuracy in Afghanistan.
GPMG	General Purpose Machine Gun: standard British medium machine gun of 7.62 mm calibre, with a rate of fire of 750 rounds per minute. May be mounted on a bipod or tripod in a static position or in a vehicle.
HE	High Explosive. Invented by Alfred Nobel in the nineteenth century. He also owned the Bofors company and his father was the inventor of plywood.
HLS/HLZ	Helicopter Landing Site or Zone.
HMG	Heavy machine gun; see Browning 50.
IED	Improvized Explosive Device. A mine made from any available materials and explosives and intended for use against both personnel and vehicles. The greatest threat to ISAF troops in Helmand.
IRT	Incident Response Team. A group of soldiers and medics at Camp Bastion whose job it was to undertake casualty evacuations across Helmand.
ISAF	International Security Assistance Force. Established under a UN mandate in 2001 as the overall organization for international military forces operating in Afghanistan. Since 2003, ISAF has been led by NATO.
JTAC	Joint Tactical Air Controller. (In US parlance, Joint Terminal Attack Controller.) Based with ground troops, the JTAC controls aircraft within his specific area; this includes movements of reconnaissance aircraft, supply helicopters and attack aircraft. He can call in and direct the last named as they make their attacks.
LMG	Light Machine Gun. A 5.56 mm weapon based on the Minimi LMG, it has a belt feed and can fire 700–1,000 rpm.
LSW	Light Support Weapon. A light machine gun, based on the SA80 rifle but with a longer and heavier barrel to provide increased muzzle velocity and accuracy; it retains the SA80's calibre of 5.56 mm. With a 30-round magazine, it has a cyclic rate of fire of 610–775 rpm.
MASCAL	Mass casualty plan. Intended to deal with a situation in which a number of casualties have been incurred.

Mastiff	A British version of the American Cougar 6 x 6 armoured patrol vehicle, this can carry six personnel plus a crew of two and offers considerable protection against mines and IEDs.
MC	Military Cross. The Army's third-level gallantry award which, since 1993, has been available to all ranks. Instituted in 1914, the MC was available to officers and Warrant Officers only, with other ranks receiving the Military Medal (MM) which was discontinued in 1993.
MiD	Mention in Despatches. The fourth level of gallantry award.
MLRS	See GMLRS.
NATO	North Atlantic Treaty Organisation. Established in 1949 and born out of the Western Union, this is an organization in which members pledge to come to the support of others should they come under attack. Originally intended to defend western Europe against Soviet aggression, it has welcomed former Soviet satellite nations into its ranks in recent years.
NDS	National Directorate of Security. The Afghan equivalent of MI5.
OMLT	Operational Mentoring and Liaison Team(s). UK troops from an OMLT Battlegroup, such as the Royal Irish, working in small groups with ANA troops.
PRR	Personal Role Radio.
PRT	Provincial Reconstruction Team(s). Composed of military and civilian personnel, these are a vital part of the process of returning Afghanistan to normality as they assist in the development and reconstruction of the country's provinces.
PSCC	Provincial Security and Co-ordination Centre. Such centres are intended to co-ordinate the operations of the ANA, ANP and NDS.
QGM	Queen's Gallantry Medal. Instituted in 1974, this is a civilian award, below the George Medal (GM), but is also available to military personnel for acts of gallantry that are not performed in the face of the enemy and for which military awards are normally not made.
QRF	Quick Reaction Force. Small groups operating as a 'fire brigade' force from forward operating bases. Also part of the IRT, with the task of ensuring that HLSs are secure during casualty evacuation operations.
SA80	The standard rifle of the Army with a 5.56 mm calibre.
SAM	Surface-to-air missile. The term covers a wide range of weaponry from shoulder-launched missiles to sophisticated equipments that

can track and destroy a high-flying aircraft. In Afghan terms this is usually the shoulder-launched version.

UAV
Unmanned Aerial Vehicle. Any of a range of aircraft controlled from a ground station and used for observation or attack.

UGL
Underslung Grenade Launcher. A Heckler & Koch AG-36 40mm grenade launcher with ladder sight fitted to an SA80 rifle.

WMIK
Pronounced Wimik, a stripped-down Land Rover with a Weapon Mount Installation Kit. The vehicle is fitted with a roll cage and can carry a selection of weapons, including a Browning 50 and a GPMG.

Bibliography

Ayton, Mark (ed), *Royal Air Force 2009. The Official RAF Annual Review*. (Key Publishing, Stamford, 2009)

Beattie, Doug, MC, with Gomm, Philip, *An Ordinary Soldier* (Simon & Schuster, London, 2008)

Bishop, Patrick, *3 Para* (Harper Perennial, London, 2008)

Fergusson James, *A Million Bullets: The Real Story of the British Army in Afghanistan* (Bantam Press, London, 2008)

Lewis, Damien, *Apache Dawn: Always Outnumbered; Never Outgunned* (Sphere, London, 2008)

Loyn, David, *Butcher and Bolt: Two Hundred Years of Foreign Engagement in Afghanistan* (Hutchinson, London, 2008)

Pigott, Peter, *Canada in Afghanistan: The War so Far* (Dundurn Press, Toronto, 2007)

Rayment, Sean, *Into the Killing Zone: The Real Story from the Frontline in Afghanistan* (Constable & Robinson, London, 2008)

Ryan, Mike, *Battlefield Afghanistan* (The History Press, Stroud, 2008)

Southby-Tailyour, Ewen, *3 Commando Brigade, Helmand, Afghanistan* (Ebury Press, London, 2008)

Journals, Magazines
The Blackthorn: Journal of the Royal Irish Regiment
The Gunner: Magazine of the Royal Artillery
Soldier: Magazine of the British Army

Websites
www.army.mod.uk – British Army official website
www.army.mod.uk/infantry – British Army infantry website
www.raf.mod.uk – Royal Air Force website
www.rn.mod.uk – Royal Navy website

Index